T E N N Y S O N
S E L E C T E D   P O E T R Y

MODERN LIBRARY COLLEGE EDITIONS

ALFRED TENNYSON

SELECTED POETRY

Edited, with an Introduction, by D O U G L A S B U S H
PROFESSOR OF ENGLISH, HARVARD UNIVERSITY

THE MODERN LIBRARY · *New York*

THE MODERN LIBRARY

is published by RANDOM HOUSE, INC.

CONTENTS

INTRODUCTION

BY DOUGLAS BUSH

THE NAME of Alfred Lord Tennyson (1809–92) commonly calls up a picture of the grand old man who had the magnificent presence of a heroic bard, the uniquely famous Poet Laureate who had become a national institution, the uncrowned king of England and of poetry, and who was buried in Westminster Abbey with such pomp and circumstance of mourning as he had celebrated in his "Ode on the Death of the Duke of Wellington." But much of Tennyson's finest poetry was written by a poor, lonely, obscure young man who had never been free from a weight of inward and outward anxieties and torments.

The mixture of high spirits and philosophizing in *The Devil and the Lady* (an extraordinary composition for a boy of fourteen), or the Byronic and Mooreish romanticism of some other juvenilia, might suggest only a carefree and bookish adolescence; but the truest notes of Tennyson's early verse were in the key of personal and metaphysical melancholy. The life of the large family in the Lincolnshire parsonage of Somersby combined happiness with acute unhappiness. The Rev. George Tennyson, who could teach his boys the classics and encourage their writing, was a disinherited and embittered son whose temperament, situation and alcoholic consolation led to fits of insane violence, and at times the sensitive young Alfred longed for death. When the father died in 1831, the family was left with small resources, and some of the poet's brothers and sisters were problems. Though the wealthy and domineering grandfather came to the rescue, Tennyson was unable to return to Cambridge and had for years to shoulder difficult responsibilities.

Then there were the religious questions which, under the increasing pressure of both science and biblical criticism, were for the first time deeply disturbing large numbers of people. Tennyson had a religious background and a temperamental strain of mysticism, but he was also, from boyhood to old age, an eager student of science. His first elaborate statement was the poem originally entitled "Supposed Confessions of a Second-rate Sensitive Mind Not in Unity with Itself"—a title of self-mocking irony that is far from flippant. The question was brought home to him with crushing force by the death (September, 1833) of his beloved friend, Arthur Hallam, who had appeared to be the brightest star in the galaxy of the Cambridge "Apostles." Apart from the fact of devoted friendship, Tennyson's situation was like that of Milton two centuries earlier. The extinction of a young life of signal goodness and promise crystallized the whole religious, ethical and metaphysical problem: is there a purpose, a reality, behind the flux of life? Is the world a divine order or is it a meaningless chaos under the sway of blind Nature? Two centuries of scientific skepticism had made positive affirmation more difficult than it was for Milton, and the young Tennyson —he was, we may remember, only twenty-four—was torn between faith and doubt. One of his early utterances after Hallam's death was apparently the lyric "Break, Break, Break." "The Two Voices," in spite of a mawkish conclusion, is a full and moving presentation of the alternatives. In "Ulysses" the poet is seeking to rise above his grief and face life with resolution. In "Tithonus" he sinks under the burden of living. And from 1833 onward Tennyson was writing the lyrics that were eventually to be gathered together as "In Memoriam" (1850).

That great work was welcomed by many Victorians as a reassuring reconciliation of science and religion, but modern readers are more inclined to see its power in its utterances of stark despair, its pictures of a boundless and timeless world of elemental forces in which man is an insignificant atom. While it may be easy for us, conditioned as we are, to acquiesce in naturalistic negations or to evade such problems altogether, Tennyson, cut adrift in "the night of fear," could not take either course. Nowadays we may discount that part of his answer that rests on ideas of evolutionary progress, but his real answer is intuitive rather than philosophical: the reality of human love is itself evidence of a higher reality. Whether we go along with him or not, in affirming faith in God and immortality he had to surmount a skepticism quite as grim and bleak as Hardy's. We should not, by the way, be misled by the apparent confidence of the prologue, "Strong Son of God, immortal Love"; it is not so much an introduction as a conclusion reached after prolonged inward turmoil. And "In Memoriam" did not end Tennyson's questionings, which appeared even in his posthumous volume of 1892.

In addition to personal and family troubles and religious problems, Tennyson early encountered another set of questions which link him with the romantic poets and critics: what is the role and function of the poet in the modern world? The great poets of the preceding generation, reacting strongly against the scientific rationalism that had made both the universe and the human soul into machines, had asserted the supremacy of the poetic imagination and its intuitive apprehension of reality. But during the same period the industrial revolution—a wholesale application of science—had begun to change an age-old way of life into the mechanized civilization we know, and both industrialism and science in general were based on facts, ideas and values antagonistic to art, to the life of the senses and the imagination. In such a world, was the poet what he had been since antiquity, the nourisher of man's real life, the leader and teacher of his fellows, or was he only an insignificant spectator on the side lines, a solitary word-spinner in the midst of a busy and alien society? Even while the romantic poets had been exalting the sacred office of the poet, it was being said that poetry was essentially primitive, that it must decline with the advance of scientific knowledge and achievement.

That problem is one theme of "Timbuctoo," which won the Chancellor's Medal at Cambridge in 1829, and which remains more interesting than most prize poems. Here the spirit of poetry and myth, which has always fed man's aspirations, foresees her surrender to the desiccating spirit of science and civilization. "The Poet," on the other hand, expresses a messianic confidence that might be called Shelleyan (though *The Defence of Poetry* was not yet published). In other poems Tennyson was preoccupied, directly or indirectly, with aspects of this theme. In "The Hesperides"—a poem of pure incantation which, while quite original, makes us think of Coleridge and Blake—he seems to be celebrating the cloistered imagination. "The Lady of Shalott," though a miniature romance, shows a weaver of dreams drawn from seclusion into the world of actuality. In "Mariana" and "Œnone" the theme of isolation may be artistic as well as personal. "The Palace of Art" is an open parable of aesthetic detachment and the higher claims of social responsibility. The Lotos-Eaters, weary of action and hardship, embrace unheroic lassitude; Ulysses—leaving civic duties to his son—rouses himself to heroic enterprise.

It was of course the claims of responsibility that won, but the seriousness of the conflict was attested by the power with which

Tennyson could render the enchantments of aesthetic ease and isolation. It was attested in another way by his clinging, in spite of scanty means, to his art and refusing to seek any gainful occupation; and his work, rich and varied as it is, might have been stronger in some respects if he had been closer to the everyday world. His poetic friend and candid critic, Edward FitzGerald, who liked Tennyson's early poems much better than "that accursed Princess" and later things (and who lived on a comfortable competence), remarked in 1850: "It is the cursed inactivity (very pleasant to me who am no Hero) of this 19th century which has spoiled Alfred, I mean spoiled him for the great work he ought now to be entering upon; the lovely and noble things he has done must remain." However, the ex-member of "The Apostles" was not likely to avert his eyes from national problems, and it was the public poet who put the liberal-conservative wisdom of Burke into the speech of Pallas in "Œnone" and into the group of political poems, and surveyed the troubled state of England in "Locksley Hall." If this last poem seems to us mainly rhetoric, it was felt by earnest readers of the age as a call to action; and if its dramatic situation seems to us Victorian theatricalism, it had lately had a sort of parallel within the Tennyson clan.

Tennyson's first independent volumes, *Poems, Chiefly Lyrical* (1830) and *Poems* (1832), were roughly handled by a number of critics, notably "Christopher North" and John Wilson Croker (who had bludgeoned Keats some years earlier). As a result, the very sensitive young poet published no book for almost a decade. The two volumes of 1842 contained new poems and a selection of old ones, altogether a large proportion of his best work, and both old and new pieces showed that the author had heeded the strictures of hostile critics and the friendly counsel of others. Such early poems as "The Lady of Shalott," "Œnone," "The Palace of Art," "The Lotos-Eaters," and "A Dream of Fair Women" were radically revised and greatly improved; and in the new poems—though this was a natural development—there was less of pretty fancy and more of ethical and social seriousness.

The year 1850 brought "In Memoriam" (the work of seventeen years), Tennyson's appointment as Poet Laureate in succession to Wordsworth, and his long-delayed marriage. From then on, or rather from the appearance of the first "Idylls of the King" (1859), he grew more and more to be regarded, on both sides of the Atlantic, as a major prophet, and, despite the shyness that was mixed with innocent enjoyment of his fame, to live in something like the public glare of a Hollywood figure—though he could still draw criticism and could receive the ambiguous tribute of parody. It is often said that the consciousness of being an oracle and instinctive responsiveness to public taste and sentiment, along with the normal conservatism of advancing age, tamed a great poet and robust personality into a purveyor of popular uplift. That common notion may have a little truth, but it is not a key to Tennyson. The weaker as well as the stronger impulses of Victorianism had been present in him from the beginning and appeared in early as well as late poems; also, he wrote many fine things up through his last decades. It might be added—to glance ahead to the chief stumbling block, the "Idylls" —that the young Tennyson, like Keats, had poetic ambitions larger than his native gifts quite warranted, and, unlike Keats, he lived to carry them out.

We may or may not share the author's fondness for "Maud" (1855), his "little *Hamlet*," which he was happy to read aloud on all occasions (and which a humble American crossed the sea to recite to him). As a monodrama of unusual complexity, and as a study of revolt and mental derangement, "Maud" was a fairly bold experiment, which alienated many of Tennyson's public. Victorian poets in general were not given to variations of style and tone within a single work, though Tennyson had essayed that in "The Princess" and, more successfully, in the short "Vision of Sin"; and the author of "Maud" was evidently aware of the new "spasmodic" poetry of the early 1850's. But both his technique and his theme were thoroughly Tennysonian developments. The hero's feverish rebellion against the established social order reminds us of "Locksley Hall" (and again of the old feud in the Tennyson clan); and a number of poems had indicated Tennyson's capacity for rendering psychological disturbance. A good many people, sick of the Crimean War, condemned "Maud" for its apparent glorification of war; but the conclusion may be thought dramatically consistent. While the poem is no *Hamlet,* the picture of a young man's shattered world and shaken mind may be more acceptable in the age of Hemingway and Faulkner than it was in 1855.

After "Maud," Tennyson's major works, in magnitude if not in lasting poetical importance, were the long-meditated tales that became "Idylls of the King." (The plays we must pass by, though they contained some crisp writing and met some success on the stage.) The "Idylls," apart from one added in 1885, were published from 1859 to 1872; the early "Morte d'Arthur," somewhat revised, became the conclusion, "The Passing of Arthur." Tennyson put a great deal of work, and a great deal of himself, into the "Idylls," which were to be his *Paradise Lost,* and they contain many fine bits; but nowadays for the most part they are—along with "Enoch Arden" (1864)—skipped by even the poet's stanchest admirers. Whether or not we have Malory's great prose in mind, we are repelled by the satiny unreality, the stylized monotony, of Tennyson's versions. In "Lancelot and Elaine," for example, the lyrical magic of "The Lady of Shalott" is diluted into a romantic novelette. Then the handling of the allegorical theme, of "Sense at war with Soul," is not what we ask of poetic myth. If Guinevere is remote from Queen Victoria, the blameless king is rather too much of a glorified Prince Albert, and at times he seems to be wearing the garment consecrated by that name. In general, Tennyson's sincere and earnest idealism fails to move us because the "Idylls" seem to be, not an exploration of human strength and weakness, but a preconceived pattern imposed upon experience; because the poems, growing as they did, do not form an integrated whole; and because the texture is unrealistically decorative and literary. Yet the "Idylls" cannot be altogether dismissed. As in "In Memoriam," though much less often, Tennyson can be impressive in his dark moods of pessimism. The Holy Grail is not the high mystical goal of medieval quests, but a lure that shows up the neurotic egoism, the craving for spurious excitement, of many who seek it; the poem is in some sense a Victorian *Waste Land.* And in "The Holy Grail," "The Last Tournament," and elsewhere, the aging idealist's vision of the decay of an old order has a power that is absent from the hectoring of "Locksley Hall Sixty Years After."

The tenor of this last remark is still more true of Tennyson's indirect treatment of modern themes in his classical poems. "Lucretius," with its dramatic interweaving of motifs and phrases from "De Rerum Natura," is immeasurably more effective than such a modern and didactic counterpart as "Despair." If "Crossing the Bar" raises some doubts, none can touch the grandly Pindaric ending of "Tiresias." The "optimistic" conclusion of "Demeter and Persephone" (the work of a poet of seventy-seven) might be called a mythological version of the

> one far-off divine event,
> To which the whole creation moves.

but we respond much more to the myth than to the pious hope. Classical symbols, though they may not lend themselves to precise interpretation, carry a concrete richness of association and suggestion, whereas direct adumbrations of "the Ideal" may be merely vague. Most of these poems are monologues, with more of the descriptive, narrative and reflective than of the dramatic; the almost Browningesque violence and the tincture of Swinburnian sexuality in "Lucretius"—which grow out of the legend Tennyson was using—are not characteristic. If at times, as in "Œnone" and "Ulysses," the modern "message" is in danger of becoming obtrusive, the poems are more than saved by their beauty of texture and allusion. "Œnone," with its refrain and its scene-painting, is in the tradition of Theocritus, though the conclusion takes fire from Aeschylus and Virgil; and Tennyson was far happier with such a story and setting than in the supposedly Theocritean idylls of contemporary English life. The idea of Ulysses' western voyage, while hinted at in the *Odyssey* (xi. 119–37), is not Homeric, and Tennyson's "romantic" version is based on the twenty-sixth canto of Dante's *Inferno;* it is of interest also, in view of the emotional origins and theme of the poem, that he evidently had in mind a soliloquy of Hamlet's (IV. iv. 32–66). "Tithonus," as we have seen, originated likewise in Tennyson's grief for Hallam, and it simply develops the theme of age and loneliness and desire for death, without any overtones except what belong to the myth. The poem is perhaps the most perfect and poignant of Tennyson's classical re-creations.

It is a commonplace that Tennyson, in many respects so thoroughly English, is the most Virgilian of English poets. "To Virgil" is as noble a tribute as any modern poet has paid to an ancient, and we think of Tennyson himself when we read of the

> Landscape-lover, lord of language
>   more than he that sang the Works and Days,
> All the chosen coin of fancy
>   flashing out from many a golden phrase;

or (in "Poets and their Bibliographies") of

> Old Virgil who would write ten lines, they say,
> At dawn, and lavish all the golden day
> To make them wealthier in their readers' eyes.

Tennyson loved and echoed Homer, but even "Ulysses," and indeed the "Specimen of a Translation of the Iliad," have the inlaid phrasing and the slowness of pace that are Virgilian rather than Homeric.

The Virgil of the nineteenth century was the Virgil of *sunt lacrimae rerum et mentem mortalia tangunt*—"Thou majestic in thy sadness at the doubtful doom of human kind"—and Tennyson had a deep strain of that Virgilian mood. Many of his finest lyrics, such as "Tears, Idle Tears," are variations on the simple universal theme of mortality and the remembrance of things past. The lyrical poems in which Tennyson feels "the Passion of the Past" range from the early "Song: 'A spirit haunts the year's last hours,'" which has an unwonted immediacy of autumnal sensation, to the "Frater Ave Atque Vale" of fifty years later, in which he recalls Catullus' tender farewell and also, probably, the recent death of his own favorite brother. Tennyson did so many different things with such inspiration or competence that we may forget that he was the greatest lyrist of the century. In lyrics, as in poems on classical themes, he was likely to show all his strength and little or nothing of his weakness. One gift that is conspicuous in his poems of both kinds, and indeed almost anywhere in his writing, is not, on a high level, so common in poetry as it is assumed to be—that is, the gift for description. Cut off by both science and religion from Wordsworthian "mysticism," Tennyson, a much closer observer than Wordsworth, described the nature that his acute senses and human emotions gave him. Even in his saddest lyrics he makes "the too much loved earth more lovely," and above all, perhaps, he is the painter of the sea. He wrote some beautiful lyrics of love, in "The Princess" and "Maud," but these do not, like the lyrics of nature and the past, seem to well up from the depths of his being.

"In Memoriam" was not planned as a whole, and is hardly unified, but Tennyson was right in his instinct for "Short swallowflights of song." Within the ritualistic stylization there is variety of manner and tone and rhythm. Tennyson can be both ornate and simple, though his simplicity is not Wordsworthian but always aware of itself. In "In Memoriam" X he does not say "in the chancel" but

> where the kneeling hamlet drains
> The chalice of the grapes of God,

a periphrasis that might be defended as Dantesque if it were not a little overrefined. In the next lyric we have such a direct image and sensation as

> And only thro' the faded leaf
> The chestnut pattering to the ground,

and yet here too there is the touch of conscious design. Tennyson's elaborateness of periphrasis or compression may approach "metaphysical wit" and result in ambiguities and obscurities that trouble expositors of "In Memoriam." Other critics have had their fun with the elegant circumlocutions that dignify Enoch Arden's fish and King Arthur's mustache. But if at times Tennyson is too "poetical," as a rule his studied refinement of phrasing is essential to the theme and the effect; and it can hardly be called more artificial than the "colloquial" style of much modern poetry. "In Memoriam," like Tennyson's other best work, has countless passages of potent rightness, whether a vision of geological change,

> There rolls the deep where grew the tree.
> O earth, what changes hast thou seen!
> There where the long street roars hath been
> The stillness of the central sea,

or the descriptive setting and mystical experience of section XCV.

Tennyson's first volumes had linked him in the eyes of critics with the Keatsian tradition, and in 1846 hostile opinion was summed up in Bulwer-Lytton's lines about "School-Miss Alfred" and his

> jingling medley of purloin'd conceits,
> Outbabying Wordsworth, and outglittering Keats—

which drew from Tennyson "The New Timon and the Poets," a revelation of an unexpected talent for stinging satire. To think of Keats and Tennyson is perhaps to think less of resemblances than of profound differences, but there is the obvious affinity in pictorial richness. Yet we cannot simply identify Tennyson with the ornate, nor indeed can we properly speak of his "style," because he has many styles. In running through the contents of even a modest volume of selections, one cannot but recognize that no other poet of the century had such a range of manner as well as of theme—from the delicate, hovering elusiveness of "The Hesperides" to the ultra-Wordsworthian and biblical plainness of "Dora," from the primitive vitality of "The Kraken" to the gnomic political poems, from the sensuous concreteness of "Early Spring" to the metaphysical abstractions of "The Higher Pantheism," from the elegiac nostalgia of many lyrics to the semi-

Horatian addresses to friends, from the gorgeous felicity of the classical poems to the earthy felicity of the "Northern Farmer," from the romantic realism of "Mariana" to the macabre realism of "Rizpah," from the painful wrestling of "The Two Voices" to the quiet assurance of "The Ancient Sage," from the purely lyrical to the philosophical poems of "In Memoriam," from the heroic stateliness of the "Ode" on Wellington to the heroic balladry of "The Revenge," from the ecstasies and hysterias of "Maud" to the ecstasies and hysterias of "The Holy Grail." . . .

The same random list, and many other titles, remind us also of Tennyson's notable mastery and variety of rhythm, and what was said of his language, of the abundant success and occasional failures of highly conscious art, may be applied to both the minutiae and the total effects of his metrical virtuosity. And, again, there is seldom anything but complete success in the blank verse of most of the classical poems and the almost infinite variety of lyric measures (which include blank verse). To us Tennyson may seem to have worked within the orthodox tradition, but he could be boldly original and, within the limits of his versatile powers, he exploited to the full the resources of the language and of his almost too sensitive ear. As his revisions help to show, Tennyson was enormously concerned with problems of craftsmanship, and his range of experimentation embraced everything from a whole work like "Maud" to the management of pauses or the letter "s." Moreover, steeped as he was in some of the chief classical poets, he gave special study to quantitative values in English.

There are examples of onomatopoeia where the piling up of sonorous vowels or harsh consonants calls attention to itself, as in the panel-pictures of "The Palace of Art" or

> The moan of doves in immemorial elms,
> And murmuring of innumerable bees.

At the opposite pole from the too obviously labored, we find what is still contrivance, but in the modern manner:

> And ghastly thro' the drizzling rain
> On the bald street breaks the blank day,

where realistic bareness is heightened by a halting rhythm and unmusical monosyllabic alliteration. Most of Tennyson's rhythms, melodious or rugged, move between these extremes. It is odd, by the way, that a poet so given to the wedding of sound and sense should have written "Locksley Hall" in trochaics because he was told the English people liked that meter; the galloping lines are in frequent conflict with the theme and mood. But one should not speak of lapses or excesses when Tennyson provides such a wealth and diversity of music. In our day ears are attuned to more brittle—but, as with matters of phrasing, by no means less artificial—rhythms and may not relish Tennyson's elaborate and exquisite prosody; yet such leaders of modern poetry as Yeats and Mr. Eliot, however remote from Tennyson, do also create rhythmical patterns that stay in one's head.

Tennyson's preoccupation with the niceties of art and accuracy of description was perhaps one way of escape from the inward and outward conflicts and frustrations that tormented him; in a world of dissolving beliefs and values, a universe of overwhelming vastness, art and nature were at least solid and sure. Tennyson was much more than a polished mirror of Victorian England; he was in the main a great artist, very often a great poet. It is easy to catalogue his deficiencies, but it is wiser to enjoy the many things he did superbly. And we should not take shallowness for granted. Beneath the beautiful surfaces there are revelations of the dark abyss in which the poet's deepest self lived. In the essential nature of his idealism and his disillusioned melancholy, his pervading sense of irreparable loss, he is very much our contemporary, the poet of an age of anxiety.

This selection aims at presenting much of Tennyson's best poetry, but a few pieces that are not among his best are admitted because they represent areas of his poetical or intellectual interest. Poems are here printed roughly in the order of composition, though the order can be only approximate because the composition of a good many poems cannot be closely dated. Sometimes, especially for poems not published fairly soon after they were written, known or conjectural dates are given along with dates of publication. More than one date of publication indicates that a poem underwent considerable revision. The text of this edition, apart from a few silent corrections, follows that of the "Cambridge Edition" by W. J. Rolfe (published by Houghton Mifflin Company). I am obliged to two Tennysonian friends, Professor James B. Munn and Dr. Edgar F. Shannon, for looking over the prefatory matter and table of contents.

BIBLIOGRAPHY

Annotated editions of complete and selected works: *Works*, ed. Hallam Lord Tennyson, Eversley Edition, 6 vols., New York, 1908; the same, 1 vol., New York, 1913; *Poetic and Dramatic Works*, ed. W. J. Rolfe, Cambridge Edition, Boston, 1898; *Early Poems*, ed. J. C. Collins, London, 1900; *Selections*, ed. W. C. and M. P. De Vane, New York, 1940; *Representative Poems*, ed. S. C. Chew, New York, 1941; *Poems*, ed. J. H. Buckley, Boston, 1958; and selections in various anthologies of Victorian poetry. Sir Charles Tennyson edited *The Devil and the Lady* (London, 1930) and *Unpublished Early Poems* (London, 1931), and the two together (Bloomington, Ind., 1964).

Bagehot, Walter. "Wordsworth, Tennyson, and Browning; or, Pure, Ornate, and Grotesque in English Poetry" (1864). *Literary Studies*. 2 vols. 1879 and later edns.

Bateson, F. W., ed. *Cambridge Bibliography of English Literature*. New York, 1941, III, 253–58. Supplement, ed. G. Watson, 1957.

Baum, Paull F. *Tennyson Sixty Years After*. Chapel Hill, 1948

Beach, Joseph W. *The Concept of Nature in Nineteenth-Century English Poetry*. New York, 1936.

Benziger, James. *Images of Eternity: Studies in the Poetry of Religious Vision from Wordsworth to T. S. Eliot*. Carbondale, Ill., 1962.

Bradley, A. C. *A Commentary on Tennyson's In Memoriam*. Third Edition, Revised. London, 1910.

———. "The Reaction against Tennyson." *A Miscellany*. London, 1929.

Buckley, Jerome H. *Tennyson: The Growth of a Poet*. Cambridge, Mass., 1960.

Bush, Douglas. *Mythology and the Romantic Tradition in English Poetry*. Cambridge, Mass., 1937.

Carr, Arthur J. "Tennyson as a Modern Poet." *University of Toronto Quarterly*, 19 (1949–50), 361–82 (repr. in Killham, below).

Eliot, T. S. "In Memoriam." *Essays Ancient and Modern*. New York, 1936 (repr. in Killham, below).

Elton, Oliver. *A Survey of English Literature, 1780–1880*. 4 vols. New York, 1920.

Gransden, K. W. *Tennyson: In Memoriam*. London, 1964.

Green, Joyce. "Tennyson's Development during the 'Ten Years' Silence' (1832–1842)." *Publications of the Modern Language Association*, 66 (1951), 662–97.

Hough, Graham. "The Natural Theology of *In Memoriam*." *Review of English Studies*, 23 (1947), 244–56.

Houghton, Walter E. *The Victorian Frame of Mind 1830–1870*. New Haven, 1957.

Johnson, E. D. H. *The Alien Vision of Victorian Poetry*. Princeton, 1952.

Killham, John. *Tennyson and The Princess: Reflections of an Age*. London, 1958.

———, ed. *Critical Essays on the Poetry of Tennyson*. London and New York, 1960. (Includes—in addition to items noted above and below—essays by G. M. Young, G. R. Stange, L. Stevenson, C. Brooks, G. Hough, L. Spitzer, *et al*.)

MacCallum, Sir M. W. *Tennyson's Idylls of the King and Arthurian Story*. New York, 1894.

Mattis, Eleanor B. *In Memoriam: The Way of a Soul*. New York, 1951.

McLuhan, H. M. "Tennyson and Picturesque Poetry." *Essays in Criticism*, 1 (1951), 262–82 (repr. in Killham, above).

Mustard, W. P. *Classical Echoes in Tennyson*. New York, 1904.

Paden, W. D. *Tennyson in Egypt: A Study of the Imagery in His Earlier Work*. Lawrence, Kan., 1942.

Pitt, Valerie. *Tennyson Laureate*. London, 1962.

Preyer, Robert. "Tennyson as an Oracular Poet." *Modern Philology*, 55 (1957–58), 239–51.

Priestley, F. E. L. "Tennyson's *Idylls*." *University of Toronto Quarterly*, 19 (1949–50), 35–49 (repr. in Killham, above).

Rader, Ralph W. *Tennyson's Maud: The Biographical Genesis*. Berkeley, 1963.

Roppen, Georg. *Evolution and Poetic Belief*. Oslo and Oxford, 1956.

Ryals, C. de L. *Theme and Symbol in Tennyson's Early Poems to 1850* Philadelphia, 1964.

Shannon, Edgar F. *Tennyson and the Reviewers*. Cambridge, Mass., 1952.

———— and W. H. Bond. "Literary Manuscripts of Alfred Tennyson in the Harvard College Library." *Harvard Library Bulletin*, 10 (1956), 254–74.

Smith, Elton E. *The Two Voices: A Tennyson Study*. Lincoln, Neb., 1964.

Stevenson, Lionel. *Darwin among the Poets*. Chicago, 1932.

Tennyson, Sir Charles. *Six Tennyson Essays*. London, 1954.

Willey, Basil. "Tennyson." *More Nineteenth Century Studies*. London, 1956.

TENNYSON
SELECTED POETRY

THE DEVIL AND THE LADY [1]

ACT II

SCENE I [MAGUS's *cottage with the wood and lake in the distance. Enter* DEVIL *and takes his station before the cottage door attired in a cap and gown.*

DEVIL. The starry fires of yon Chrystalline vault
Are waning, and the airy-footed Night
Will soon withdraw the dismal solitude
Of her capacious pall, wherewith she clouds
Yon mighty and illimitable sky,
Placing a death-like colour in all things,
Monopolizing all the varied Earth
With her dim mantle—

                                    [*A pause*
                    Oh! ye eyes of Heaven,
Ye glorious inextinguishable lights,
High blazing mid the lone solemnity   10
Of night and silence, shall the poor worm, Man,
The creature of this solitary earth,
Presume to think his destiny enroll'd
In your almighty everlasting fires?
Shall this poor thing of melancholy clay,
This lone ephemeris of one small hour,
Proudly suppose his little fate inscribed
In the magnificent stars? What have the worlds
Of yon o'er arching Heav'n—the ample spheres
Of never-ending space, to do with Man?   20
And some romantick visionaries have deem'd
This petty clod the centre of all worlds.
Nay—even the Sun himself, the gorgeous Sun,
Pays homage to it. Ha! Ha! Ha! Poor Man,
Thou summer midge!—Oh, ye shine bravely now

---

[1] The two passages here given from *The Devil and the Lady by Alfred Tennyson, Edited by Charles Tennyson his Grandson* (Copyright 1930, Macmillan and Company, Limited, London) are used with the permission of The Macmillan Company, New York and London, and Sir Charles Tennyson.

The unfinished play was mostly written when the poet was fourteen.

Through the deep purple of the summer sky,
I know that ye are Earths as fair and fairer
And mightier than this I tread upon—
For I have scaled your mountains, to whose cones
Of most insuperable altitude   30
This Earth's most glorious Eminences and heights
All pil'd and heap'd upon each other's brows,
And massed and kneaded to one common substance,
Were but a molehill.
And I have swum your boundless seas, whose waves
Were each an ocean of this little orb,
Yet know I not your natures, or if that
Which we call palpable and visible
Is condensation of firm particles.
O suns and spheres and stars and belts and systems,   40
Are ye or are ye not?
Are ye realities or semblances
Of that which men call real?
Are ye true substance? are ye anything
Except delusive shows and physical points
Endow'd with some repulsive potency?
Could the Omnipotent fill all space, if ye
Or the least atom in ye or the least
Division of that atom (if least can dwell
In infinite divisibility) should be impenetrable?   50
I have some doubt if ye exist when none
Are by to view ye; if your Being alone
Be in the mind and the intelligence
Of the created? should some great decree
Annihilate the sentient principle
Would ye or would ye not be non-existent?
'Tis a shrewd doubt. . . .

ACT III (*From* SCENE II)

MAGUS. Half the powers o' th' other world
Were leagued against my journeying: but had not
The irresistible and lawless might
Of brazen-handed fix'd Fatality
Oppos'd me, I had done it. The black storm,
From out whose mass of volum'd vapour sprang
The lively curling thunderbolt had ceas'd

Long ere from out the dewy depth of Pines
Emerging on the hollow'd banks, that bound
The leapings of the saucy tide, I stood—   10
The mighty waste of moaning waters lay
So goldenly in moonlight, whose clear lamp
With its long line of vibratory lustre
Trembled on the dun surface, that my Spirit
Was buoyant with rejoicings. Each hoar wave
With crisped undulation arching rose,
Thence falling in white ridge with sinuous slope
Dash'd headlong to the shore and spread along
The sands its tender fringe of creamy spray.
Thereat my shallop lightly I unbound,   20
Spread my white sail and rode exulting on
The placid murmurings of each feathery wave
That hurried into sparkles round the cleaving
Of my dark Prow; but scarcely had I past
The third white line of breakers when a squall
Fell on me from the North, an inky Congress
O' the Republican clouds unto the zenith
Rush'd from th' horizon upwards with the speed
Of their own thunder-bolts.
The seas divided and dim Phantasies   30
Came thronging thickly round me, with hot eyes
Unutterable things came flitting by me;
Semblance of palpability was in them,
Albeit the wavering lightnings glitter'd thro'
Their shadow'd immaterialities.
Black shapes clung to my boat; a sullen owl
Perch'd on the Prow, and overhead the hum
As of infernal Spirits in mid Heaven
Holding aerial council caught mine ear.
Then came a band of melancholy sprites,   40
White as their shrouds and motionlessly pale
Like some young Ashwood when the argent Moon
Looks in upon its many silver stems. . . .
                            [1823–24; publ. 1930]

TIMBUCTOO

"Deep in that lion-haunted inland lies
A mystic city, goal of high emprise."
CHAPMAN.[1]

I STOOD upon the Mountain which o'erlooks
The narrow seas, whose rapid interval
Parts Afric from green Europe, when the Sun
Had fall'n below th' Atlantic, and above
The silent heavens were blench'd with faery light,
Uncertain whether faery light or cloud,
Flowing Southward, and the chasms of deep, deep blue
Slumber'd unfathomable, and the stars
Were flooded over with clear glory and pale.
I gazed upon the sheeny coast beyond,   10
There where the Giant of old Time infix'd
The limits of his prowess, pillars high
Long time erased from earth: even as the Sea
When weary of wild inroad buildeth up
Huge mounds whereby to stay his yeasty waves.
And much I mused on legends quaint and old
Which whilome won the hearts of all on earth
Toward their brightness, ev'n as flame draws air;
But had their being in the heart of man
As air is th' life of flame: and thou wert then   20
A center'd glory-circled memory,
Divinest Atalantis, whom the waves
Have buried deep, and thou of later name,
Imperial Eldorado, roof'd with gold:
Shadows to which, despite all shocks of change,
All on-set of capricious accident,
Men clung with yearning hope which would not die.
As when in some great city where the walls
Shake, and the streets with ghastly faces throng'd,
Do utter forth a subterranean voice,   30
Among the inner columns far retired
At midnight, in the lone Acropolis,

[1] These two lines do not seem to be George Chapman's and may have been Tennyson's own.

Before the awful Genius of the place
Kneels the pale Priestess in deep faith, the while
Above her head the weak lamp dips and winks
Unto the fearful summoning without:
Nathless she ever clasps the marble knees,
Bathes the cold hands with tears, and gazeth on
Those eyes which wear no light but that wherewith
Her phantasy informs them.
                              Where are ye,   **40**
Thrones of the Western wave, fair Islands green?
Where are your moonlight halls, your cedarn glooms,
The blossoming abysses of your hills?
Your flowering capes, and your gold-sanded bays
Blown round with happy airs of odorous winds?
Where are the infinite ways, which, seraph-trod,
Wound thro' your great Elysian solitudes,
Whose lowest deeps were, as with visible love,
Fill'd with Divine effulgence, circumfused,
Flowing between the clear and polish'd stems,   **50**
And ever circling round their emerald cones
In coronals and glories, such as gird
The unfading foreheads of the Saints in Heaven?
For nothing visible, they say, had birth
In that blest ground, but it was play'd about
With its peculiar glory. Then I raised
My voice and cried, "Wide Afric, doth thy Sun
Lighten, thy hills enfold a city as fair
As those which starr'd the night o' the elder world?
Or is the rumour of thy Timbuctoo   **60**
A dream as frail as those of ancient time?"
    A curve of whitening, flashing, ebbing light!
A rustling of white wings! the bright descent
Of a young Seraph! and he stood beside me
There on the ridge, and look'd into my face
With his unutterable, shining orbs.
So that with hasty motion I did veil
My vision with both hands, and saw before me
Such colour'd spots as dance athwart the eyes
Of those that gaze upon the noonday Sun.   **70**
Girt with a zone of flashing gold beneath
His breast, and compass'd round about his brow
With triple arch of ever-changing bows,

And circled with the glory of living light
And alternation of all hues, he stood.
   "O child of man, why muse you here alone
Upon the Mountain, on the dreams of old
Which fill'd the earth with passing loveliness,
Which flung strange music on the howling winds,
And odours rapt from remote Paradise?   80
Thy sense is clogg'd with dull mortality;
Thy spirit fetter'd with the bond of clay:
Open thine eyes and see."
                  I look'd, but not
Upon his face, for it was wonderful
With its exceeding brightness, and the light
Of the great Angel Mind which look'd from out
The starry glowing of his restless eyes.
I felt my soul grow mighty, and my spirit
With supernatural excitation bound
Within me, and my mental eye grew large   90
With such a vast circumference of thought,
That in my vanity I seem'd to stand
Upon the outward verge and bound alone
Of full beatitude. Each failing sense,
As with a momentary flash of light,
Grew thrillingly distinct and keen. I saw
The smallest grain that dappled the dark earth,
The indistinctest atom in deep air,
The Moon's white cities, and the opal width
Of her small glowing lakes, her silver heights   100
Unvisited with dew of vagrant cloud,
And the unsounded, undescended depth
Of her black hollows. The clear galaxy
Shorn of its hoary lustre, wonderful,
Distinct and vivid with sharp points of light,
Blaze within blaze, an unimagin'd depth
And harmony of planet-girded suns
And moon-encircled planets, wheel in wheel,
Arch'd the wan sapphire. Nay—the hum of men,
Or other things talking in unknown tongues,   110
And notes of busy life in distant worlds
Beat like a far wave on my anxious ear.
   A maze of piercing, trackless, thrilling thoughts,
Involving and embracing each with each,

Rapid as fire, inextricably link'd,
Expanding momently with every sight
And sound which struck the palpitating sense,
The issue of strong impulse, hurried through
The riven rapt brain; as when in some large lake
From pressure of descendant crags, which lapse   120
Disjointed, crumbling from their parent slope
At slender interval, the level calm
Is ridg'd with restless and increasing spheres
Which break upon each other, each th' effect
Of separate impulse, but more fleet and strong
Than its precursor, till the eye in vain
Amid the wild unrest of swimming shade
Dappled with hollow and alternate rise
Of interpenetrated arc, would scan
Definite round.

         I know not if I shape   130
These things with accurate similitude
From visible objects, for but dimly now,
Less vivid than a half-forgotten dream,
The memory of that mental excellence
Comes o'er me, and it may be I entwine
The indecision of my present mind
With its past clearness, yet it seems to me
As even then the torrent of quick thought
Absorbed me from the nature of itself
With its own fleetness. Where is he that, borne   140
Adown the sloping of an arrowy stream,
Could link his shallop to the fleeting edge,
And muse midway with philosophic calm
Upon the wondrous laws which regulate
The fierceness of the bounding element?
    My thoughts which long had grovell'd in the slime
Of this dull world, like dusky worms which house
Beneath unshaken waters, but at once
Upon some earth-awakening day of Spring
Do pass from gloom to glory, and aloft   150
Winnow the purple, bearing on both sides
Double display of star-lit wings, which burn
Fan-like and fibred with intensest bloom;
Ev'n so my thoughts, erewhile so low, now felt
Unutterable buoyancy and strength

To bear them upward through the trackless fields
Of undefin'd existence far and free.
    Then first within the South methought I saw
A wilderness of spires, and chrystal pile
Of rampart upon rampart, dome on dome,   **160**
Illimitable range of battlement
On battlement, and the imperial height
Of canopy o'ercanopied.
                Behind
In diamond light upsprung the dazzling peaks
Of Pyramids, as far surpassing earth's
As heaven than earth is fairer. Each aloft
Upon his narrow'd eminence bore globes
Of wheeling suns, or stars, or semblances
Of either, showering circular abyss
Of radiance. But the glory of the place   **170**
Stood out a pillar'd front of burnish'd gold,
Interminably high, if gold it were
Or metal more etherial, and beneath
Two doors of blinding brilliance, where no gaze
Might rest, stood open, and the eye could scan,
Through length of porch and valve and boundless hall,
Part of a throne of fiery flame, wherefrom
The snowy skirting of a garment hung,
And glimpse of multitudes of multitudes
That minister'd around it—if I saw   **180**
These things distinctly, for my human brain
Stagger'd beneath the vision, and thick night
Came down upon my eyelids, and I fell.
    With ministering hand he raised me up:
Then with a mournful and ineffable smile,
Which but to look on for a moment fill'd
My eyes with irresistible sweet tears,
In accents of majestic melody,
Like a swoln river's gushings in still night
Mingled with floating music, thus he spake: **190**
    "There is no mightier Spirit than I to sway
The heart of man: and teach him to attain
By shadowing forth the Unattainable;
And step by step to scale that mighty stair
Whose landing-place is wrapt about with clouds

Of glory of heaven.[1] With earliest light of Spring,
And in the glow of sallow Summertide,
And in red Autumn when the winds are wild
With gambols, and when full-voiced Winter roofs
The headland with inviolate white snow,   200
I play about his heart a thousand ways,
Visit his eyes with visions, and his ears
With harmonies of wind and wave and wood,—
Of winds which tell of waters, and of waters
Betraying the close kisses of the wind—
And win him unto me: and few there be
So gross of heart who have not felt and known
A higher than they see: They with dim eyes
Behold me darkling. Lo! I have given thee
To understand my presence, and to feel   210
My fullness; I have fill'd thy lips with power.
I have raised thee nigher to the spheres of heaven,
Man's first, last home: and thou with ravish'd sense
Listenest the lordly music flowing from
Th' illimitable years. I am the Spirit,
The permeating life which courseth through
All th' intricate and labyrinthine veins
Of the great vine of Fable, which, outspread
With growth of shadowing leaf and clusters rare,
Reacheth to every corner under heaven,   220
Deep-rooted in the living soil of truth;
So that men's hopes and fears take refuge in
The fragrance of its complicated glooms,
And cool impleachèd twilights. Child of man,
See'st thou yon river, whose translucent wave,
Forth issuing from the darkness, windeth through
The argent streets o' th' city, imaging
The soft inversion of her tremulous domes,
Her gardens frequent with the stately palm,
Her pagods hung with music of sweet bells,   230
Her obelisks of rangèd chrysolite,
Minarets and towers? Lo! how he passeth by,
And gulphs himself in sands, as not enduring

---

[1] "Be ye perfect even as your Father in heaven is perfect." [Tennyson's note]

To carry through the world those waves, which bore
The reflex of my city in their depths.
Oh city! oh latest throne! where I was raised
To be a mystery of loveliness
Unto all eyes, the time is well-nigh come
When I must render up this glorious home
To keen Discovery: soon yon brilliant towers   240
Shall darken with the waving of her wand;
Darken, and shrink and shiver into huts,
Black specks amid a waste of dreary sand,
Low-built, mud-wall'd, barbarian settlements.
How chang'd from this fair city!"
                                 Thus far the Spirit:
Then parted heaven-ward on the wing: and I
Was left alone on Calpe, and the moon
Had fallen from the night, and all was dark!
                              [1824–29; publ. 1829]

SUPPOSED CONFESSIONS

OF A SECOND-RATE SENSITIVE MIND

O God! my God! have mercy now.
I faint, I fall. Men say that Thou
Didst die for me, for such as *me*,
Patient of ill, and death, and scorn,
And that my sin was as a thorn
Among the thorns that girt Thy brow,
Wounding Thy soul.—That even now,
In this extremest misery
Of ignorance, I should require
A sign! and if a bolt of fire   10
Would rive the slumbrous summer noon
While I do pray to Thee alone,
Think my belief would stronger grow!
Is not my human pride brought low?
The boastings of my spirit still?
The joy I had in my free-will
All cold, and dead, and corpse-like grown?
And what is left to me but Thou,
And faith in Thee? Men pass me by;

Christians with happy countenances— 20
And children all seem full of Thee!
And women smile with saint-like glances
Like Thine own mother's when she bow'd
Above Thee, on that happy morn
When angels spake to men aloud,
And Thou and peace to earth were born.
Good-will to me as well as all—
I one of them; my brothers they;
Brothers in Christ—a world of peace
And confidence, day after day; 30
And trust and hope till things should cease,
And then one Heaven receive us all.

How sweet to have a common faith!
To hold a common scorn of death!
And at a burial to hear
The creaking cords which wound and eat
Into my human heart, whene'er
Earth goes to earth, with grief, not fear,
With hopeful grief, were passing sweet!

Thrice happy state again to be 40
The trustful infant on the knee,
Who lets his rosy fingers play
About his mother's neck, and knows
Nothing beyond his mother's eyes!
They comfort him by night and day;
They light his little life alway;
He hath no thought of coming woes;
He hath no care of life or death;
Scarce outward signs of joy arise,
Because the Spirit of happiness 50
And perfect rest so inward is;
And loveth so his innocent heart,
Her temple and her place of birth,
Where she would ever wish to dwell,
Life of the fountain there, beneath
Its salient springs, and far apart,
Hating to wander out on earth,
Or breathe into the hollow air,
Whose chillness would make visible

Her subtil, warm, and golden breath,   60
Which mixing with the infant's blood,
Fulfils him with beatitude.
O, sure it is a special care
Of God, to fortify from doubt,
To arm in proof, and guard about
With triple-mailed trust, and clear
Delight, the infant's dawning year.

Would that my gloomed fancy were
As thine, my mother, when with brows
Propt on thy knees, my hands upheld   70
In thine, I listen'd to thy vows,
For me outpour'd in holiest prayer—
For me unworthy!—and beheld
Thy mild deep eyes upraised, that knew
The beauty and repose of faith,
And the clear spirit shining thro'.
O, wherefore do we grow awry
From roots which strike so deep? why dare
Paths in the desert? Could not I
Bow myself down, where thou hast knelt,   80
To the earth—until the ice would melt
Here, and I feel as thou hast felt?
What devil had the heart to scathe
Flowers thou hadst rear'd—to brush the dew
From thine own lily, when thy grave
Was deep, my mother, in the clay?
Myself? Is it thus? Myself? Had I
So little love for thee? But why
Prevail'd not thy pure prayers? Why pray
To one who heeds not, who can save   90
But will not? Great in faith, and strong
Against the grief of circumstance
Wert thou, and yet unheard. What if
Thou pleadest still, and seest me drive
Thro' utter dark a full-sail'd skiff,
Unpiloted i' the echoing dance
Of reboant whirlwinds, stooping low
Unto the death, not sunk! I know
At matins and at evensong,
That thou, if thou wert yet alive,   100

In deep and daily prayers wouldst strive
To reconcile me with thy God.
Albeit, my hope is gray, and cold
At heart, thou wouldest murmur still—
"Bring this lamb back into Thy fold,
My Lord, if so it be Thy will."
Wouldst tell me I must brook the rod
And chastisement of human pride;
That pride, the sin of devils, stood,
Betwixt me and the light of God;   110
That hitherto I had defied
And had rejected God—that grace
Would drop from His o'er-brimming love,
As manna on my wilderness,
If I would pray—that God would move
And strike the hard, hard rock, and thence,
Sweet in their utmost bitterness,
Would issue tears of penitence
Which would keep green hope's life. Alas!
I think that pride hath now no place   120
Nor sojourn in me. I am void,
Dark, formless, utterly destroyed.

Why not believe then? Why not yet
Anchor thy frailty there, where man
Hath moor'd and rested? Ask the sea
At midnight, when the crisp slope waves
After a tempest rib and fret
The broad-imbased beach, why he
Slumbers not like a mountain tarn?
Wherefore his ridges are not curls   130
And ripples of an inland mere?
Wherefore he moaneth thus, nor can
Draw down into his vexed pools
All that blue heaven which hues and paves
The other? I am too forlorn,
Too shaken: my own weakness fools
My judgment, and my spirit whirls,
Moved from beneath with doubt and fear.

"Yet," said I, in my morn of youth,
The unsunn'd freshness of my strength,   140

When I went forth in quest of truth,
"It is man's privilege to doubt,
If so be that from doubt at length
Truth may stand forth unmoved of change,
An image with profulgent brows
And perfect limbs, as from the storm
Of running fires and fluid range
Of lawless airs, at last stood out
This excellence and solid form
Of constant beauty. For the ox   **150**
Feeds in the herb, and sleeps, or fills
The horned valleys all about,
And hollows of the fringed hills
In summer heats, with placid lows
Unfearing, till his own blood flows
About his hoof. And in the flocks
The lamb rejoiceth in the year,
And raceth freely with his fere,
And answers to his mother's calls
From the flower'd furrow. In a time   **160**
Of which he wots not, run short pains
Thro' his warm heart; and then, from whence
He knows not, on his light there falls
A shadow; and his native slope,
Where he was wont to leap and climb,
Floats from his sick and filmed eyes,
And something in the darkness draws
His forehead earthward, and he dies.
Shall man live thus, in joy and hope
As a young lamb, who cannot dream,   **170**
Living, but that he shall live on?
Shall we not look into the laws
Of life and death, and things that seem,
And things that be, and analyze
Our double nature, and compare
All creeds till we have found the one,
If one there be?" Ay me! I fear
All may not doubt, but everywhere
Some must clasp idols. Yet, my God,
Whom call I idol? Let Thy dove   **180**
Shadow me over, and my sins
Be unremember'd, and Thy love

Enlighten me. O, teach me yet
Somewhat before the heavy clod
Weighs on me, and the busy fret
Of that sharp-headed worm begins
In the gross blackness underneath.

O weary life! O weary death!
O spirit and heart made desolate!
O damned vacillating state!   **190**

[publ. 1830]

THE KRAKEN

Below the thunders of the upper deep,
Far, far beneath in the abysmal sea,
His ancient, dreamless, uninvaded sleep
The Kraken sleepeth: faintest sunlights flee
About his shadowy sides; above him swell
Huge sponges of millennial growth and height;
And far away into the sickly light,
From many a wondrous grot and secret cell
Unnumber'd and enormous polypi
Winnow with giant arms the slumbering green.   **10**
There hath he lain for ages, and will lie
Battening upon huge sea-worms in his sleep,
Until the latter fire shall heat the deep;
Then once by man and angels to be seen,
In roaring he shall rise and on the surface die.

[publ. 1830]

MARIANA

"Mariana in the moated grange."
Measure for Measure.

With blackest moss the flower-plots
    Were thickly crusted, one and all;
The rusted nails fell from the knots
    That held the pear to the gable-wall.

The broken sheds look'd sad and strange:
   Unlifted was the clinking latch;
  Weeded and worn the ancient thatch
Upon the lonely moated grange.
     She only said, "My life is dreary,
      He cometh not," she said;
     She said, "I am aweary, aweary,
      I would that I were dead!"

Her tears fell with the dews at even;
   Her tears fell ere the dews were dried;
She could not look on the sweet heaven,
   Either at morn or eventide.
After the flitting of the bats,
   When thickest dark did trance the sky,
   She drew her casement-curtain by,
And glanced athwart the glooming flats.
     She only said, "The night is dreary,
      He cometh not," she said;
     She said, "I am aweary, aweary,
      I would that I were dead!"

Upon the middle of the night,
   Waking she heard the night-fowl crow;
The cock sung out an hour ere light;
   From the dark fen the oxen's low
Came to her; without hope of change,
   In sleep she seem'd to walk forlorn,
   Till cold winds woke the gray-eyed morn
About the lonely moated grange.
     She only said, "The day is dreary,
      He cometh not," she said;
     She said, "I am aweary, aweary,
      I would that I were dead!"

About a stone-cast from the wall
   A sluice with blacken'd waters slept,
And o'er it many, round and small,
   The cluster'd marish-mosses crept.
Hard by a poplar shook alway,
   All silver-green with gnarled bark:
   For leagues no other tree did mark

The level waste, the rounding gray.
    She only said, "My life is dreary,
      He cometh not," she said;
    She said, "I am aweary, aweary,
      I would that I were dead!"

And ever when the moon was low,
    And the shrill winds were up and away,   50
In the white curtain, to and fro,
    She saw the gusty shadow sway.
But when the moon was very low,
    And wild winds bound within their cell,
    The shadow of the poplar fell
Upon her bed, across her brow.
    She only said, "The night is dreary,
      He cometh not," she said;
    She said, "I am aweary, aweary,
      I would that I were dead!"   60

All day within the dreamy house,
    The doors upon their hinges creak'd;
The blue fly sung in the pane; the mouse
    Behind the mouldering wainscot shriek'd,
Or from the crevice peer'd about.
    Old faces glimmer'd thro' the doors,
    Old footsteps trod the upper floors,
Old voices called her from without.
    She only said, "My life is dreary,
      He cometh not," she said;   70
    She said, "I am aweary, aweary,
      I would that I were dead!"

The sparrow's chirrup on the roof,
    The slow clock ticking, and the sound
Which to the wooing wind aloof
    The poplar made, did all confound
Her sense; but most she loathed the hour
    When the thick-moted sunbeam lay
    Athwart the chambers, and the day
Was sloping toward his western bower.   80
    Then, said she, "I am very dreary,
      He will not come," she said;

She wept, "I am aweary, aweary,
Oh God, that I were dead!"
[publ. 1830]

RECOLLECTIONS OF THE ARABIAN NIGHTS

WHEN the breeze of a joyful dawn blew free
In the silken sail of infancy,
The tide of time flow'd back with me,
   The forward-flowing tide of time;
And many a sheeny summer-morn,
Adown the Tigris I was borne,
By Bagdat's shrines of fretted gold,
High-walled gardens green and old;
True Mussulman was I and sworn,
   For it was in the golden prime   10
      Of good Haroun Alraschid.

Anight my shallop, rustling thro'
The low and bloomed foliage, drove
The fragrant, glistening deeps, and clove
The citron-shadows in the blue;
By garden porches on the brim,
The costly doors flung open wide,
Gold glittering thro' lamplight dim,
And broider'd sofas on each side.
   In sooth it was a goodly time,   20
   For it was in the golden prime
      Of good Haroun Alraschid.

Often, where clear-stemm'd platans guard
The outlet, did I turn away
The boat-head down a broad canal
From the main river sluiced, where all
The sloping of the moonlit sward
Was damask-work, and deep inlay
Of braided blooms unmown, which crept
Adown to where the water slept.   30
   A goodly place, a goodly time,

For it was in the golden prime
   Of good Haroun Alraschid.

A motion from the river won
Ridged the smooth level, bearing on
My shallop thro' the star-strown calm,
Until another night in night
I enter'd, from the clearer light,
Imbower'd vaults of pillar'd palm,
Imprisoning sweets, which, as they clomb   **40**
Heavenward, were stay'd beneath the dome
   Of hollow boughs. A goodly time,
    For it was in the golden prime
      Of good Haroun Alraschid.

Still onward; and the clear canal
Is rounded to as clear a lake.
From the green rivage many a fall
Of diamond rillets musical,
Thro' little crystal arches low
Down from the central fountain's flow   **50**
Fallen silver-chiming, seemed to shake
The sparkling flints beneath the prow.
   A goodly place, a goodly time,
    For it was in the golden prime
      Of good Haroun Alraschid.

Above thro' many a bowery turn
A walk with vari-colored shells
Wander'd engrain'd. On either side
All round about the fragrant marge
From fluted vase, and brazen urn   **60**
In order, eastern flowers large,
Some dropping low their crimson bells
Half-closed, and others studded wide
   With disks and tiars, fed the time
    With odor in the golden prime
      Of good Haroun Alraschid.

Far off, and where the lemon grove
In closest coverture upsprung,

The living airs of middle night
Died round the bulbul as he sung;   '70
Not he, but something which possess'd
The darkness of the world, delight,
Life, anguish, death, immortal love,
Ceasing not, mingled, unrepress'd,
    Apart from place, withholding time,
    But flattering the golden prime
      Of good Haroun Alraschid.

Black the garden-bowers and grots
Slumber'd; the solemn palms were ranged
Above, unwoo'd of summer wind;   80
A sudden splendor from behind
Flush'd all the leaves with rich gold-green,
And, flowing rapidly between
Their interspaces, counterchanged
The level lake with diamond-plots
    Of dark and bright. A lovely time,
    For it was in the golden prime
      Of good Haroun Alraschid.

Dark-blue the deep sphere overhead,
Distinct with vivid stars inlaid,   90
Grew darker from that under-flame;
So, leaping lightly from the boat,
With silver anchor left afloat,
In marvel whence that glory came
Upon me, as in sleep I sank
In cool soft turf upon the bank,
    Entranced with that place and time,
    So worthy of the golden prime
      Of good Haroun Alraschid.

Thence thro' the garden I was drawn—   100
A realm of pleasance, many a mound,
And many a shadow-chequer'd lawn
Full of the city's stilly sound,
And deep myrrh-thickets blowing round
The stately cedar, tamarisks,
Thick rosaries of scented thorn,
Tall orient shrubs, and obelisks

Graven with emblems of the time,
In honor of the golden prime
    Of good Haroun Alraschid. 110

With dazed vision unawares
From the long alley's latticed shade
Emerged, I came upon the great
Pavilion of the Caliphat.
Right to the carven cedarn doors,
Flung inward over spangled floors,
Broad-based flights of marble stairs
Ran up with golden balustrade,
    After the fashion of the time,
    And humor of the golden prime 120
      Of good Haroun Alraschid.

The fourscore windows all alight
As with the quintessence of flame,
A million tapers flaring bright
From twisted silvers look'd to shame
The hollow-vaulted dark, and stream'd
Upon the mooned domes aloof
In inmost Bagdat, till there seem'd
Hundreds of crescents on the roof
    Of night new-risen, that marvellous time 130
    To celebrate the golden prime
      Of good Haroun Alraschid.

Then stole I up, and trancedly
Gazed on the Persian girl alone,
Serene with argent-lidded eyes
Amorous, and lashes like to rays
Of darkness, and a brow of pearl
Tressed with redolent ebony,
In many a dark delicious curl,
Flowing beneath her rose-hued zone; 140
    The sweetest lady of the time,
    Well worthy of the golden prime
      Of good Haroun Alraschid.

Six columns, three on either side
Pure silver, underpropt a rich

Throne of the massive ore, from which
Down-droop'd, in many a floating fold,
Engarlanded and diaper'd
With inwrought flowers, a cloth of gold.
Thereon, his deep eye laughter-stirr'd   **150**
With merriment of kingly pride,
 Sole star of all that place and time,
 I saw him—in his golden prime,
  THE GOOD HAROUN ALRASCHID.
         [publ. 1830]

SONG

I

A SPIRIT haunts the year's last hours
Dwelling amid these yellowing bowers.
  To himself he talks;
For at eventide, listening earnestly,
At his work you may hear him sob and sigh
  In the walks;
 Earthward he boweth the heavy stalks
Of the mouldering flowers.
  Heavily hangs the broad sunflower
   Over its grave i' the earth so chilly;   **10**
  Heavily hangs the hollyhock
   Heavily hangs the tiger-lily.

II

The air is damp, and hush'd, and close,
As a sick man's room when he taketh repose
  An hour before death;
My very heart faints and my whole soul grieves
At the moist rich smell of the rotting leaves,
  And the breath
 Of the fading edges of box beneath,
And the year's last rose.   **20**
  Heavily hangs the broad sunflower
   Over its grave i' the earth so chilly;

Heavily hangs the hollyhock,
   Heavily hangs the tiger-lily.
                    [publ. 1830]

THE POET

THE poet in a golden clime was born,
   With golden stars above;
Dower'd with the hate of hate, the scorn of scorn,
   The love of love.

He saw thro' life and death, thro' good and ill,
   He saw thro' his own soul.
The marvel of the everlasting will,
    An open scroll,

Before him lay; with echoing feet he threaded
    The secretest walks of fame: **10**
The viewless arrows of his thoughts were headed
    And wing'd with flame,

Like Indian reeds blown from his silver tongue,
   And of so fierce a flight,
From Calpe unto Caucasus they sung,
    Filling with light

And vagrant melodies the winds which bore
    Them earthward till they lit;
Then, like the arrow-seeds of the field flower,
    The fruitful wit   **20**

Cleaving took root, and springing forth anew
    Where'er they fell, behold,
Like to the mother plant in semblance, grew
    A flower all gold,

And bravely furnish'd all abroad to fling
    The winged shafts of truth,
To throng with stately blooms the breathing spring
    Of Hope and Youth.

So many minds did gird their orbs with beams,
    Tho' one did fling the fire;   30
Heaven flow'd upon the soul in many dreams
    Of high desire.

Thus truth was multiplied on truth, the world
    Like one great garden show'd,
And thro' the wreaths of floating dark upcurl'd,
    Rare sunrise flow'd.

And Freedom rear'd in that august sunrise
    Her beautiful bold brow,
When rites and forms before his burning eyes
    Melted like snow.   40

There was no blood upon her maiden robes
    Sunn'd by those orient skies;
But round about the circles of the globes
    Of her keen eyes

And in her raiment's hem was traced in flame
    WISDOM, a name to shake
All evil dreams of power—a sacred name.
    And when she spake,

Her words did gather thunder as they ran,
    And as the lightning to the thunder   50
Which follows it, riving the spirit of man,
    Making earth wonder,

So was their meaning to her words. No sword
    Of wrath her right arm whirl'd,
But one poor poet's scroll, and with *his* word
    She shook the world.

                  [publ. 1830]

THE POET'S MIND

I

Vex not thou the poet's mind
  With thy shallow wit;
Vex not thou the poet's mind,
  For thou canst not fathom it.
Clear and bright it should be ever,
Flowing like a crystal river,
Bright as light, and clear as wind.

II

Dark-brow'd sophist, come not anear;
  All the place is holy ground;
  Hollow smile and frozen sneer   10
    Come not here.
    Holy water will I pour
    Into every spicy flower
Of the laurel-shrubs that hedge it around.
The flowers would faint at your cruel cheer.
  In your eye there is death,
  There is frost in your breath
  Which would blight the plants.
  Where you stand you cannot hear
    From the groves within   20
    The wild-bird's din.
In the heart of the garden the merry bird chants.
It would fall to the ground if you came in.
  In the middle leaps a fountain
    Like sheet lightning,
    Ever brightening
  With a low melodious thunder;
All day and all night it is ever drawn
  From the brain of the purple mountain
  Which stands in the distance yonder.   30
It springs on a level of bowery lawn,
And the mountain draws it from heaven above,
And it sings a song of undying love;

And yet, tho' its voice be so clear and full,
You never would hear it, your ears are so dull;
So keep where you are; you are foul with sin;
It would shrink to the earth if you came in.

[publ. 1830]

THE DYING SWAN

I

THE plain was grassy, wild and bare,
Wide, wild, and open to the air,
Which had built up everywhere
  An under-roof of doleful gray.
With an inner voice the river ran,
Adown it floated a dying swan,
    And loudly did lament.
  It was the middle of the day.
Ever the weary wind went on,
    And took the reed-tops as it went.   10

II

Some blue peaks in the distance rose,
And white against the cold-white sky
Shone out their crowning snows.
  One willow over the river wept,
And shook the wave as the wind did sigh;
Above in the wind was the swallow,
    Chasing itself at its own wild will,
    And far thro' the marish green and still
    The tangled water-courses slept,
Shot over with purple, and green, and yellow.   20

III

The wild swan's death-hymn took the soul
Of that waste place with joy
Hidden in sorrow. At first to the ear
The warble was low, and full and clear;
And floating about the under-sky,

Prevailing in weakness, the coronach stole
Sometimes afar, and sometimes anear;
But anon her awful jubilant voice,
With a music strange and manifold,
Flow'd forth on a carol free and bold;   30
As when a mighty people rejoice
With shawms, and with cymbals, and harps of gold,
And the tumult of their acclaim is roll'd
Thro' the open gates of the city afar,
To the shepherd who watcheth the evening star.
And the creeping mosses and clambering weeds,
And the willow-branches hoar and dank,
And the wavy swell of the soughing reeds,
And the wave-worn horns of the echoing bank,
And the silvery marish-flowers that throng   40
The desolate creeks and pools among,
Were flooded over with eddying song.
                                        [publ. 1830]

THE HESPERIDES

"Hesperus and his daughters three
That sing about the golden tree."
                                        Comus.

THE North wind fall'n, in the new-starréd night
Zidonian Hanno, voyaging beyond
The hoary promontory of Soloë,
Past Thymiaterion, in calméd bays,
Between the southern and the western Horn,
Heard neither warbling of the nightingale,
Nor melody o' the Libyan lotus flute
Blown seaward from the shore; but from a slope
That ran bloom-bright into the Atlantic blue,
Beneath a highland leaning down a weight   10
Of cliffs, and zoned below with cedar shade,
Came voices, like the voices in a dream,
Continuous, till he reached the outer sea.

SONG

I

The golden apple, the golden apple, the hallowed fruit
Guard it well, guard it warily,
Singing airily,
Standing about the charméd root.
Round about all is mute,
As the snow-field on the mountain-peaks,
As the sand-field at the mountain-foot.   20
Crocodiles in briny creeks
Sleep and stir not: all is mute.
If ye sing not, if ye make false measure,
We shall lose eternal pleasure,
Worth eternal want of rest.
Laugh not loudly: watch the treasure
Of the wisdom of the West.
In a corner wisdom whispers. Five and three
(Let it not be preached abroad) make an awful mystery.
For the blossom unto threefold music bloweth;   30
Evermore it is born anew;
And the sap to threefold music floweth,
From the root
Drawn in the dark,
Up to the fruit,
Creeping under the fragrant bark,
Liquid gold, honeysweet, thro' and thro'.
Keen-eyed Sisters, singing airily,
Looking warily
Every way,   40
Guard the apple night and day,
Lest one from the East come and take it away.

II

Father Hesper, Father Hesper, watch, watch, ever and aye,
Looking under silver hair with a silver eye.
Father, twinkle not thy steadfast sight;

Kingdoms lapse, and climates change, and races die;
Honor comes with mystery;
Hoarded wisdom brings delight.
Number, tell them over and number
How many the mystic fruit-tree holds,   50
Lest the red-combed dragon slumber
Rolled together in purple folds.
Look to him, father, lest he wink, and the golden apple be stol'n
      away,
For his ancient heart is drunk with overwatchings night and day,
Round about the hallowed fruit-tree curled—
Sing away, sing aloud evermore in the wind, without stop,
Lest his scaléd eyelid drop,
For he is older than the world.
If he waken, we waken,
Rapidly levelling eager eyes.   60
If he sleep, we sleep,
Dropping the eyelid over the eyes.
If the golden apple be taken,
The world will be overwise.
Five links, a golden chain, are we,
Hesper, the dragon, and sisters three,
Bound about the golden tree.

                                    III

Father Hesper, Father Hesper, watch, watch, night and day,
Lest the old wound of the world be healéd,
The glory unsealéd,   70
The golden apple stol'n away,
And the ancient secret revealéd.
Look from west to east along:
Father, old Himala weakens, Caucasus is bold and strong.
Wandering waters unto wandering waters call;
Let them clash together, foam and fall.
Out of watchings, out of wiles,
Comes the bliss of secret smiles.
All things are not told to all.
Half-round the mantling night is drawn,   80
Purple-fringéd with even and dawn.
Hesper hateth Phosphor, evening hateth morn.

IV

Every flower and every fruit the redolent breath
Of this warm sea-wind ripeneth,
Arching the billow in his sleep;
But the land-wind wandereth,
Broken by the highland-steep,
Two streams upon the violet deep;
For the western sun and the western star,
And the low west-wind, breathing afar,   90
The end of day and beginning of night
Make the apple holy and bright;
Holy and bright, round and full, bright and blest,
Mellowed in a land of rest;
Watch it warily day and night;
All good things are in the west.
Till mid noon the cool east light
Is shut out by the round of the tall hillbrow;
But when the full-faced sunset yellowly
Stays on the flowering arch of the bough,   100
The luscious fruitage clustereth mellowly,
Golden-kernelled, golden-cored,
Sunset-ripened above on the tree.
The world is wasted with fire and sword,
But the apple of gold hangs over the sea.
Five links, a golden chain are we,
Hesper, the dragon, and sisters three,
Daughters three,
Bound about
All round about   110
The gnarléd bole of the charméd tree.
The golden apple, the golden apple, the hallowed fruit,
Guard it well, guard it warily,
Watch it warily,
Singing airily,
Standing about the charméd root.

[publ. 1832]

SIR LAUNCELOT AND QUEEN GUINEVERE

A FRAGMENT

LIKE souls that balance joy and pain,
With tears and smiles from heaven again
The maiden Spring upon the plain
Came in a sunlit fall of rain.
    In crystal vapor everywhere
Blue isles of heaven laugh'd between,
And far, in forest-deeps unseen,
The topmost elm-tree gather'd green
    From draughts of balmy air.

Sometimes the linnet piped his song;   10
Sometimes the throstle whistled strong;
Sometimes the sparhawk, wheel'd along,
Hush'd all the groves from fear of wrong;
    By grassy capes with fuller sound
In curves the yellowing river ran,
And drooping chestnut-buds began
To spread into the perfect fan,
    Above the teeming ground.

Then, in the boyhood of the year,
Sir Launcelot and Queen Guinevere   20
Rode thro' the coverts of the deer,
With blissful treble ringing clear.
    She seem'd a part of joyous Spring;
A gown of grass-green silk she wore,
Buckled with golden clasps before;
A light-green tuft of plumes she bore
    Closed in a golden ring.

Now on some twisted ivy-net,
Now by some tinkling rivulet,
In mosses mixt with violet   30
Her cream-white mule his pastern set;
    And fleeter now she skimm'd the plains

Than she whose elfin prancer springs
By night to eery warblings,
When all the glimmering moorland rings
    With jingling bridle-reins.

As she fled fast thro' sun and shade,
The happy winds upon her play'd,
Blowing the ringlet from the braid.
She look'd so lovely, as she sway'd   **40**
    The rein with dainty finger-tips,
A man had given all other bliss,
And all his worldly worth for this,
To waste his whole heart in one kiss
    Upon her perfect lips.
           [1830; publ. 1842]

THE LADY OF SHALOTT

PART I

ON EITHER side the river lie
Long fields of barley and of rye,
That clothe the wold and meet the sky;
And thro' the field the road runs by
    To many-tower'd Camelot;
And up and down the people go,
Gazing where the lilies blow
Round an island there below,
    The island of Shalott.

Willows whiten, aspens quiver,   **10**
Little breezes dusk and shiver
Thro' the wave that runs for ever
By the island in the river
    Flowing down to Camelot.
Four gray walls, and four gray towers,
Overlook a space of flowers,
And the silent isle imbowers
    The Lady of Shalott.

By the margin, willow-veil'd,
Slide the heavy barges trail'd   **20**

By slow horses; and unhail'd
The shallop flitteth silken-sail'd
      Skimming down to Camelot:
But who hath seen her wave her hand?
Or at the casement seen her stand?
Or is she known in all the land,
      The Lady of Shalott?

Only reapers, reaping early
In among the bearded barley,
Hear a song that echoes cheerly   30
From the river winding clearly,
      Down to tower'd Camelot;
And by the moon the reaper weary,
Piling sheaves in uplands airy,
Listening, whispers " 'Tis the fairy
      Lady of Shalott."

PART II

There she weaves by night and day
A magic web with colors gay.
She has heard a whisper say,
A curse is on her if she stay   40
      To look down to Camelot.
She knows not what the curse may be,
And so she weaveth steadily,
And little other care hath she,
      The Lady of Shalott.

And moving thro' a mirror clear
That hangs before her all the year,
Shadows of the world appear.
There she sees the highway near
      Winding down to Camelot;   50
There the river eddy whirls,
And there the surly village-churls,
And the red cloaks of market girls,
      Pass onward from Shalott.

Sometimes a troop of damsels glad,
An abbot on an ambling pad,
Sometimes a curly shepherd-lad,

Or long-hair'd page in crimson clad,
    Goes by to tower'd Camelot;
And sometimes thro' the mirror blue   60
The knights come riding two and two:
She hath no loyal knight and true,
    The Lady of Shalott.

But in her web she still delights
To weave the mirror's magic sights,
For often thro' the silent nights
A funeral, with plumes and lights
    And music, went to Camelot;
Or when the moon was overhead,
Came two young lovers lately wed: 70
"I am half sick of shadows," said
    The Lady of Shalott.

PART III

A bow-shot from her bower-eaves,
He rode between the barley-sheaves,
The sun came dazzling thro' the leaves,
And flamed upon the brazen greaves
    Of bold Sir Lancelot.
A red-cross knight for ever kneel'd
To a lady in his shield,
That sparkled on the yellow field,   80
    Beside remote Shalott.

The gemmy bridle glitter'd free,
Like to some branch of stars we see
Hung in the golden Galaxy.
The bridle bells rang merrily
    As he rode down to Camelot;
And from his blazon'd baldric slung
A mighty silver bugle hung,
And as he rode his armor rung,
    Beside remote Shalott.   90

All in the blue unclouded weather
Thick-jewell'd shone the saddle-leather,
The helmet and the helmet-feather

Burn'd like one burning flame together,
    As he rode down to Camelot;
As often thro' the purple night,
Below the starry clusters bright,
Some bearded meteor, trailing light,
    Moves over still Shalott.

His broad clear brow in sunlight glow'd;   100
On burnish'd hooves his war-horse trode;
From underneath his helmet flow'd
His coal-black curls as on he rode,
    As he rode down to Camelot.
From the bank and from the river
He flash'd into the crystal mirror,
"Tirra lirra," by the river
    Sang Sir Lancelot.

She left the web, she left the loom,
She made three paces thro' the room,   110
She saw the water-lily bloom,
She saw the helmet and the plume,
    She look'd down to Camelot.
Out flew the web and floated wide;
The mirror crack'd from side to side;
"The curse is come upon me," cried
    The Lady of Shalott.

PART IV

In the stormy east-wind straining,
The pale yellow woods were waning,
The broad stream in his banks complaining,   120
Heavily the low sky raining
    Over tower'd Camelot;
Down she came and found a boat
Beneath a willow left afloat,
And round about the prow she wrote
    The Lady of Shalott.

And down the river's dim expanse
Like some bold seër in a trance,
Seeing all his own mischance—

With a glassy countenance   130
   Did she look to Camelot.
And at the closing of the day
She loosed the chain, and down she lay;
The broad stream bore her far away,
   The Lady of Shalott.

Lying, robed in snowy white
That loosely flew to left and right—
The leaves upon her falling light—
Thro' the noises of the night
   She floated down to Camelot;   140
And as the boat-head wound along
The willowy hills and fields among,
They heard her singing her last song,
   The Lady of Shalott.

Heard a carol, mournful, holy,
Chanted loudly, chanted lowly,
Till her blood was frozen slowly,
And her eyes were darken'd wholly,
   Turn'd to tower'd Camelot.
For ere she reach'd upon the tide   150
The first house by the water-side,
Singing in her song she died,
   The Lady of Shalott.

Under tower and balcony,
By garden-wall and gallery,
A gleaming shape she floated by,
Dead-pale between the houses high,
   Silent into Camelot.
Out upon the wharfs they came,
Knight and burgher, lord and dame,   160
And round the prow they read her name,
   The Lady of Shalott.

Who is this? and what is here?
And in the lighted palace near
Died the sound of royal cheer;
And they cross'd themselves for fear,
   All the knights at Camelot:

But Lancelot mused a little space;
He said, "She has a lovely face;
God in his mercy lend her grace,   170
    The Lady of Shalott."
              [publ. 1832, 1842]

ŒNONE [1]

THERE lies a vale in Ida, lovelier
Than all the valleys of Ionian hills.
The swimming vapor slopes athwart the glen,
Puts forth an arm, and creeps from pine to pine,
And loiters, slowly drawn. On either hand
The lawns and meadow-ledges midway down
Hang rich in flowers, and far below them roars
The long brook falling thro' the cloven ravine
In cataract after cataract to the sea.
Behind the valley topmost Gargarus   10
Stands up and takes the morning; but in front
The gorges, opening wide apart, reveal
Troas and Ilion's column'd citadel,
The crown of Troas.
            Hither came at noon
Mournful Œnone, wandering forlorn
Of Paris, once her playmate on the hills.

[1] For comparison with the revised version of 1842, a few lines may
be quoted from the original text of 1832:

    There is a dale in Ida, lovelier
    Than any in old Ionia, beautiful
    With emerald slopes of sunny sward, that lean
    Above the loud glenriver, which hath worn
    A path thro' steepdown granite walls below
    Mantled with flowering tendriltwine. In front
    The cedarshadowy valleys open wide.
    Far-seen, high over all the Godbuilt wall
    And many a snowycolumned range divine,
    Mounted with awful sculptures—men and Gods,
    The work of Gods—bright in the darkblue sky
    The windy citadel of Ilion
    Shone, like the crown of Troas.

Her cheek had lost the rose, and round her neck
Floated her hair or seem'd to float in rest.
She, leaning on a fragment twined with vine,
Sang to the stillness, till the mountain-shade   20
Sloped downward to her seat from the upper cliff.

"O mother Ida, many-fountain'd Ida,
Dear mother Ida, harken ere I die.
For now the noonday quiet holds the hill;
The grasshopper is silent in the grass;
The lizard, with his shadow on the stone,
Rests like a shadow, and the winds are dead.
The purple flower droops, the golden bee
Is lily-cradled; I alone awake.
My eyes are full of tears, my heart of love,   30
My heart is breaking, and my eyes are dim,
And I am all aweary of my life.

"O mother Ida, many-fountain'd Ida.
Dear mother Ida, harken ere I die.
Hear me, O earth, hear me, O hills, O caves
That house the cold crown'd snake! O mountain brooks,
I am the daughter of a River-God,
Hear me, for I will speak, and build up all
My sorrow with my song, as yonder walls
Rose slowly to a music slowly breathed,   40
A cloud that gather'd shape; for it may be
That, while I speak of it, a little while
My heart may wander from its deeper woe.

"O mother Ida, many-fountain'd Ida,
Dear mother Ida, harken ere I die.
I waited underneath the dawning hills;
Aloft the mountain lawn was dewy-dark,
And dewy-dark aloft the mountain pine.
Beautiful Paris, evil-hearted Paris,
Leading a jet-black goat white-horn'd, white-hooved,   50
Came up from reedy Simois all alone.

"O mother Ida, harken ere I die.
Far-off the torrent call'd me from the cleft;
Far up the solitary morning smote

The streaks of virgin snow. With down-dropt eyes
I sat alone; white-breasted like a star
Fronting the dawn he moved; a leopard skin
Droop'd from his shoulder, but his sunny hair
Cluster'd about his temples like a God's;
And his cheek brighten'd as the foam-bow brightens   60
When the wind blows the foam, and all my heart
Went forth to embrace him coming ere he came.

"Dear mother Ida, harken ere I die.
He smiled, and opening out his milk-white palm
Disclosed a fruit of pure Hesperian gold,
That smelt ambrosially, and while I look'd
And listen'd, the full-flowing river of speech
Came down upon my heart:
                          " 'My own Œnone,
Beautiful-brow'd Œnone, my own soul,
Behold this fruit, whose gleaming rind ingraven   70
"For the most fair," would seem to award it thine,
As lovelier than whatever Oread haunt
The knolls of Ida, loveliest in all grace
Of movement, and the charm of married brows.'

"Dear mother Ida, harken ere I die.
He prest the blossom of his lips to mine,
And added, 'This was cast upon the board,
When all the full-faced presence of the Gods
Ranged in the halls of Peleus; whereupon
Rose feud, with question unto whom 't were due;   80
But light-foot Iris brought it yester-eve,
Delivering, that to me, by common voice
Elected umpire, Herè comes to-day,
Pallas and Aphrodite, claiming each
This meed of fairest. Thou, within the cave
Behind yon whispering tuft of oldest pine,
Mayst well behold them unbeheld, unheard
Hear all, and see thy Paris judge of Gods.'

"Dear mother Ida, harken ere I die.
It was the deep midnoon; one silvery cloud   90
Had lost his way between the piny sides
Of this long glen. Then to the bower they came,

Naked they came to that smooth-swarded bower,
And at their feet the crocus brake like fire,
Violet, amaracus, and asphodel,
Lotos and lilies; and a wind arose,
And overhead the wandering ivy and vine,
This way and that, in many a wild festoon
Ran riot, garlanding the gnarled boughs
With bunch and berry and flower thro' and thro'.   100

"O mother Ida, harken ere I die.
On the tree-tops a crested peacock lit,
And o'er him flow'd a golden cloud, and lean'd
Upon him, slowly dropping fragrant dew.
Then first I heard the voice of her to whom
Coming thro' heaven, like a light that grows
Larger and clearer, with one mind the Gods
Rise up for reverence. She to Paris made
Proffer of royal power, ample rule
Unquestion'd, overflowing revenue   110
Wherewith to embellish state, 'from many a vale
And river-sunder'd champaign clothed with corn,
Or labor'd mine undrainable of ore.
Honor,' she said, 'and homage, tax and toll,
From many an inland town and haven large,
Mast-throng'd beneath her shadowing citadel
In glassy bays among her tallest towers.'

"O mother Ida, harken ere I die.
Still she spake on and still she spake of power,
'Which in all action is the end of all;   120
Power fitted to the season; wisdom-bred
And throned of wisdom—from all neighbor crowns
Alliance and allegiance, till thy hand
Fail from the sceptre-staff. Such boon from me,
From me, heaven's queen, Paris, to thee king-born,
A shepherd all thy life but yet king-born,
Should come most welcome, seeing men, in power
Only, are likest Gods, who have attain'd
Rest in a happy place and quiet seats
Above the thunder, with undying bliss   130
In knowledge of their own supremacy.'

"Dear mother Ida, harken ere I die.
She ceased, and Paris held the costly fruit
Out at arm's-length, so much the thought of power
Flatter'd his spirit; but Pallas where she stood
Somewhat apart, her clear and bared limbs
O'erthwarted with the brazen-headed spear
Upon her pearly shoulder leaning cold,
The while, above, her full and earnest eye
Over her snow-cold breast and angry cheek   140
Kept watch, waiting decision, made reply:

" 'Self-reverence, self-knowledge, self-control,
These three alone lead life to sovereign power.
Yet not for power (power of herself
Would come uncall'd for) but to live by law,
Acting the law we live by without fear;
And, because right is right, to follow right
Were wisdom in the scorn of consequence.'

"Dear mother Ida, harken ere I die.
Again she said: 'I woo thee not with gifts.   150
Sequel of guerdon could not alter me
To fairer. Judge thou me by what I am,
So shalt thou find me fairest.
                            Yet, indeed,
If gazing on divinity disrobed
Thy mortal eyes are frail to judge of fair,
Unbias'd by self-profit, O, rest thee sure
That I shall love thee well and cleave to thee,
So that my vigor, wedded to thy blood,
Shall strike within thy pulses, like a God's,
To push thee forward thro' a life of shocks,   160
Dangers, and deeds, until endurance grow
Sinew'd with action, and the full-grown will,
Circled thro' all experiences, pure law,
Commeasure perfect freedom.'
                            "Here she ceas'd,
And Paris ponder'd, and I cried, 'O Paris,
Give it to Pallas!' but he heard me not,
Or hearing would not hear me, woe is me!

"O mother Ida, many-fountain'd Ida,
Dear mother Ida, harken ere I die.
Idalian Aphrodite beautiful,   **170**
Fresh as the foam, new-bathed in Paphian wells,
With rosy slender fingers backward drew
From her warm brows and bosom her deep hair
Ambrosial, golden round her lucid throat
And shoulder; from the violets her light foot
Shone rosy-white, and o'er her rounded form
Between the shadows of the vine-bunches
Floated the glowing sunlights, as she moved.

"Dear mother Ida, harken ere I die.
She with a subtle smile in her mild eyes,   **180**
The herald of her triumph, drawing nigh
Half-whisper'd in his ear, 'I promise thee
The fairest and most loving wife in Greece.'
She spoke and laugh'd; I shut my sight for fear;
But when I look'd, Paris had raised his arm,
And I beheld great Herè's angry eyes,
As she withdrew into the golden cloud,
And I was left alone within the bower;
And from that time to this I am alone,
And I shall be alone until I die.   **190**

"Yet, mother Ida, harken ere I die.
Fairest—why fairest wife? am I not fair?
My love hath told me so a thousand times.
Methinks I must be fair, for yesterday,
When I past by, a wild and wanton pard,
Eyed like the evening star, with playful tail
Crouch'd fawning in the weed. Most loving is she?
Ah me, my mountain shepherd, that my arms
Were wound about thee, and my hot lips prest
Close, close to thine in that quick-falling dew   **200**
Of fruitful kisses, thick as autumn rains
Flash in the pools of whirling Simois!

"O mother, hear me yet before I die.
They came, they cut away my tallest pines,
My tall dark pines, that plumed the craggy ledge
High over the blue gorge. and all between

The snowy peak and snow-white cataract
Foster'd the callow eaglet—from beneath
Whose thick mysterious boughs in the dark morn
The panther's roar came muffled, while I sat   210
Low in the valley. Never, never more
Shall lone Œnone see the morning mist
Sweep thro' them; never see them overlaid
With narrow moonlit slips of silver cloud,
Between the loud stream and the trembling stars.

"O mother, hear me yet before I die.
I wish that somewhere in the ruin'd folds,
Among the fragments tumbled from the glens,
Or the dry thickets, I could meet with her
The Abominable, that uninvited came   220
Into the fair Peleïan banquet-hall,
And cast the golden fruit upon the board,
And bred this change; that I might speak my mind,
And tell her to her face how much I hate
Her presence, hated both of Gods and men.

"O mother, hear me yet before I die.
Hath he not sworn his love a thousand times,
In this green valley, under this green hill,
Even on this hand, and sitting on this stone?
Seal'd it with kisses? water'd it with tears?   230
O happy tears, and how unlike to these!
O happy heaven, how canst thou see my face?
O happy earth, how canst thou bear my weight?
O death, death, death, thou ever-floating cloud,
There are enough unhappy on this earth,
Pass by the happy souls, that love to live;
I pray thee, pass before my light of life,
And shadow all my soul, that I may die.
Thou weighest heavy on the heart within,
Weigh heavy on my eyelids; let me die.   240

"O mother, hear me yet before I die.
I will not die alone, for fiery thoughts
Do shape themselves within me, more and more,
Whereof I catch the issue, as I hear
Dead sounds at night come from the inmost hills,

Like footsteps upon wool. I dimly see
My far-off doubtful purpose, as a mother
Conjectures of the features of her child
Ere it is born. Her child!—a shudder comes
Across me: never child be born of me,   250
Unblest, to vex me with his father's eyes!

"O mother, hear me yet before I die.
Hear me, O earth. I will not die alone,
Lest their shrill happy laughter come to me
Walking the cold and starless road of death
Uncomforted, leaving my ancient love
With the Greek woman. I will rise and go
Down into Troy, and ere the stars come forth
Talk with the wild Cassandra, for she says
A fire dances before her, and a sound   260
Rings ever in her ears of armed men.
What this may be I know not, but I know
That, wheresoe'er I am by night and day,
All earth and air seem only burning fire."
                              [publ. 1832, 1842]

THE PALACE OF ART

TO ———

WITH THE FOLLOWING POEM

I SEND you here a sort of allegory—
For you will understand it—of a soul,
A sinful soul possess'd of many gifts,
A spacious garden full of flowering weeds,
A glorious devil, large in heart and brain,
That did love beauty only—beauty seen
In all varieties of mould and mind—
And knowledge for its beauty; or if good,
Good only for its beauty, seeing not
That Beauty, Good, and Knowledge are three sisters   10
That doat upon each other, friends to man,
Living together under the same roof,
And never can be sunder'd without tears.

And he that shuts Love out. in turn shall be
Shut out from Love, and on her threshold lie
.iowling in outer darkness. Not for this
Was common clay ta'en from the common earth
Moulded by God, and temper'd with the tears
Of angels to the perfect shape of man.

THE PALACE OF ART

I BUILT my soul a lordly pleasure-house,
    Wherein at ease for aye to dwell.
I said, "O Soul, make merry and carouse,
    Dear soul, for all is well."

A huge crag-platform, smooth as burnish'd brass,
    I chose. The ranged ramparts bright
From level meadow-bases of deep grass
    Suddenly scaled the light.

Thereon I built it firm. Of ledge or shelf
    The rock rose clear, or winding stair.   10
My soul would live alone unto herself
    In her high palace there.

And "while the world runs round and round," I said,
    "Reign thou apart, a quiet king,
Still as, while Saturn whirls, his steadfast shade
    Sleeps on his luminous ring."

To which my soul made answer readily:
    "Trust me, in bliss I shall abide
In this great mansion, that is built for me,
    So royal-rich and wide."   20

        .   .   .   .

Four courts I made, East, West and South an North,
    In each a squared lawn, wherefrom
The golden gorge of dragons spouted forth
    A flood of fountain-foam.

And round the cool green courts there ran a row
   Of cloisters, branch'd like mighty woods,
Echoing all night to that sonorous flow
    Of spouted fountain-floods;

And round the roofs a gilded gallery
   That lent broad verge to distant lands,   30
Far as the wild swan wings, to where the sky
    Dipt down to sea and sands.

From those four jets four currents in one swell
   Across the mountain stream'd below
In misty folds, that floating as they fell
    Lit up a torrent-bow.

And high on every peak a statue seem'd
   To hang on tiptoe, tossing up
A cloud of incense of all odor steam'd
    From out a golden cup.   40

So that she thought, "And who shall gaze upon
   My palace with unblinded eyes,
While this great bow will waver in the sun,
    And that sweet incense rise?"

For that sweet incense rose and never fail'd,
   And, while day sank or mounted higher,
The light aerial gallery, golden-rail'd,
    Burnt like a fringe of fire.

Likewise the deep-set windows, stain'd and traced,
   Would seem slow-flaming crimson fires   50
From shadow'd grots of arches interlaced,
    And tipt with frost-like spires.

    .   .   .   '   .   .   .   .

Full of long-sounding corridors it was,
   That over-vaulted grateful gloom,
Thro' which the livelong day my soul did pass,
    Well-pleased, from room to room.

Full of great rooms and small the palace stood,
   All various, each a perfect whole
From living Nature, fit for every mood
   And change of my still soul.   60

For some were hung with arras green and blue,
   Showing a gaudy summer-morn,
Where with puff'd cheek the belted hunter blew
   His wreathed bugle-horn.

One seem'd all dark and red—a tract of sand,
   And some one pacing there alone,
Who paced for ever in a glimmering land,
   Lit with a low large moon.

One show'd an iron coast and angry waves.
   You seem'd to hear them climb and fall   70
And roar rock-thwarted under bellowing caves,
   Beneath the windy wall.

And one, a full-fed river winding slow
   By herds upon an endless plain,
The ragged rims of thunder brooding low,
   With shadow-streaks of rain.

And one, the reapers at their sultry toil.
   In front they bound the sheaves. Behind
Were realms of upland, prodigal in oil,
   And hoary to the wind.   80

And one a foreground black with stones and slags;
   Beyond, a line of heights; and higher
All barr'd with long white cloud the scornful crags;
   And highest, snow and fire.

And one, an English home—gray twilight pour'd
   On dewy pastures, dewy trees,
Softer than sleep—all things in order stored,
   A haunt of ancient Peace.

Nor these alone, but every landscape fair,
   As fit for every mood of mind,   90

Or gay, or grave, or sweet, or stern, was there,
   Not less than truth design'd.

.   .   .   .

Or the maid-mother by a crucifix,
   In tracts of pasture sunny-warm,
Beneath branch-work of costly sardonyx
   Sat smiling, babe in arm.

Or in a clear-wall'd city on the sea,
   Near gilded organ-pipes, her hair
Wound with white roses, slept Saint Cecily;
   An angel look'd at her.   **100**

Or thronging all one porch of Paradise
   A group of Houris bow'd to see
The dying Islamite, with hands and eyes
   That said, We wait for thee.

Or mythic Uther's deeply-wounded son
   In some fair space of sloping greens
Lay, dozing in the vale of Avalon,
   And watch'd by weeping queens.

Or hollowing one hand against his ear,
   To list a foot-fall, ere he saw   **110**
The wood-nymph, stay'd the Ausonian king to hear
   Of wisdom and of law.

Or over hills with peaky tops engrail'd,
   And many a tract of palm and rice,
The throne of Indian Cama slowly sail'd
   A summer fann'd with spice.

Or sweet Europa's mantle blew unclasp'd,
   From off her shoulder backward borne;
From one hand droop'd a crocus; one hand grasp'd
   The mild bull's golden horn.   **120**

Or else flush'd Ganymede, his rosy thigh
   Half-buried in the eagle's down,

Sole as a flying star shot thro' the sky
    Above the pillar'd town.

Nor these alone; but every legend fair
    Which the supreme Caucasian mind
Carved out of Nature for itself was there,
    Not less than life design'd.

    .   .   .   .

Then in the towers I placed great bells that swung,
    Moved of themselves, with silver sound;   **130**
And with choice paintings of wise men I hung
    The royal dais round.

For there was Milton like a seraph strong,
    Beside him Shakespeare bland and mild;
And there the world-worn Dante grasp'd his song,
    And somewhat grimly smiled.

And there the Ionian father of the rest;
    A million wrinkles carved his skin;
A hundred winters snow'd upon his breast,
    From cheek and throat and chin.   **140**

Above, the fair hall-ceiling stately-set
    Many an arch high up did lift,
And angels rising and descending met
    With interchange of gift.

Below was all mosaic choicely plann'd
    With cycles of the human tale
Of this wide world, the times of every land
    So wrought they will not fail.

The people here, a beast of burden slow,
    Toil'd onward, prick'd with goads and stings;   **150**
Here play'd, a tiger, rolling to and fro
    The heads and crowns of kings;

Here rose, an athlete, strong to break or bind
    All force in bonds that might endure,

And here once more like some sick man declined,
    And trusted any cure.

But over these she trod; and those great bells
    Began to chime. She took her throne;
She sat betwixt the shining oriels,
    To sing her songs alone.   **160**

And thro' the topmost oriels' colored flame
    Two godlike faces gazed below;
Plato the wise, and large-brow'd Verulam,
    The first of those who know.

And all those names that in their motion were
    Full-welling fountain-heads of change,
Betwixt the slender shafts were blazon'd fair
    In diverse raiment strange;

Thro' which the lights, rose, amber, emerald, blue,
    Flush'd in her temples and her eyes,   **170**
And from her lips, as morn from Memnon, drew
    Rivers of melodies.

No nightingale delighteth to prolong
    Her low preamble all alone,
More than my soul to hear her echo'd song
    Throb thro' the ribbed stone;

Singing and murmuring in her feastful mirth,
    Joying to feel herself alive,
Lord over Nature, lord of the visible earth,
    Lord of the senses five;   **180**

Communing with herself: "All these are mine,
    And let the world have peace or wars,
'Tis one to me." She—when young night divine
    Crown'd dying day with stars,

Making sweet close of his delicious toils—
    Lit light in wreaths and anadems,
And pure quintessences of precious oils
    In hollow'd moons of gems,

To mimic heaven; and clapt her hands and cried,
   "I marvel if my still delight   **196**
In this great house so royal-rich and wide
    Be flatter'd to the height.

"O all things fair to sate my various eyes!
   O shapes and hues that please me well!
O silent faces of the Great and Wise,
    My Gods, with whom I dwell!

"O Godlike isolation which art mine,
   I can but count thee perfect gain,
What time I watch the darkening droves of swine
    That range on yonder plain.   **200**

"In filthy sloughs they roll a prurient skin,
   They graze and wallow, breed and sleep;
And oft some brainless devil enters in,
    And drives them to the deep."

Then of the moral instinct would she prate
   And of the rising from the dead,
As hers by right of full-accomplish'd Fate;
    And at the last she said:

"I take possession of man's mind and deed.
   I care not what the sects may brawl.   **210**
I sit as God holding no form of creed,
    But contemplating all."

   .   .   .   .

Full oft the riddle of the painful earth
   Flash'd thro' her as she sat alone,
Yet not the less held she her solemn mirth,
    And intellectual throne.

And so she throve and prosper'd; so three years
   She prosper'd; on the fourth she fell,
Like Herod, when the shout was in his ears,
    Struck thro' with pangs of hell.   **220**

Lest she should fail and perish utterly,
    God, before whom ever lie bare
The abysmal deeps of personality,
        Plagued her with sore despair.

When she would think, where'er she turn'd her sight
    The airy hand confusion wrought,
Wrote, "Mene, mene," and divided quite
        The kingdom of her thought.

Deep dread and loathing of her solitude
    Fell on her, from which mood was born   230
Scorn of herself; again, from out that mood
        Laughter at her self-scorn.

"What! is not this my place of strength," she said,
    "My spacious mansion built for me,
Whereof the strong foundation-stones were laid
        Since my first memory?"

But in dark corners of her palace stood
    Uncertain shapes; and unawares
On white-eyed phantasms weeping tears of blood,
        And horrible nightmares,   240

And hollow shades enclosing hearts of flame,
    And, with dim fretted foreheads all,
On corpses three-months-old at noon she came,
        That stood against the wall.

A spot of dull stagnation, without light
    Or power of movement, seem'd my soul,
Mid onward-sloping motions infinite
        Making for one sure goal;

A still salt pool, lock'd in with bars of sand,
    Left on the shore, that hears all night   250
The plunging seas draw backward from the land
        Their moon-led waters white;

A star that with the choral starry dance
    Join'd not, but stood, and standing saw

The hollow orb of moving Circumstance
    Roll'd round by one fix'd law.

Back on herself her serpent pride had curl'd.
    "No voice," she shriek'd in that lone hall,
"No voice breaks thro' the stillness of this world;
    One deep, deep silence all!"   260

She, mouldering with the dull earth's mouldering sod,
    Inwrapt tenfold in slothful shame,
Lay there exiled from eternal God,
    Lost to her place and name;

And death and life she hated equally,
    And nothing saw, for her despair,
But dreadful time, dreadful eternity,
    No comfort anywhere;

Remaining utterly confused with fears,
    And ever worse with growing time,   270
And ever unrelieved by dismal tears,
    And all alone in crime.

Shut up as in a crumbling tomb, girt round
    With blackness as a solid wall,
Far off she seem'd to hear the dully sound
    Of human footsteps fall:

As in strange lands a traveller walking slow,
    In doubt and great perplexity,
A little before moonrise hears the low
    Moan of an unknown sea;   280

And knows not if it be thunder, or a sound
    Of rocks thrown down, or one deep cry
Of great wild beasts; then thinketh, "I have found
    A new land, but I die."

She howl'd aloud, "I am on fire within.
    There comes no murmur of reply.
What is it that will take away my sin,
    And save me lest I die?"

So when four years were wholly finished,
 She threw her royal robes away.   **290**
"Make me a cottage in the vale," she said,
 "Where I may mourn and pray.

"Yet pull not down my palace towers, that are
 So lightly, beautifully built;
Perchance I may return with others there
 When I have purged my guilt."
         [publ. 1832, 1842]

THE LOTOS-EATERS

"COURAGE!" he said, and pointed toward the land,
"This mounting wave will roll us shoreward soon."
In the afternoon they came unto a land
In which it seemed always afternoon.
All round the coast the languid air did swoon,
Breathing like one that hath a weary dream.
Full-faced above the valley stood the moon;
And, like a downward smoke, the slender stream
Along the cliff to fall and pause and fall did seem.

A land of streams! some, like a downward smoke,   **10**
Slow-dropping veils of thinnest lawn, did go;
And some thro' wavering lights and shadows broke,
Rolling a slumbrous sheet of foam below.
They saw the gleaming river seaward flow
From the inner land; far off, three mountain-tops,
Three silent pinnacles of aged snow,
Stood sunset-flush'd; and, dew'd with showery drops,
Up-clomb the shadowy pine above the woven copse.

The charmed sunset linger'd low adown
In the red West; thro' mountain clefts the dale   **20**
Was seen far inland, and the yellow down
Border'd with palm, and many a winding vale
And meadow, set with slender galingale;
A land where all things always seem'd the same!

And round about the keel with faces pale,
Dark faces pale against that rosy flame,
The mild-eyed melancholy Lotos-eaters came.

Branches they bore of that enchanted stem,
Laden with flower and fruit, whereof they gave
To each, but whoso did receive of them   30
And taste, to him the gushing of the wave
Far far away did seem to mourn and rave
On alien shores; and if his fellow spake,
His voice was thin, as voices from the grave;
And deep-asleep he seem'd, yet all awake,
And music in his ears his beating heart did make.

They sat them down upon the yellow sand,
Between the sun and moon upon the shore;
And sweet it was to dream of Fatherland,
Of child, and wife, and slave; but evermore   40
Most weary seem'd the sea, weary the oar,
Weary the wandering fields of barren foam.
Then some one said, "We will return no more;"
And all at once they sang, "Our island home
Is far beyond the wave; we will no longer roam."

CHORIC SONG

I

THERE is sweet music here that softer falls
Than petals from blown roses on the grass,
Or night-dews on still waters between walls
Of shadowy granite, in a gleaming pass;
Music that gentlier on the spirit lies,
Than tired eyelids upon tired eyes;
Music that brings sweet sleep down from the blissful skies.
Here are cool mosses deep,
And thro' the moss the ivies creep,
And in the stream the long-leaved flowers weep,   10
And from the craggy ledge the poppy hangs in sleep.

II

Why are we weigh'd upon with heaviness,
And utterly consumed with sharp distress,
While all things else have rest from weariness?
All things have rest: why should we toil alone,
We only toil, who are the first of things,
And make perpetual moan,
Still from one sorrow to another thrown;
Nor ever fold our wings,
And cease from wanderings,   20
Nor steep our brows in slumber's holy balm;
Nor harken what the inner spirit sings,
  'There is no joy but calm!"—
Why should we only toil, the roof and crown of things?

III

Lo! in the middle of the wood,
The folded leaf is woo'd from out the bud
With winds upon the branch, and there
Grows green and broad, and takes no care,
Sun-steep'd at noon, and in the moon
Nightly dew-fed; and turning yellow   30
Falls, and floats adown the air.
Lo! sweeten'd with the summer light,
The full-juiced apple, waxing over-mellow,
Drops in a silent autumn night.
All its allotted length of days
The flower ripens in its place,
Ripens and fades, and falls, and hath no toil,
Fast-rooted in the fruitful soil.

IV

Hateful is the dark-blue sky,
Vaulted o'er the dark-blue sea.   40
Death is the end of life; ah, why
Should life all labor be?
Let us alone. Time driveth onward fast,
And in a little while our lips are dumb.

Let us alone. What is it that will last?
All things are taken from us, and become
Portions and parcels of the dreadful past.
Let us alone. What pleasure can we have
To war with evil? Is there any peace
In ever climbing up the climbing wave? 50
All things have rest, and ripen toward the grave
In silence—ripen, fall, and cease:
Give us long rest or death, dark death, or dreamful ease.

v

How sweet it were, hearing the downward stream,
With half-shut eyes ever to seem
Falling asleep in a half-dream!
To dream and dream, like yonder amber light,
Which will not leave the myrrh-bush on the height;
To hear each other's whisper'd speech;
Eating the Lotos day by day, 60
To watch the crisping ripples on the beach,
And tender curving lines of creamy spray;
To lend our hearts and spirits wholly
To the influence of mild-minded melancholy;
To muse and brood and live again in memory,
With those old faces of our infancy
Heap'd over with a mound of grass,
Two handfuls of white dust, shut in an urn of brass!

vi

Dear is the memory of our wedded lives,
And dear the last embraces of our wives 70
And their warm tears; but all hath suffer'd change;
For surely now our household hearths are cold,
Our sons inherit us, our looks are strange,
And we should come like ghosts to trouble joy.
Or else the island princes over-bold
Have eat our substance, and the minstrel sings
Before them of the ten years' war in Troy,
And our great deeds, as half-forgotten things.
Is there confusion in the little isle?
Let what is broken so remain. 80

The Gods are hard to reconcile;
'Tis hard to settle order once again.
There *is* confusion worse than death,
Trouble on trouble, pain on pain,
Long labor unto aged breath,
Sore tasks to hearts worn out by many wars
And eyes grown dim with gazing on the pilot-stars.

VII

But, propt on beds of amaranth and moly,
How sweet—while warm airs lull us, blowing lowly—
With half-dropt eyelid still,   90
Beneath a heaven dark and holy,
To watch the long bright river drawing slowly
His waters from the purple hill—
To hear the dewy echoes calling
From cave to cave thro' the thick-twined vine—
To watch the emerald-color'd water falling
Thro' many a woven acanthus-wreath divine!
Only to hear and see the far-off sparkling brine,
Only to hear were sweet, stretch'd out beneath the pine.

VIII

The Lotos blooms below the barren peak,   100
The Lotos blows by every winding creek;
All day the wind breathes low with mellower tone;
Thro' every hollow cave and alley lone
Round and round the spicy downs the yellow Lotos-dust is
    blown.
We have had enough of action, and of motion we,
Roll'd to starboard, roll'd to larboard, when the surge was seeth-
    ing free,
Where the wallowing monster spouted his foam-fountains in
    the sea.
Let us swear an oath, and keep it with an equal mind,
In the hollow Lotos-land to live and lie reclined
On the hills like Gods together, careless of mankind.   110
For they lie beside their nectar, and the bolts are hurl'd
Far below them in the valleys, and the clouds are lightly curl'd
Round their golden houses, girdled with the gleaming world;

Where they smile in secret, looking over wasted lands,
Blight and famine, plague and earthquake, roaring deeps and
    fiery sands,
Clanging fights, and flaming towns, and sinking ships, and pray-
    ing hands.
But they smile, they find a music centred in a doleful song
Steaming up, a lamentation and an ancient tale of wrong,
Like a tale of little meaning tho' the words are strong;
Chanted from an ill-used race of men that cleave the soil,   120
Sow the seed, and reap the harvest with enduring toil,
Storing yearly little dues of wheat, and wine and oil;
Till they perish and they suffer—some, 'tis whisper'd—down in
    hell
Suffer endless anguish, others in Elysian valleys dwell,
Resting weary limbs at last on beds of asphodel.
Surely, surely, slumber is more sweet than toil, the shore
Than labor in the deep mid-ocean, wind and wave and oar;
O, rest ye, brother mariners, we will not wander more.
                        [publ. 1832, 1842]

A DREAM OF FAIR WOMEN

I READ, before my eyelids dropt their shade,
    "The Legend of Good Women," long ago
Sung by the morning star of song, who made
      His music heard below;

Dan Chaucer, the first warbler, whose sweet breath
    Preluded those melodious bursts that fill
The spacious times of great Elizabeth
      With sounds that echo still.

And, for a while, the knowledge of his art
    Held me above the subject, as strong gales   10
Hold swollen clouds from raining, tho' my heart,
      Brimful of those wild tales,

Charged both mine eyes with tears. In every land
    I saw, wherever light illumineth,

Beauty and anguish walking hand in hand
    The downward slope to death.

Those far-renowned brides of ancient song
    Peopled the hollow dark, like burning stars,
And I heard sounds of insult, shame, and wrong,
    And trumpets blown for wars;   20

And clattering flints batter'd with clanging hoofs;
    And I saw crowds in column'd sanctuaries,
And forms that pass'd at windows and on roofs
    Of marble palaces;

Corpses across the threshold, heroes tall
    Dislodging pinnacle and parapet
Upon the tortoise creeping to the wall,
    Lances in ambush set;

And high shrine-doors burst thro' with heated blasts
    That run before the fluttering tongues of fire;   30
White surf wind-scatter'd over sails and masts,
    And ever climbing higher;

Squadrons and squares of men in brazen plates,
    Scaffolds, still sheets of water, divers woes,
Ranges of glimmering vaults with iron grates,
    And hush'd seraglios.

So shape chased shape as swift as, when to land
    Bluster the winds and tides the selfsame way,
Crisp foam-flakes scud along the level sand,
    Torn from the fringe of spray.   40

I started once, or seem'd to start in pain,
    Resolved on noble things, and strove to speak,
As when a great thought strikes along the brain
    And flushes all the cheek.

And once my arm was lifted to hew down
    A cavalier from off his saddle-bow,
That bore a lady from a leaguer'd town;
    And then, I know not how.

All those sharp fancies, by down-lapsing thought
    Stream'd onward, lost their edges, and did creep   50
Roll'd on each other, rounded, smooth'd, and brought
      Into the gulfs of sleep.

At last methought that I had wander'd far
    In an old wood; fresh-wash'd in coolest dew
The maiden splendors of the morning star
      Shook in the steadfast blue.

Enormous elm-tree boles did stoop and lean
    Upon the dusky brushwood underneath
Their broad curved branches, fledged with clearest green,
      New from its silken sheath.   60

The dim red Morn had died, her journey done,
    And with dead lips smiled at the twilight plain,
Half-fallen across the threshold of the sun,
      Never to rise again.

There was no motion in the dumb dead air,
    Not any song of bird or sound of rill;
Gross darkness of the inner sepulchre
      Is not so deadly still

As that wide forest. Growths of jasmine turn'd
    Their humid arms festooning tree to tree,   70
And at the root thro' lush green grasses burn'd
      The red anemone.

I knew the flowers, I knew the leaves, I knew
    The tearful glimmer of the languid dawn
On those long, rank, dark wood-walks drench'd in dew,
      Leading from lawn to lawn.

The smell of violets, hidden in the green,
    Pour'd back into my empty soul and frame
The times when I remember to have been
      Joyful and free from blame.   80

And from within me a clear undertone
    Thrill'd thro' mine ears in that unblissful clime,

"Pass freely thro'; the wood is all thine own
    Until the end of time."

At length I saw a lady within call,
    Stiller than chisell'd marble, standing there;
A daughter of the gods, divinely tall,
    And most divinely fair.

Her loveliness with shame and with surprise
    Froze my swift speech; she turning on my face   **90**
The star-like sorrows of immortal eyes,
    Spoke slowly in her place:

"I had great beauty; ask thou not my name:
    No one can be more wise than destiny.
Many drew swords and died. Where'er I came
    I brought calamity."

"No marvel, sovereign lady: in fair field
    Myself for such a face had boldly died,"
I answer'd free; and turning I appeal'd
    To one that stood beside.   **100**

But she, with sick and scornful looks averse,
    To her full height her stately stature draws;
"My youth," she said, "was blasted with a curse:
    This woman was the cause.

"I was cut off from hope in that sad place
    Which men call'd Aulis in those iron years:
My father held his hand upon his face;
    I, blinded with my tears,

"Still strove to speak: my voice was thick with sighs
    As in a dream. Dimly I could descry   **110**
The stern black-bearded kings with wolfish eyes,
    Waiting to see me die.

"The high masts flicker'd as they lay afloat;
    The crowds, the temples, waver'd, and the shore;
The bright death quiver'd at the victim's throat—
    Touch'd—and I knew no more."

Whereto the other with a downward brow:
  "I would the white cold heavy-plunging foam,
Whirl'd by the wind, had roll'd me deep below,
    Then when I left my home."   120

Her slow full words sank thro' the silence drear,
  As thunder-drops fall on a sleeping sea:
Sudden I heard a voice that cried, "Come here,
    That I may look on thee."

I turning saw, throned on a flowery rise,
  One sitting on a crimson scarf unroll'd;
A queen, with swarthy cheeks and bold black eyes,
    Brow-bound with burning gold.

She, flashing forth a haughty smile, began:
  "I govern'd men by change, and so I sway'd   130
All moods. 'Tis long since I have seen a man.
    Once, like the moon, I made

The ever-shifting currents of the blood
  According to my humor ebb and flow.
I have no men to govern in this wood:
    That makes my only woe.

"Nay—yet it chafes me that I could not bend
  One will; nor tame and tutor with mine eye
That dull cold-blooded Cæsar. Prythee, friend,
    Where is Mark Antony?   140

"The man, my lover, with whom I rode sublime
  On Fortune's neck; we sat as God by God:
The Nilus would have risen before his time
    And flooded at our nod.

"We drank the Libyan Sun to sleep, and lit
  Lamps which out-burn'd Canopus. O, my life
In Egypt! O, the dalliance and the wit,
    The flattery and the strife,

"And the wild kiss, when fresh from war's alarms,
  My Hercules, my Roman Antony,   150

My mailed Bacchus leapt into my arms,
    Contented there to die!

"And there he died: and when I heard my name
    Sigh'd forth with life I would not brook my fear
Of the other; with a worm I balk'd his fame.
    What else was left? look here!"—

With that she tore her robe apart, and half
    The polish'd argent of her breast to sight
Laid bare. Thereto she pointed with a laugh,
    Showing the aspick's bite.—   160

"I died a Queen. The Roman soldier found
    Me lying dead, my crown about my brows,
A name for ever!—lying robed and crown'd,
    Worthy a Roman spouse."

Her warbling voice, a lyre of widest range
    Struck by all passion, did fall down and glance
From tone to tone, and glided thro' all change
    Of liveliest utterance.

When she made pause I knew not for delight;
    Because with sudden motion from the ground   170
She raised her piercing orbs, and fill'd with light
    The interval of sound.

Still with their fires Love tipt his keenest darts;
    As once they drew into two burning rings
All beams of Love, melting the mighty hearts
    Of captains and of kings.

Slowly my sense undazzled. Then I heard
    A noise of some one coming thro' the lawn,
And singing clearer than the crested bird
    That claps his wings at dawn: 180

"The torrent brooks of hallow'd Israel
    From craggy hollows pouring, late and soon,
Sound all night long, in falling thro' the dell,
    Far-heard beneath the moon.

"The balmy moon of blessed Israel
   Floods all the deep-blue gloom with beams divine;
All night the splinter'd crags that wall the dell
     With spires of silver shine."

As one that museth where broad sunshine laves
   The lawn by some cathedral, thro' the door   **190**
Hearing the holy organ rolling waves
     Of sound on roof and floor

Within, and anthem sung, is charm'd and tied
   To where he stands,—so stood I, when that flow
Of music left the lips of her that died
     To save her father's vow;

The daughter of the warrior Gileadite,
   A maiden pure; as when she went along
From Mizpeh's tower'd gate with welcome light,
     With timbrel and with song.   **200**

My words leapt forth: "Heaven heads the count of crimes
   With that wild oath." She render'd answer high:
"Not so, nor once alone; a thousand times
     I would be born and die.

"Single I grew, like some green plant, whose root
   Creeps to the garden water-pipes beneath,
Feeding the flower; but ere my flower to fruit
     Changed, I was ripe for death.

"My God, my land, my father—these did move
   Me from my bliss of life that Nature gave,   **210**
Lower'd softly with a threefold cord of love
     Down to a silent grave.

"And I went mourning, 'No fair Hebrew boy
   Shall smile away my maiden blame among
The Hebrew mothers'—emptied of all joy,
     Leaving the dance and song,

"Leaving the olive-gardens far below,
   Leaving the promise of my bridal bower,

The valleys of grape-loaded vines that glow
    Beneath the battled tower.   220

"The light white cloud swam over us. Anon
    We heard the lion roaring from his den;
We saw the large white stars rise one by one,
    Or, from the darken'd glen,

"Saw God divide the night with flying flame,
    And thunder on the everlasting hills.
I heard Him, for He spake, and grief became
    A solemn scorn of ills.

"When the next moon was roll'd into the sky,
    Strength came to me that equall'd my desire.   230
How beautiful a thing it was to die
    For God and for my sire!

"It comforts me in this one thought to dwell,
    That I subdued me to my father's will;
Because the kiss he gave me, ere I fell,
    Sweetens the spirit still.

"Moreover it is written that my race
    Hew'd Ammon, hip and thigh, from Aroer
On Arnon unto Minneth." Here her face
    Glow'd, as I look'd at her.   240

She lock'd her lips; she left me where I stood:
    "Glory to God," she sang, and past afar,
Thridding the sombre boskage of the wood,
    Toward the morning-star.

Losing her carol I stood pensively,
    As one that from a casement leans his head,
When midnight bells cease ringing suddenly,
    And the old year is dead.

"Alas! alas!" a low voice, full of care,
    Murmur'd beside me: "Turn and look on me;   250
I am that Rosamond, whom men call fair,
    If what I was I be.

"Would I had been some maiden coarse and poor!
    O me, that I should ever see the light!
Those dragon eyes of anger'd Eleanor
        Do hunt me, day and night."

She ceased in tears, fallen from hope and trust;
    To whom the Egyptian: "O, you tamely died!
You should have clung to Fulvia's waist, and thrust
        The dagger thro' her side."   260

With that sharp sound the white dawn's creeping beams,
    Stolen to my brain, dissolved the mystery
Of folded sleep. The captain of my dreams
        Ruled in the eastern sky.

Morn broaden'd on the borders of the dark
    Ere I saw her who clasp'd in her last trance
Her murder'd father's head, or Joan of Arc,
        A light of ancient France;

Or her who knew that Love can vanquish Death,
    Who kneeling, with one arm about her king,   270
Drew forth the poison with her balmy breath,
        Sweet as new buds in spring.

No memory labors longer from the deep
    Gold-mines of thought to lift the hidden ore
That glimpses, moving up, than I from sleep
        To gather and tell o'er

Each little sound and sight. With what dull pain
    Compass'd, how eagerly I sought to strike
Into that wondrous track of dreams again!
        But no two dreams are like.   280

As when a soul laments, which hath been blest,
    Desiring what is mingled with past years,
In yearnings that can never be exprest
        By signs or groans or tears;

Because all words, tho' cuil'd with choicest art,
    Failing to give the bitter of the sweet,

Wither beneath the palate, and the heart
    Faints, faded by its heat.

                          [publ. 1832, 1842]

TO J.S.[1]

THE wind that beats the mountain blows
    More softly round the open wold,
And gently comes the world to those
    That are cast in gentle mould.

And me this knowledge bolder made,
    Or else I had not dared to flow
In these words toward you, and invade
    Even with a verse your holy woe.

'Tis strange that those we lean on most,
    Those in whose laps our limbs are nursed,   10
Fall into shadow, soonest lost;
    Those we love first are taken first.

God gives us love. Something to love
    He lends us; but, when love is grown
To ripeness, that on which it throve
    Falls off, and love is left alone.

This is the curse of time. Alas!
    In grief I am not all unlearn'd;
Once thro' mine own doors Death did pass;
    One went who never hath return'd.   20

He will not smile—not speak to me
    Once more. Two years his chair is seen
Empty before us. That was he
    Without whose life I had not been.

[1] James Spedding, one of Tennyson's Cambridge circle (who was destined to be the devoted editor of Bacon); his brother Edward, who died young, was also a friend of Tennyson's.

Your loss is rarer; for this star
    Rose with you thro' a little arc
Of heaven, nor having wander'd far
    Shot on the sudden into dark.

I knew your brother; his mute dust
    I honor and his living worth;   **30**
A man more pure and bold and just
    Was never born into the earth.

I have not look'd upon you nigh
    Since that dear soul hath fallen asleep.
Great Nature is more wise than I;
    I will not tell you not to weep.

And tho' mine own eyes fill with dew,
    Drawn from the spirit thro' the brain,
I will not even preach to you,
    "Weep, weeping dulls the inward pain."   **40**

Let Grief be her own mistress still.
    She loveth her own anguish deep
More than much pleasure. Let her will
    Be done—to weep or not to weep.

I will not say, "God's ordinance
    Of death is blown in every wind;"
For that is not a common chance
    That takes away a noble mind.

His memory long will live alone
    In all our hearts, as mournful light   **50**
That broods above the fallen sun,
    And dwells in heaven half the night.

Vain solace! Memory standing near
    Cast down her eyes, and in her throat
Her voice seem'd distant, and a tear
    Dropt on the letters as I wrote.

I wrote I know not what. In truth,
    How *should* I soothe you any way,

Who miss the brother of your youth?
    Yet something I did wish to say;   60

For he too was a friend to me.
    Both are my friends, and my true breast
Bleedeth for both; yet it may be
    That only silence suiteth best.

Words weaker than your grief would make
    Grief more. 'T were better I should cease
Although myself could almost take
    The place of him that sleeps in peace.

Sleep sweetly, tender heart, in peace;
    Sleep, holy spirit, blessed soul,   70
While the stars burn, the moons increase,
    And the great ages onward roll.

Sleep till the end, true soul and sweet.
    Nothing comes to thee new or strange.
Sleep full of rest from head to feet;
    Lie still, dry dust, secure of change.
                    [publ. 1832]

BREAK, BREAK, BREAK

BREAK, break, break,
    On thy cold gray stones, O Sea!
And I would that my tongue could utter
    The thoughts that arise in me.

O, well for the fisherman's boy,
    That he shouts with his sister at play!
O, well for the sailor lad,
    That he sings in his boat on the bay!

And the stately ships go on
    To their haven under the hill;   10
But O for the touch of a vanish'd hand,
    And the sound of a voice that is still!

Break, break, break,
  At the foot of thy crags, O Sea!
But the tender grace of a day that is **dead**
  Will never come back to me.
           [1833–34; publ. 1842]

THE TWO VOICES

A STILL small voice spake unto me,
"Thou art so full of misery,
Were it not better not to be?"

Then to the still small voice I said:
"Let me not cast in endless shade
What is so wonderfully made."

To which the voice did urge reply:
"To-day I saw the dragon-fly
Come from the wells where he did lie.

"An inner impulse rent the veil   **10**
Of his old husk; from head to tail
Came out clear plates of sapphire mail.

"He dried his wings; like gauze they grew;
Thro' crofts and pastures wet with dew
A living flash of light he flew."

I said: "When first the world began,
Young Nature thro' five cycles ran,
And in the sixth she moulded man.

"She gave him mind, the lordliest
Proportion, and, above the rest,   **20**
Dominion in the head and breast."

Thereto the silent voice replied:
"Self-blinded are you by your pride,
Look up thro' night; the world is wide.

"This truth within thy mind rehearse,
That in a boundless universe
Is boundless better, boundless worse.

"Think you this mould of hopes and fears
Could find no statelier than his peers
In yonder hundred million spheres?"   30

It spake, moreover, in my mind:
"Tho' thou wert scatter'd to the wind,
Yet is there plenty of the kind."

Then did my response clearer fall:
"No compound of this earthly ball
Is like another, all in all."

To which he answer'd scoffingly:
"Good soul! suppose I grant it thee,
Who'll weep for thy deficiency?

"Or will one beam be less intense,   40
When thy peculiar difference
Is cancell'd in the world of sense?"

I would have said, "Thou canst not know,"
But my full heart, that work'd below,
Rain'd thro' my sight its overflow.

Again the voice spake unto me:
"Thou art so steep'd in misery,
Surely 't were better not to be.

"Thine anguish will not let thee sleep,   50
Nor any train of reason keep;
Thou canst not think, but thou wilt weep."

I said: "The years with change advance;
If I make dark my countenance,
I shut my life from happier chance.

"Some turn this sickness yet might take,
Even yet." But he: "What drug can make
A wither'd palsy cease to shake?"

I wept: "Tho' I should die, I know
That all about the thorn will blow
In tufts of rosy-tinted snow;   60

"And men, thro' novel spheres of thought
Still moving after truth long sought,
Will learn new things when I am not."

"Yet," said the secret voice, "some time,
Sooner or later, will gray prime
Make thy grass hoar with early rime.

"Not less swift souls that yearn for light,
Rapt after heaven's starry flight,
Would sweep the tracts of day and night.

"Not less the bee would range her cells,   70
The furzy prickle fire the dells,
The foxglove cluster dappled bells."

I said that "all the years invent;
Each month is various to present
The world with some development.

"Were this not well, to bide mine hour,
Tho' watching from a ruin'd tower
How grows the day of human power?"

"The highest-mounted mind," he said,
"Still sees the sacred morning spread   80
The silent summit overhead.

"Will thirty seasons render plain
Those lonely lights that still remain,
Just breaking over land and main?

"Or make that morn, from his cold crown
And crystal silence creeping down,
Flood with full daylight glebe and town?

"Forerun thy peers, thy time, and let
Thy feet, millenniums hence, be set
In midst of knowledge, dream'd not yet.   90

"Thou hast not gain'd a real height,
Nor art thou nearer to the light,
Because the scale is infinite.

" 'T were better not to breathe or speak,
Than cry for strength, remaining weak,
And seem to find, but still to seek.

"Moreover, but to seem to find
Asks what thou lackest, thought resign'd,
A healthy frame, a quiet mind."

I said: "When I am gone away,   100
'He dared not tarry,' men will say,
Doing dishonor to my clay."

"This is more vile," he made reply,
"To breathe and loathe, to live and sigh,
Than once from dread of pain to die.

"Sick art thou—a divided will
Still heaping on the fear of ill
The fear of men, a coward still.

"Do men love thee? Art thou so bound
To men that how thy name may sound   110
Will vex thee lying underground?

"The memory of the wither'd leaf
In endless time is scarce more brief
Than of the garner'd autumn-sheaf.

"Go, vexed spirit, sleep in trust;
The right ear that is fill'd with dust
Hears little of the false or just."

"Hard task, to pluck resolve," I cried,
"From emptiness and the waste wide
Of that abyss, or scornful pride!   **120**

"Nay—rather yet that I could raise
One hope that warm'd me in the days
While still I yearn'd for human praise.

"When, wide in soul and bold of tongue,
Among the tents I paused and sung,
The distant battle flash'd and rung.

"I sung the joyful Pæan clear,
And, sitting, burnish'd without fear
The brand, the buckler, and the spear—

"Waiting to strive a happy strife,   **130**
To war with falsehood to the knife,
And not to lose the good of life—

"Some hidden principle to move,
To put together, part and prove,
And mete the bounds of hate and love—

"As far as might be, to carve out
Free space for every human doubt,
That the whole mind might orb about—

"To search thro' all I felt or saw,
The springs of life, the depths of awe,   **140**
And reach the law within the law;

"At least, not rotting like a weed,
But, having sown some generous seed,
Fruitful of further thought and deed,

"To pass, when Life her light withdraws,
Not void of righteous self-applause,
Nor in a merely selfish cause—

"In some good cause, not in mine own,
To perish, wept for, honor'd, known,
And like a warrior overthrown;   150

"Whose eyes are dim with glorious tears,
When, soil'd with noble dust, he hears
His country's war-song thrill his ears:

"Then dying of a mortal stroke,
What time the foeman's line is broke,
And all the war is roll'd in smoke."

"Yea!" said the voice, "thy dream was good,
While thou abodest in the bud.
It was the stirring of the blood.

"If Nature put not forth her power   160
About the opening of the flower,
Who is it that could live an hour?

"Then comes the check, the change, the fall,
Pain rises up, old pleasures pall.
There is one remedy for all.

"Yet hadst thou, thro' enduring pain,
Link'd month to month with such a chain
Of knitted purport, all were vain

"Thou hadst not between death and birth
Dissolved the riddle of the earth.   170
So were thy labor little worth.

"That men with knowledge merely play'd,
I told thee—hardly nigher made,
Tho' scaling slow from grade to grade;

"Much less this dreamer, deaf and blind,
Named man, may hope some truth to find,
That bears relation to the mind.

"For every worm beneath the moon
Draws different threads, and late and soon
Spins, toiling out his own cocoon.   180

"Cry, faint not: either Truth is born
Beyond the polar gleam forlorn,
Or in the gateways of the morn.

"Cry, faint not, climb: the summits slope
Beyond the furthest flights of hope,
Wrapt in dense cloud from base to cope.

"Sometimes a little corner shines,
As over rainy mist inclines
A gleaming crag with belts of pines.

"I will go forward, sayest thou,   190
I shall not fail to find her now.
Look up, the fold is on her brow.

"If straight thy track, or if oblique,
Thou know'st not. Shadows thou dost strike,
Embracing cloud, Ixion-like;

"And owning but a little more
Than beasts, abidest lame and poor,
Calling thyself a little lower

"Than angels. Cease to wail and brawl!
Why inch by inch to darkness crawl?   200
There is one remedy for all."

"O dull, one-sided voice," said I,
"Wilt thou make everything a lie,
To flatter me that I may die?

"I know that age to age succeeds,
Blowing a noise of tongues and deeds,
A dust of systems and of creeds.

"I cannot hide that some have striven,
Achieving calm, to whom was given
The joy that mixes man with Heaven;   210

"Who, rowing hard against the stream,
Saw distant gates of Eden gleam,
And did not dream it was a dream;

"But heard, by secret transport led,
Even in the charnels of the dead,
The murmur of the fountain-head—

"Which did accomplish their desire,
Bore and forebore, and did not tire,
Like Stephen, an unquenched fire.

"He heeded not reviling tones,   220
Nor sold his heart to idle moans,
Tho' cursed and scorn'd, and bruised with stones;

"But looking upward, full of grace,
He pray'd, and from a happy place
God's glory smote him on the face."

The sullen answer slid betwixt:
"Not that the grounds of hope were fix'd,
The elements were kindlier mix'd."

I said: "I toil beneath the curse,
But, knowing not the universe,   230
I fear to slide from bad to worse;

"And that, in seeking to undo
One riddle, and to find the true,
I knit a hundred others new;

"Or that this anguish fleeting hence,
Unmanacled from bonds of sense,
Be fix'd and frozen to permanence:

"For I go, weak from suffering here;
Naked I go, and void of cheer:
What is it that I may not fear?"   240

"Consider well," the voice replied,
"His face that two hours since hath died;
Wilt thou find passion, pain or pride?

"Will he obey when one commands?
Or answer should one press his hands?
He answers not, nor understands.

"His palms are folded on his breast;
There is no other thing express'd
But long disquiet merged in rest.

"His lips are very mild and meek;   250
Tho' one should smite him on the cheek,
And on the mouth, he will not speak.

"His little daughter, whose sweet face
He kiss'd, taking his last embrace,
Becomes dishonor to her race—

"His sons grow up that bear his name,
Some grow to honor, some to shame,—
But he is chill to praise or blame.

"He will not hear the north-wind rave,
Nor, moaning, household shelter crave   260
From winter rains that beat his grave.

"High up the vapors fold and swim;
About him broods the twilight dim;
The place he knew forgetteth him."

"If all be dark, vague voice," I said,
"These things are wrapt in doubt and dread,
Nor canst thou show the dead are dead.

"The sap dries up: the plant declines.
A deeper tale my heart divines.
Know I not death? the outward signs?   270

"I found him when my years were few;
A shadow on the graves I knew,
And darkness in the village yew.

"From grave to grave the shadow crept;
In her still place the morning wept;
Touch'd by his feet the daisy slept.

"The simple senses crown'd his head:
'Omega! thou art Lord,' they said,
'We find no motion in the dead!'

"Why, if man rot in dreamless ease,   280
Should that plain fact, as taught by these,
Not make him sure that he shall cease?

"Who forged that other influence,
That heat of inward evidence,
By which he doubts against the sense?

"He owns the fatal gift of eyes,
That read his spirit blindly wise,
Not simple as a thing that dies.

"Here sits he shaping wings to fly;
His heart forebodes a mystery;   290
He names the name Eternity.

"That type of Perfect in his mind
In Nature can he nowhere find.
He sows himself on every wind.

'He seems to hear a Heavenly Friend,
And thro' thick veils to apprehend
A labor working to an end.

"The end and the beginning vex
His reason: many things perplex,
With motions, checks, and counterchecks.   300

"He knows a baseness in his blood
At such strange war with something good,
He may not do the thing he would.

"Heaven opens inward, chasms yawn,
Vast images in glimmering dawn,
Half shown, are broken and withdrawn.

"Ah! sure within him and without,
Could his dark wisdom find it out,
There must be answer to his doubt,

"But thou canst answer not again.   310
With thine own weapon art thou slain,
Or thou wilt answer but in vain.

"The doubt would rest, I dare not solve,
In the same circle we revolve.
Assurance only breeds resolve."

As when a billow, blown against,
Falls back, the voice with which I fenced
A little ceased, but recommenced:

"Where wert thou when thy father play'd
In his free field, and pastime made,   326
A merry boy in sun and shade?

"A merry boy they call'd him then,
He sat upon the knees of men
In days that never come again;

"Before the little ducts began
To feed thy bones with lime, and ran
Their course, till thou wert also man:

"Who took a wife, who rear'd his race,
Whose wrinkles gather'd on his face,
Whose troubles number with his days;   330

"A life of nothings, nothing worth,
From that first nothing ere his birth
To that last nothing under earth!"

"These words," I said, "are like the rest;
No certain clearness, but at best
A vague suspicion of the breast:

"But if I grant, thou mightst defend
The thesis which thy words intend—
That to begin implies to end;

"Yet how should I for certain hold,   340
Because my memory is so cold,
That I first was in human mould?

"I cannot make this matter plain,
But I would shoot, howe'er in vain,
A random arrow from the brain.

"It may be that no life is found,
Which only to one engine bound
Falls off, but cycles always round.

"As old mythologies relate,
Some draught of Lethe might await   350
The slipping thro' from state to state;

"As here we find in trances, men
Forget the dream that happens then,
Until they fall in trance again;

"So might we, if our state were such
As one before, remember much,
For those two likes might meet and touch.

"But, if I lapsed from nobler place,
Some legend of a fallen race
Alone might hint of my disgrace;   360

"Some vague emotion of delight
In gazing up an Alpine height,
Some yearning toward the lamps of night;

"Or if thro' lower lives I came—
Tho' all experience past became
Consolidate in mind and frame—

"I might forget my weaker lot;
For is not our first year forgot?
The haunts of memory echo not.

"And men, whose reason long was blind,   370
From cells of madness unconfined,
Oft lose whole years of darker mind.

"Much more, if first I floated free,
As naked essence, must I be
Incompetent of memory;

"For memory dealing but with time,
And he with matter, could she climb
Beyond her own material prime?

"Moreover, something is or seems,
That touches me with mystic gleams,   380
Like glimpses of forgotten dreams—

"Of something felt, like something here;
Of something done, I know not where;
Such as no language may declare."

The still voice laugh'd. "I talk," said he.
"Not with thy dreams. Suffice it thee
Thy pain is a reality."

"But thou," said I, "hast missed thy mark,
Who sought'st to wreck my mortal ark,
By making all the horizon dark.   390

"Why not set forth, if I should do
This rashness, that which might ensue
With this old soul in organs new?

"Whatever crazy sorrow saith,
No life that breathes with human breath
Has ever truly long'd for death.

" 'T is life, whereof our nerves are scant,
O, life, not death, for which we pant;
More life, and fuller, that I want."

I ceased, and sat as one forlorn.   400
Then said the voice, in quiet scorn,
"Behold, it is the Sabbath morn."

And I arose, and I released
The casement, and the light increased
With freshness in the dawning east.

Like soften'd airs that blowing steal,
When meres begin to uncongeal,
The sweet church bells began to peal.

On to God's house the people prest;   410
Passing the place where each must rest,
Each enter'd like a welcome guest.

One walk'd between his wife and child,
With measured footfall firm and mild,
And now and then he gravely smiled.

The prudent partner of his blood
Lean'd on him, faithful, gentle, good,
Wearing the rose of womanhood.

And in their double love secure,
The little maiden walk'd demure,
Pacing with downward eyelids pure. 420

These three made unity so sweet,
My frozen heart began to beat,
Remembering its ancient heat.

I blest them, and they wander'd on;
I spoke, but answer came there none;
The dull and bitter voice was gone.

A second voice was at mine ear,
A little whisper silver-clear,
A murmur, "Be of better cheer."

As from some blissful neighborhood, 430
A notice faintly understood,
"I see the end, and know the good."

A little hint to solace woe,
A hint, a whisper breathing low,
"I may not speak of what I know."

Like an Æolian harp that wakes
No certain air, but overtakes
Far thought with music that it makes;

Such seem'd the whisper at my side:
"What is it thou knowest, sweet voice?" I cried. 440
"A hidden hope," the voice replied;

So heavenly-toned, that in that hour
From out my sullen heart a power
Broke, like the rainbow from the shower,

To feel, altho' no tongue can prove,
That every cloud, that spreads above
And veileth love, itself is love.

And forth into the fields I went,
And Nature's living motion lent
The pulse of hope to discontent.   459

I wonder'd at the bounteous hours,
The slow result of winter showers;
You scarce could see the grass for flowers.

I wonder'd, while I paced along;
The woods were fill'd so full with song,
There seem'd no room for sense of wrong;

And all so variously wrought,
I marvell'd how the mind was brought
To anchor by one gloomy thought;

And wherefore rather I made choice   460
To commune with that barren voice,
Than him that said, "Rejoice! Rejoice!"
                          [1833; publ. 1842]

ULYSSES

IT LITTLE profits that an idle king,
By this still hearth, among these barren crags,
Match'd with an aged wife, I mete and dole
Unequal laws unto a savage race,
That hoard, and sleep, and feed, and know not me.
I cannot rest from travel; I will drink
Life to the lees. All times I have enjoy'd
Greatly, have suffer'd greatly, both with those
That loved me, and alone; on shore, and when
Thro' scudding drifts the rainy Hyades   10
Vext the dim sea. I am become a name;
For always roaming with a hungry heart
Much have I seen and known,—cities of men

And manners, climates, councils, governments,
Myself not least, but honor'd of them all,—
And drunk delight of battle with my peers,
Far on the ringing plains of windy Troy.
I am a part of all that I have met;
Yet all experience is an arch wherethro'
Gleams that untravell'd world whose margin fades   20
For ever and for ever when I move.
How dull it is to pause, to make an end,
To rust unburnish'd, not to shine in use!
As tho' to breathe were life! Life piled on life
Were all too little, and of one to me
Little remains; but every hour is saved
From that eternal silence, something more,
A bringer of new things; and vile it were
For some three suns to store and hoard myself,
And this gray spirit yearning in desire   30
To follow knowledge like a sinking star,
Beyond the utmost bound of human thought.

   This is my son, mine own Telemachus,
To whom I leave the sceptre and the isle,—
Well-loved of me, discerning to fulfil
This labor, by slow prudence to make mild
A rugged people, and thro' soft degrees
Subdue them to the useful and the good.
Most blameless is he, centred in the sphere
Of common duties, decent not to fail   40
In offices of tenderness, and pay
Meet adoration to my household gods,
When I am gone. He works his work, I mine.

   There lies the port; the vessel puffs her sail;
There gloom the dark, broad seas. My mariners,
Souls that have toil'd, and wrought, and thought with me,—
That ever with a frolic welcome took
The thunder and the sunshine, and opposed
Free hearts, free foreheads,—you and I are old;
Old age hath yet his honor and his toil.   50
Death closes all; but something ere the end,
Some work of noble note, may yet be done,
Not unbecoming men that strove with Gods.
The lights begin to twinkle from the rocks;
The long day wanes; the slow moon climbs; the deep

Moans round with many voices. Come, my friends,
'Tis not too late to seek a newer world.
Push off, and sitting well in order smite
The sounding furrows; for my purpose holds
To sail beyond the sunset, and the baths   60
Of all the western stars, until I die.
It may be that the gulfs will wash us down;
It may be we shall touch the Happy Isles,
And see the great Achilles, whom we knew.
Tho' much is taken, much abides; and tho'
We are not now that strength which in old days
Moved earth and heaven, that which we are, we are,—
One equal temper of heroic hearts,
Made weak by time and fate, but strong in will
To strive, to seek, to find, and not to yield.   70

[1833; publ. 1842]

TITHONUS

THE woods decay, the woods decay and fall,
The vapors weep their burthen to the ground,
Man comes and tills the field and lies beneath,
And after many a summer dies the swan.
Me only cruel immortality
Consumes; I wither slowly in thine arms,   ,
Here at the quiet limit of the world,
A white-hair'd shadow roaming like a dream
The ever-silent spaces of the East,
Far-folded mists, and gleaming halls of morn.   10
   Alas! for this gray shadow, once a man—
So glorious in his beauty and thy choice,
Who madest him thy chosen, that he seem'd
To his great heart none other than a God!
I ask'd thee, "Give me immortality."
Then didst thou grant mine asking with a smile,
Like wealthy men who care not how they give.
But thy strong Hours indignant work'd their wills,
And beat me down and marr'd and wasted me,
And tho' they could not end me, left me maim'd   20
To dwell in presence of immortal youth,

Immortal age beside immortal youth,
And all I was in ashes. Can thy love,
Thy beauty, make amends, tho' even now,
Close over us, the silver star, thy guide,
Shines in those tremulous eyes that fill with tears
To hear me? Let me go; take back thy gift.
Why should a man desire in any way
To vary from the kindly race of men,
Or pass beyond the goal of ordinance   30
Where all should pause, as is most meet for all?

A soft air fans the cloud apart; there comes
A glimpse of that dark world where I was born.
Once more the old mysterious glimmer steals
From thy pure brows, and from thy shoulders pure,
And bosom beating with a heart renew'd.
Thy cheek begins to redden thro' the gloom,
Thy sweet eyes brighten slowly close to mine,
Ere yet they blind the stars, and the wild team
Which love thee, yearning for thy yoke, arise,   40
And shake the darkness from their loosen'd manes,
And beat the twilight into flakes of fire.

Lo! ever thus thou growest beautiful
In silence, then before thine answer given
Departest, and thy tears are on my cheek.

Why wilt thou ever scare me with thy tears,
And make me tremble lest a saying learnt,
In days far-off, on that dark earth, be true?
"The Gods themselves cannot recall their gifts."

Ay me! ay me! with what another heart   50
In days far-off, and with what other eyes
I used to watch—if I be he that watch'd—
The lucid outline forming round thee; saw
The dim curls kindle into sunny rings;
Changed with thy mystic change, and felt my blood
Glow with the glow that slowly crimson'd all
Thy presence and thy portals, while I lay,
Mouth, forehead, eyelids, growing dewy-warm
With kisses balmier than half-opening buds
Of April, and could hear the lips that kiss'd   60
Whispering I knew not what of wild and sweet,
Like that strange song I heard Apollo sing,
While Ilion like a mist rose into towers.

Yet hold me not for ever in thine East;
How can my nature longer mix with thine?
Coldly thy rosy shadows bathe me, cold
Are all thy lights, and cold my wrinkled feet
Upon thy glimmering thresholds, when the steam
Floats up from those dim fields about the homes
Of happy men that have the power to die,   70
And grassy barrows of the happier dead.
Release me, and restore me to the ground.
Thou seest all things, thou wilt see my grave;
Thou wilt renew thy beauty morn by morn,
I earth in earth forget these empty courts,
And thee returning on thy silver wheels.

          [1833–34; rev. 1859; publ. 1860[1]]

TIRESIAS [2]

TO E. FITZGERALD

OLD FITZ, who from your suburb grange,
   Where once I tarried for a while,
Glance at the wheeling orb of change,
   And greet it with a kindly smile;
Whom yet I see as there you sit
   Beneath your sheltering garden-tree,
And watch your doves about you flit,
   And plant on shoulder, hand, and knee,
Or on your head their rosy feet,
   As if they knew your diet spares   10
Whatever moved in that full sheet
   Let down to Peter at his prayers;
Who live on milk and meal and grass;
   And once for ten long weeks I tried
Your table of Pythagoras,

[1] A full critical study of the early and late versions has been made
by Mary J. Donahue, *PMLA* 64 (1949), 400–16.
[2] The narrative poem was partly written at the time of *Ulysses*, in
1833, the dedication shortly before FitzGerald's death (June 14,
1883); the epilogue was added before the *Tiresias* volume was published.

And seem'd at first "a thing enskied,"
As Shakespeare has it, airy-light
   To float above the ways of men,
Then fell from that half-spiritual height
   Chill'd, till I tasted flesh again   20
One night when earth was winter-black,
   And all the heavens flash'd in frost;
And on me, half-asleep, came back
   That wholesome heat the blood had lost,
And set me climbing icy capes
   And glaciers, over which there roll'd
To meet me long-arm'd vines with grapes
   Of Eshcol hugeness; for the cold
Without, and warmth within me, wrought
   To mould the dream; but none can say   30
That Lenten fare makes Lenten thought
   Who reads your golden Eastern lay,
Than which I know no version done
   In English more divinely well;
A planet equal to the sun
   Which cast it, that large infidel
Your Omar; and your Omar drew
   Full-handed plaudits from our best
In modern letters, and from two,
   Old friends outvaluing all the rest,   40
Two voices heard on earth no more;
   But we old friends are still alive,
And I am nearing seventy-four,
   While you have touch'd at seventy-five,
And so I send a birthday line
   Of greeting; and my son, who dipt
In some forgotten book of mine
   With sallow scraps of manuscript,
And dating many a year ago,
   Has hit on this, which you will take,   50
My Fitz, and welcome, as I know,
   Less for its own than for the sake
Of one recalling gracious times,
   When, in our younger London days,
You found some merit in my rhymes,
   And I more pleasure in your praise.

TIRESIAS

I WISH I were as in the years of old,
While yet the blessed daylight made itself
Ruddy thro' both the roofs of sight, and woke
These eyes, now dull, but then so keen to seek
The meanings ambush'd under all they saw,
The flight of birds, the flame of sacrifice,
What omens may foreshadow fate to man
And woman, and the secret of the Gods.

     My son, the Gods, despite of human prayer,
Are slower to forgive than human kings.   10
The great God Arês burns in anger still
Against the guiltless heirs of him from Tyre,
Our Cadmus, out of whom thou art, who found
Beside the springs of Dircê, smote, and still'd
Thro' all its folds the multitudinous beast,
The dragon, which our trembling fathers call'd
The God's own son.

             A tale, that told to me,
When but thine age, by age as winter-white
As mine is now, amazed, but made me yearn
For larger glimpses of that more than man   20
Which rolls the heavens, and lifts and lays the deep,
Yet loves and hates with mortal hates and loves,
And moves unseen among the ways of men.

     Then, in my wanderings all the lands that lie
Subjected to the Heliconian ridge
Have heard this footstep fall, altho' my wont
Was more to scale the highest of the heights
With some strange hope to see the nearer God.

     One naked peak—the sister of the Sun
Would climb from out the dark, and linger there   30
To silver all the valleys with her shafts—
There once, but long ago, five-fold thy term
Of years, I lay; the winds were dead for heat;
The noonday crag made the hand burn; and sick
For shadow—not one bush was near—I rose,
Following a torrent till its myriad falls
Found silence in the hollows underneath.

There in a secret olive-glade I saw
Pallas Athene climbing from the bath
In anger; yet one glittering foot disturb'd 40
The lucid well; one snowy knee was prest
Against the margin flowers; a dreadful light
Came from her golden hair, her golden helm
And all her golden armor on the grass,
And from her virgin breast, and virgin eyes
Remaining fixt on mine, till mine grew dark
For ever, and I heard a voice that said,
"Henceforth be blind, for thou hast seen too much,
And speak the truth that no man may believe."
    Son, in the hidden world of sight that lives 50
Behind this darkness, I behold her still,
Beyond all work of those who carve the stone,
Beyond all dreams of Godlike womanhood,
Ineffable beauty, out of whom, at a glance,
And as it were, perforce, upon me flash'd
The power of prophesying—but to me
No power—so chain'd and coupled with the curse
Of blindness and their unbelief who heard
And heard not, when I spake of famine, plague,
Shrine-shattering earthquake, fire, flood, thunderbolt, 60
And angers of the Gods for evil done
And expiation lack'd—no power on Fate
Theirs, or mine own! for when the crowd would roar
For blood, for war, whose issue was their doom,
To cast wise words among the multitude
Was flinging fruit to lions; nor, in hours
Of civil outbreak, when I knew the twain
Would each waste each, and bring on both the yoke
Of stronger states, was mine the voice to curb
The madness of our cities and their kings. 70
    Who ever turn'd upon his heel to hear
My warning that the tyranny of one
Was prelude to the tyranny of all?
My counsel that the tyranny of all
Led backward to the tyranny of one?
    This power hath work'd no good to aught that lives,
And these blind hands were useless in their wars.
O, therefore, that the unfulfill'd desire,
The grief for ever born from griefs to be,

The boundless yearning of the prophet's heart—   80
Could *that* stand forth, and like a statue, rear'd
To some great citizen, win all praise from all
Who past it, saying, "That was he!"
                              In vain!
Virtue must shape itself in deed, and those
Whom weakness or necessity have cramp'd
Within themselves, immerging, each, his urn
In his own well, draws solace as he may.

  Menœceus, thou hast eyes, and I can hear
Too plainly what full tides of onset sap
Our seven high gates, and what a weight of war   90
Rides on those ringing axles! jingle of bits,
Shouts, arrows, tramp of the horn-footed horse
That grind the glebe to powder! Stony showers
Of that ear-stunning hail of Arês crash
Along the sounding walls. Above, below,
Shock after shock, the song-built towers and gates
Reel, bruised and butted with the shuddering
War-thunder of iron rams; and from within
The city comes a murmur void of joy,
Lest she be taken captive—maidens, wives,   100
And mothers with their babblers of the dawn,
And oldest age in shadow from the night,
Falling about their shrines before their Gods,
And wailing, "Save us."
                              And they wail to thee!
These eyeless eyes, that cannot see thine own,
See this, that only in thy virtue lies
The saving of our Thebes; for, yesternight,
To me, the great God Arês, whose one bliss
Is war and human sacrifice—himself
Blood-red from battle, spear and helmet tipt   110
With stormy light as on a mast at sea,
Stood out before a darkness, crying, "Thebes,
Thy Thebes shall fall and perish, for I loathe
The seed of Cadmus—yet if one of these
By his own hand—if one of these—"
                              My son,
No sound is breathed so potent to coerce,
And to conciliate, as their names who dare
For that sweet mother land which gave them birth

Nobly to do, nobly to die. Their names,
Graven on memorial columns, are a song 120
Heard in the future; few, but more than wall
And rampart, their examples reach a hand
Far thro' all years, and everywhere they meet
And kindle generous purpose, and the strength
To mould it into action pure as theirs.
    Fairer thy fate than mine, if life's best end
Be to end well! and thou refusing this,
Unvenerable will thy memory be
While men shall move the lips; but if thou dare—
Thou, one of these, the race of Cadmus—then 130
No stone is fitted in yon marble girth
Whose echo shall not tongue thy glorious doom,
Nor in this pavement but shall ring thy name
To every hoof that clangs it, and the springs
Of Dircê laving yonder battle-plain,
Heard from the roofs by night, will murmur thee
To thine own Thebes, while Thebes thro' thee shall stand
Firm-based with all her Gods.
               The Dragon's cave
Half hid, they tell me, now in flowing vines—
Where once he dwelt and whence he roll'd himself 140
At dead of night—thou knowest, and that smooth rock
Before it, altar-fashion'd, where of late
The woman-breasted Sphinx, with wings drawn back,
Folded her lion paws, and look'd to Thebes.
There blanch the bones of whom she slew, and these
Mixt with her own, because the fierce beast found
A wiser than herself, and dash'd herself
Dead in her rage; but thou art wise enough,
Tho' young, to love thy wiser, blunt the curse
Of Pallas, hear, and tho' I speak the truth 150
Believe I speak it, let thine own hand strike
Thy youthful pulses into rest and quench
The red God's anger, fearing not to plunge
Thy torch of life in darkness, rather—thou
Rejoicing that the sun, the moon, the stars
Send no such light upon the ways of men
As one great deed.
           Thither, my son, and there
Thou, that hast never known the embrace of love,

Offer thy maiden life.
               This useless hand!
I felt one warm tear fall upon it. Gone!   **160**
He will achieve his greatness.
                   But for me,
I would that I were gather'd to my rest,
And mingled with the famous kings of old,
On whom about their ocean-islets flash
The faces of the Gods—the wise man's word,
Here trampled by the populace underfoot,
There crown'd with worship—and these eyes will find
The men I knew, and watch the chariot whirl
About the goal again, and hunters race
The shadowy lion, and the warrior-kings,   **170**
In height and prowess more than human, strive
Again for glory, while the golden lyre
Is ever sounding in heroic ears
Heroic hymns, and every way the vales
Wind, clouded with the grateful incense-fume
Of those who mix all odor to the Gods
On one far height in one far-shining fire.

"One height and one far-shining fire!"
    And while I fancied that my friend
For this brief idyll would require   **180**
    A less diffuse and opulent end,
And would defend his judgment well,
    If I should deem it over nice—
The tolling of his funeral bell
    Broke on my Pagan Paradise,
And mixt the dream of classic times,
    And all the phantoms of the dream,
With present grief, and made the rhymes,
    That miss'd his living welcome, seem
Like would-be guests an hour too late,   **190**
    Who down the highway moving on
With easy laughter find the gate
    Is bolted, and the master gone.
Gone into darkness, that full light
    Of friendship! past, in sleep, away
By night, into the deeper night!

The deeper night? A clearer day
Than our poor twilight dawn on earth—
    If night, what barren toil to be!
What life, so maim'd by night, were worth
    Our living out? Not mine to me
Remembering all the golden hours
    Now silent, and so many dead,
And him the last; and laying flowers,
    This wreath, above his honor'd head,
And praying that, when I from hence
    Shall fade with him into the unknown,
My close of earth's experience
    May prove as peaceful as his own.

[1833 f.; publ. 1885]

YOU ASK ME, WHY, THO' ILL AT EASE

You ask me, why, tho' ill at ease,
    Within this region I subsist,
    Whose spirits falter in the mist,
And languish for the purple seas.

It is the land that freemen till,
    That sober-suited Freedom chose,
    The land, where girt with friends or foes
A man may speak the thing he will;

A land of settled government,
    A land of just and old renown,
    Where Freedom slowly broadens down
From precedent to precedent;

Where faction seldom gathers head,
    But, by degrees to fullness wrought,
    The strength of some diffusive thought
Hath time and space to work and spread.

Should banded unions persecute
    Opinion, and induce a time

When single thought is civil crime,
And individual freedom mute,   20

Tho' power should make from land to land
    The name of Britain trebly great—
    Tho' every channel of the State
Should fill and choke with golden sand—

Yet waft me from the harbor-mouth,
    Wild wind! I seek a warmer sky,
    And I will see before I die
The palms and temples of the South.
                    [1833–34; publ. 1842]

OF OLD SAT FREEDOM ON THE HEIGHTS

OF OLD sat Freedom on the heights,
    The thunders breaking at her feet;
Above her shook the starry lights;
    She heard the torrents meet.

There in her place she did rejoice,
    Self-gather'd in her prophet-mind,
But fragments of her mighty voice
    Came rolling on the wind.

Then stept she down thro' town and field
    To mingle with the human race,   10
And part by part to men reveal'd
    The fullness of her face—

Grave mother of majestic works,
    From her isle-altar gazing down,
Who, Godlike, grasps the triple forks,
    And, king-like, wears the crown.

Her open eyes desire the truth.
    The wisdom of a thousand years
Is in them. May perpetual youth
    Keep dry their light from tears;   20

That her fair form may stand and shine,
  Make bright our days and light our dreams,
Turning to scorn with lips divine
  'The falsehood of extremes!
                    [1833–34; publ. 1842]

LOVE THOU THY LAND,
WITH LOVE FAR-BROUGHT

LOVE thou thy land, with love far-brought
  From out the storied past, and used
  Within the present, but transfused
Thro' future time by power of thought;

True love turn'd round on fixed poles,
  Love, that endures not sordid ends,
  For English natures, freemen, friends,
Thy brothers and immortal souls.

But pamper not a hasty time,
  Nor feed with crude imaginings   **10**
  The herd, wild hearts and feeble wings
That every sophister can lime.

Deliver not the tasks of might
  To weakness, neither hide the ray
  From those, not blind, who wait for day,
Tho' sitting girt with doubtful light.

Make knowledge circle with the winds;
  But let her herald, Reverence, fly
  Before her to whatever sky
Bear seed of men and growth of minds.   **20**

Watch what main-currents draw the years;
  Cut Prejudice against the grain.
  But gentle words are always gain;
Regard the weakness of thy peers.

Nor toil for title, place, or touch
    Of pension, neither count on praise—
    It grows to guerdon after-days.
Nor deal in watch-words overmuch;

Not clinging to some ancient saw,
    Not master'd by some modern term,   30
    Not swift nor slow to change, but firm;
And in its season bring the law,

That from Discussion's lip may fall
    With Life that, working strongly, binds—
    Set in all lights by many minds,
To close the interests of all.

For Nature also, cold and warm,
    And moist and dry, devising long,
    Thro' many agents making strong,
Matures the individual form.   40

Meet is it changes should control
    Our being, lest we rust in ease.
    We all are changed by still degrees,
All but the basis of the soul.

So let the change which comes be free
    To ingroove itself with that which flies,
    And work, a joint of state, that plies
Its office, moved with sympathy.

A saying hard to shape in act;
    For all the past of Time reveals   50
    A bridal dawn of thunder-peals,
Wherever Thought hath wedded Fact.

Even now we hear with inward strife
    A motion toiling in the gloom—
    The Spirit of the years to come
Yearning to mix himself with Life.

A slow-develop'd strength awaits
    Completion in a painful school;

Phantoms of other forms of rule,
New Majesties of mighty States—   60

The warders of the growing hour,
    But vague in vapor, hard to mark;
    And round them sea and air are dark
With great contrivances of Power.

Of many changes, aptly join'd,
    Is bodied forth the second whole.
    Regard gradation, lest the soul
Of Discord race the rising wind;

A wind to puff your idol-fires,
    And heap their ashes on the head;   70
    To shame the boast so often made,
That we are wiser than our sires.

O, yet, if Nature's evil star
    Drive men in manhood, as in youth,
    To follow flying steps of Truth
Across the brazen bridge of war—

If New and Old, disastrous feud,
    Must ever shock, like armed foes,
    And this be true, till Time shall close,
That Principles are rain'd in blood;   80

Not yet the wise of heart would cease
    To hold his hope thro' shame and guilt,
    But with his hand against the hilt,
Would pace the troubled land, like Peace;

Not less, tho' dogs of Faction bay,
    Would serve his kind in deed and word,
    Certain, if knowledge bring the sword,
That knowledge takes the sword away—

Would love the gleams of good that broke
    From either side, nor veil his eyes;   90
    And if some dreadful need should rise
Would strike, and firmly, and one stroke.

To-morrow yet would reap to-day,
  As we bear blossom of the dead;
   Earn well the thrifty months, nor wea
Raw Haste, half-sister to Delay.
                [1833–34; publ. 1842]

ST. AGNES' EVE

DEEP on the convent-roof the snows
  Are sparkling to the moon;
My breath to heaven like vapor goes;
  May my soul follow soon!
The shadows of the convent-towers
  Slant down the snowy sward,
Still creeping with the creeping hours
  That lead me to my Lord.
Make Thou my spirit pure and clear
  As are the frosty skies,
Or this first snowdrop of the year   10
  That in my bosom lies.

As these white robes are soil'd and dark,
  To yonder shining ground;
As this pale taper's earthly spark,
  To yonder argent round;
So shows my soul before the Lamb,
  My spirit before Thee;
So in mine earthly house I am,
  To that I hope to be.   20
Break up the heavens, O Lord! and far,
  Thro' all yon starlight keen,
Draw me, thy bride, a glittering star,
  In raiment white and clean.

He lifts me to the golden doors;
  The flashes come and go;
All heaven bursts her starry floors,
  And strows her lights below,
And deepens on and up! the gates
  Roll back, and far within   30

For me the Heavenly Bridegroom waits,
   To make me pure of sin.
The Sabbaths of Eternity,
   One Sabbath deep and wide—
A light upon the shining sea—
   The Bridegroom with his bride!
              [1834; publ. 1836]

THE EPIC

AT FRANCIS ALLEN'S on the Christmas-eve,—
The game of forfeits done—the girls all kiss'd
Beneath the sacred bush and past away—
The parson Holmes, the poet Everard Hall,
The host, and I sat round the wassail-bowl,
Then half-way ebb'd; and there we held a talk,
How all the old honor had from Christmas gone,
Or gone or dwindled down to some odd games
In some odd nooks like this; till I, tired out
With cutting eights that day upon the pond,   10
Where, three times slipping from the outer edge,
I bump'd the ice into three several stars,
Fell in a doze; and half-awake I heard
The parson taking wide and wider sweeps,
Now harping on the church-commissioners,
Now hawking at geology and schism,
Until I woke, and found him settled down
Upon the general decay of faith
Right thro' the world: "at home was little left,
And none abroad; there was no anchor, none,   20
To hold by." Francis, laughing, clapt his hand
On Everard's shoulder, with "I hold by him."
"And I," quoth Everard, "by the wassail-bowl."
"Why yes," I said, "we knew your gift that way
At college; but another which you had—
I mean of verse (for so we held it then),
What came of that?" "You know," said Frank, "he burnt
His epic, his King Arthur, some twelve books"—
And then to me demanding why: "O, sir,
He thought that nothing new was said, or else   30

Something so said 't was nothing—that a truth
Looks freshest in the fashion of the day;
God knows; he has a mint of reasons; ask.
It pleased *me* well enough." "Nay, nay," said Hall,
"Why take the style of those heroic times?
For nature brings not back the mastodon,
Nor we those times; and why should any man
Remodel models? these twelve books of mine
Were faint Homeric echoes, nothing-worth,
Mere chaff and draff, much better burnt." "But I,"   **46**
Said Francis, "pick'd the eleventh from this hearth.
And have it; keep a thing, its use will come.
I hoard it as a sugar-plum for Holmes."
He laugh'd, and I, tho' sleepy, like a horse
That hears the corn-bin open, prick'd my ears;
For I remember'd Everard's college fame
When we were Freshmen. Then at my request
He brought it; and the poet, little urged,
But with some prelude of disparagement,
Read, mouthing out his hollow oes and aes,   **50**
Deep-chested music, and to this result.

MORTE D'ARTHUR

So ALL day long the noise of battle roll'd
Among the mountains by the winter sea,
Until King Arthur's table, man by man,
Had fallen in Lyonnesse about their lord,
King Arthur; then, because his wound was deep,
The bold Sir Bedivere uplifted him,
Sir Bedivere, the last of all his knights,
And bore him to a chapel nigh the field,
A broken chancel with a broken cross,   **60**
That stood on a dark strait of barren land.
On one side lay the ocean, and on one
Lay a great water, and the moon was full.
  Then spake King Arthur to Sir Bedivere:
"The sequel of to-day unsolders all
The goodliest fellowship of famous knights
Whereof this world holds record. Such a sleep

They sleep—the men I loved. I think that we
Shall never more, at any future time,
Delight our souls with talk of knightly deeds, 70
Walking about the gardens and the halls
Of Camelot, as in the days that were.
I perish by this people which I made,—
Tho' Merlin sware that I should come again
To rule once more—but let what will be be,
I am so deeply smitten thro' the helm
That without help I cannot last till morn.
Thou therefore take my brand Excalibur,
Which was my pride; for thou rememberest how
In those old days, one summer noon, an arm 80
Rose up from out the bosom of the lake,
Clothed in white samite, mystic, wonderful,
Holding the sword—and how I row'd across
And took it, and have worn it, like a king;
And, wheresoever I am sung or told
In aftertime, this also shall be known.
But now delay not; take Excalibur,
And fling him far into the middle mere;
Watch what thou seest, and lightly bring me word."

To him replied the bold Sir Bedivere: 90
"It is not meet, Sir King, to leave thee thus,
Aidless, alone, and smitten thro' the helm.
A little thing may harm a wounded man.
Yet I thy hest will all perform at full,
Watch what I see, and lightly bring thee word."

So saying, from the ruin'd shrine he stept
And in the moon athwart the place of tombs,
Where lay the mighty bones of ancient men,
Old knights, and over them the sea-wind sang
Shrill, chill, with flakes of foam. He, stepping down 100
By zigzag paths and juts of pointed rock,
Came on the shining levels of the lake.

There drew he forth the brand Excalibur,
And o'er him, drawing it, the winter moon,
Brightening the skirts of a long cloud, ran forth
And sparkled keen with frost against the hilt;
For all the haft twinkled with diamond sparks,
Myriads of topaz-lights, and jacinth-work
Of subtlest jewellery. He gazed so long

That both his eyes were dazzled, as he stood, 110
This way and that dividing the swift mind,
In act to throw; but at the last it seem'd
Better to leave Excalibur conceal'd
There in the many-knotted water-flags,
That whistled stiff and dry about the marge.
So strode he back slow to the wounded king.
　Then spake King Arthur to Sir Bedivere:
"Hast thou perform'd my mission which I gave?
What is it thou hast seen, or what hast heard?"
　And answer made the bold Sir Bedivere: 120
"I heard the ripple washing in the reeds,
And the wild water lapping on the crag."
　To whom replied King Arthur, faint and pale:
"Thou hast betray'd thy nature and thy name,
Not rendering true answer, as beseem'd
Thy fealty, nor like a noble knight;
For surer sign had follow'd, either hand,
Or voice, or else a motion of the mere.
This is a shameful thing for men to lie.
Yet now, I charge thee, quickly go again 130
As thou art lief and dear, and do the thing
I bade thee, watch, and lightly bring me word."
　Then went Sir Bedivere the second time
Across the ridge, and paced beside the mere,
Counting the dewy pebbles, fix'd in thought;
But when he saw the wonder of the hilt,
How curiously and strangely chased, he smote
His palms together, and he cried aloud:
　"And if indeed I cast the brand away,
Surely a precious thing, one worthy note, 140
Should thus be lost forever from the earth,
Which might have pleased the eyes of many men.
What good should follow this, if this were done?
What harm, undone? deep harm to disobey,
Seeing obedience is the bond of rule.
Were it well to obey then, if a king demand
An act unprofitable, against himself?
The king is sick, and knows not what he does.
What record, or what relic of my lord
Should be to aftertime, but empty breath 150
And rumors of a doubt? but were this kept,

Stored in some treasure-house of mighty kings,
Some one might show it at a joust of arms,
Saying, 'King Arthur's sword, Excalibur,
Wrought by the lonely maiden of the lake;
Nine years she wrought it, sitting in the deeps
Upon the hidden bases of the hills.'
So might some old man speak in the aftertime
To all the people, winning reverence;
But now much honor and much fame were lost." 160
  So spake he, clouded with his own conceit,
And hid Excalibur the second time,
And so strode back slow to the wounded king.
  Then spoke King Arthur, breathing heavily:
"What is it thou hast seen, or what hast heard?"
  And answer made the bold Sir Bedivere:
"I heard the water lapping on the crag,
And the long ripple washing in the reeds."
  To whom replied King Arthur, much in wrath:
"Ah, miserable and unkind, untrue, 170
Unknightly, traitor-hearted! Woe is me!
Authority forgets a dying king,
Laid widow'd of the power in his eye
That bow'd the will. I see thee what thou art,
For thou, the latest-left of all my knights,
In whom should meet the offices of all,
Thou wouldst betray me for the precious hilt;
Either from lust of gold, or like a girl
Valuing the giddy pleasure of the eyes.
Yet, for a man may fail in duty twice, 180
And the third time may prosper, get thee hence;
But, if thou spare to fling Excalibur,
I will arise and slay thee with my hands."
  Then quickly rose Sir Bedivere, and ran,
And, leaping down the ridges lightly, plunged
Among the bulrush-beds, and clutch'd the sword,
And strongly wheel'd and threw it. The great brand
Made lightnings in the splendor of the moon,
And flashing round and round, and whirl'd in an arch,
Shot like a streamer of the northern morn, 190
Seen where the moving isles of winter shock
By night, with noises of the northern sea.
So flash'd and fell the brand Excalibur;

But ere he dipt the surface, rose an arm
Cloth'd in white samite, mystic, wonderful,
And caught him by the hilt, and brandish'd him
Three times, and drew him under in the mere.
And lightly went the other to the king.

Then spoke King Arthur, drawing thicker breath:
"Now see I by thine eyes that this is done. 200
Speak out; what is it thou hast heard, or seen?"

And answer made the bold Sir Bedivere:
"Sir King, I closed mine eyelids, lest the gems
Should blind my purpose, for I never saw,
Nor shall see, here or elsewhere, till I die,
Not tho' I live three lives of mortal men,
So great a miracle as yonder hilt.
Then with both hands I flung him, wheeling him;
But when I look'd again, behold an arm,
Clothed in white samite, mystic, wonderful, 210
That caught him by the hilt, and brandish'd him
Three times, and drew him under in the mere."

And answer made King Arthur, breathing hard:
"My end draws nigh; 'tis time that I were gone.
Make broad thy shoulders to receive my weight,
And bear me to the margin; yet I fear
My wound hath taken cold, and I shall die."

So saying, from the pavement he half rose,
Slowly, with pain, reclining on his arm,
And looking wistfully with wide blue eyes 220
As in a picture. Him Sir Bedivere
Remorsefully regarded thro' his tears,
And would have spoken, but he found not words,
Then took with care, and kneeling on one knee,
O'er both his shoulders drew the languid hands,
And rising bore him thro' the place of tombs.

But, as he walk'd, King Arthur panted hard,
Like one that feels a nightmare on his bed
When all the house is mute. So sigh'd the king,
Muttering and murmuring at his ear, "Quick, quick! 230
I fear it is too late, and I shall die."
But the other swiftly strode from ridge to ridge,
Clothed with his breath, and looking, as he walk'd,
Larger than human on the frozen hills.
He heard the deep behind him, and a cry

Before. His own thought drove him like a goad.
Dry clash'd his harness in the icy caves
And barren chasms, and all to left and right
The bare black cliff clang'd round him, as he based
His feet on juts of slippery crag that rang   240
Sharp-smitten with the dint of armed heels—
And on a sudden, lo! the level lake,
And the long glories of the winter moon.
    Then saw they how there hove a dusky barge,
Dark as a funeral scarf from stem to stern,
Beneath them; and descending they were ware
That all the decks were dense with stately forms
Black-stoled, black-hooded, like a dream—by these
Three queens with crowns of gold—and from them rose
A cry that shiver'd to the tingling stars,   250
And, as it were one voice, an agony
Of lamentation, like a wind that shrills
All night in a waste land, where no one comes,
Or hath come, since the making of the world.
    Then murmur'd Arthur, "Place me in the barge,"
And to the barge they came. There those three queens
Put forth their hands, and took the king, and wept.
But she that rose the tallest of them all
And fairest laid his head upon her lap,
And loosed the shatter'd casque, and chafed his hands,   260
And call'd him by his name, complaining loud,
And dropping bitter tears against his brow
Striped with dark blood; for all his face was white
And colorless, and like the wither'd moon
Smote by the fresh beam of the springing east;
And all his greaves and cuisses dash'd with drops
Of onset; and the light and lustrous curls—
That made his forehead like a rising sun
High from the dais-throne—were parch'd with dust;
Or, clotted into points and hanging loose,   270
Mix'd with the knightly growth that fringed his lips.
So like a shatter'd column lay the king;
Not like that Arthur who, with lance in rest,
From spur to plume a star of tournament,
Shot thro' the lists at Camelot, and charged
Before the eyes of ladies and of kings.
    Then loudly cried the bold Sir Bedivere:

"Ah! my Lord Arthur, whither shall I go?
Where shall I hide my forehead and my eyes?
For now I see the true old times are dead,   280
When every morning brought a noble chance,
And every chance brought out a noble knight.
Such times have been not since the light that led
The holy Elders with the gift of myrrh.
But now the whole ROUND TABLE is dissolved
Which was an image of the mighty world;
And I, the last, go forth companionless,
And the days darken round me, and the years,
Among new men, strange faces, other minds."
    And slowly answer'd Arthur from the barge: 290
"The old order changeth, yielding place to new,
And God fulfils himself in many ways,
Lest one good custom should corrupt the world.
Comfort thyself: what comfort is in me?
I have lived my life, and that which I have done
May He within himself make pure! but thou,
If thou shouldst never see my face again,
Pray for my soul. More things are wrought by prayer
Than this world dreams of. Wherefore, let thy voice
Rise like a fountain for me night and day.   300
For what are men better than sheep or goats
That nourish a blind life within the brain,
If, knowing God, they lift not hands of prayer
Both for themselves and those who call them friend?
For so the whole round earth is every way
Bound by gold chains about the feet of God.
But now farewell. I am going a long way
With these thou seest—if indeed I go—
For all my mind is clouded with a doubt—
To the island-valley of Avilion;   310
Where falls not hail, or rain, or any snow,
Nor ever wind blows loudly, but it lies
Deep-meadow'd, happy, fair with orchard lawns
And bowery hollows crown'd with summer sea,
Where I will heal me of my grievous wound."
    So said he, and the barge with oar and sail
Moved from the brink, like some full-breasted swan
That, fluting a wild carol ere her death,
Ruffles her pure cold plume, and takes the flood
With swarthy webs. Long stood Sir Bedivere   320

Revolving many memories, till the hull
Look'd one black dot against the verge of dawn,
And on the mere the wailing died away.

Here ended Hall, and our last light, that long
Had wink'd and threaten'd darkness, flared and fell;
At which the parson, sent to sleep with sound,
And waked with silence, grunted "Good!" but we
Sat rapt: it was the tone with which he read—
Perhaps some modern touches here and there
Redeem'd it from the charge of nothingness—   330
Or else we loved the man, and prized his work;
I know not; but we sitting, as I said,
The cock crew loud, as at that time of year
The lusty bird takes every hour for dawn.
Then Francis, muttering, like a man ill-used,
"There now—that's nothing!" drew a little back,
And drove his heel into the smoulder'd log,
That sent a blast of sparkles up the flue.
And so to bed, where yet in sleep I seem'd
To sail with Arthur under looming shores,   340
Point after point; till on to dawn, when dreams
Begin to feel the truth and stir of day,
To me, methought, who waited with the crowd,
There came a bark that, blowing forward, bore
King Arthur, like a modern gentleman
Of stateliest port; and all the people cried,
"Arthur is come again: he cannot die."
Then those that stood upon the hills behind
Repeated—"Come again, and thrice as fair;"
And, further inland, voices echoed—"Come   350
With all good things, and war shall be no more."
At this a hundred bells began to peal,
That with the sound I woke, and heard indeed
The clear church-bells ring in the Christmas morn.
                                    [1834–35; publ. 1842]

DORA

WITH farmer Allan at the farm abode
William and Dora. William was his son,

And she his niece. He often look'd at them,
And often thought, "I'll make them man and wife."
Now Dora felt her uncle's will in all,
And yearn'd toward William; but the youth, because
He had been always with her in the house,
Thought not of Dora.
                                    Then there came a day
When Allan call'd his son, and said: "My son,
I married late, but I would wish to see   10
My grandchild on my knees before I die;
And I have set my heart upon a match.
Now therefore look to Dora; she is well
To look to; thrifty too beyond her age.
She is my brother's daughter; he and I
Had once hard words, and parted, and he died
In foreign lands; but for his sake I bred
His daughter Dora. Take her for your wife;
For I have wish'd this marriage, night and day,
For many years." But William answer'd short: 20
"I cannot marry Dora; by my life,
I will not marry Dora!" Then the old man
Was wroth, and doubled up his hands, and said:
"You will not, boy! you dare to answer thus!
But in my time a father's word was law,
And so it shall be now for me. Look to it;
Consider, William, take a month to think,
And let me have an answer to my wish,
Or, by the Lord that made me, you shall pack,
And never more darken my doors again."   30
But William answer'd madly, bit his lips,
And broke away. The more he look'd at her
The less he liked her; and his ways were harsh;
But Dora bore them meekly. Then before
The month was out he left his father's house,
And hired himself to work within the fields;
And half in love, half spite, he woo'd and wed
A laborer's daughter, Mary Morrison.
    Then, when the bells were ringing, Allan call'd
His niece and said: "My girl, I love you well;   40
But if you speak with him that was my son,
Or change a word with her he calls his wife,
My home is none of yours. My will is law."

And Dora promised, being meek. She thought,
"It cannot be; my uncle's mind will change!"
    And days went on, and there was born a boy
To William; then distresses came on him,
And day by day he pass'd his father's gate,
Heart-broken, and his father help'd him not.
But Dora stored what little she could save,   **50**
And sent it them by stealth, nor did they know
Who sent it; till at last a fever seized
On William, and in harvest time he died.
    Then Dora went to Mary. Mary sat
And look'd with tears upon her boy, and thought
Hard things of Dora. Dora came and said:
"I have obey'd my uncle until now,
And I have sinn'd, for it was all thro' me
This evil came on William at the first.
But, Mary, for the sake of him that's gone,   **60**
And for your sake, the woman that he chose,
And for this orphan, I am come to you.
You know there has not been for these five years
So full a harvest. Let me take the boy,
And I will set him in my uncle's eye
Among the wheat; that when his heart is glad
Of the full harvest, he may see the boy,
And bless him for the sake of him that's gone."
    And Dora took the child, and went her way
Across the wheat, and sat upon a mound   **70**
That was unsown, where many poppies grew.
Far off the farmer came into the field
And spied her not, for none of all his men
Dare tell him Dora waited with the child;
And Dora would have risen and gone to him,
But her heart fail'd her; and the reapers reap'd,
And the sun fell, and all the land was dark.
    But when the morrow came, she rose and took
The child once more, and sat upon the mound;
And made a little wreath of all the flowers   **80**
That grew about, and tied it round his hat
To make him pleasing in her uncle's eye.
Then when the farmer pass'd into the field
He spied her, and he left his men at work,
And came and said: "Where were you yesterday?

Whose child is that? What are you doing here?"
So Dora cast her eyes upon the ground,
And answer'd softly, "This is William's child!"
"And did I not," said Allan, "did I not   90
Forbid you, Dora?" Dora said again:
"Do with me as you will, but take the child,
And bless him for the sake of him that's gone!"
And Allan said: "I see it is a trick
Got up betwixt you and the woman there.
I must be taught my duty, and by you!
You knew my word was law, and yet you dared
To slight it. Well—for I will take the boy;
But go you hence, and never see me more."

So saying, he took the boy that cried aloud
And struggled hard. The wreath of flowers fell   100
At Dora's feet. She bow'd upon her hands,
And the boy's cry came to her from the field
More and more distant. She bow'd down her head,
Remembering the day when first she came,
And all the things that had been. She bow'd down
And wept in secret; and the reapers reap'd,
And the sun fell, and all the land was dark.

Then Dora went to Mary's house, and stood
Upon the threshold. Mary saw the boy
Was not with Dora. She broke out in praise   110
To God, that help'd her in her widowhood.
And Dora said: "My uncle took the boy;
But, Mary, let me live and work with you:
He says that he will never see me more."
Then answer'd Mary: "This shall never be,
That thou shouldst take my trouble on thyself;
And, now I think, he shall not have the boy,
For he will teach him hardness, and to slight
His mother. Therefore thou and I will go,
And I will have my boy, and bring him home;   120
And I will beg of him to take thee back.
But if he will not take thee back again,
Then thou and I will live within one house,
And work for William's child, until he grows
Of age to help us."
             So the women kiss'd

Each other, and set out, and reach'd the farm.
The door was off the latch; they peep'd, and saw
The boy set up betwixt his grandsire's knees,
Who thrust him in the hollows of his arm,
And clapt him on the hands and on the cheeks, 130
Like one that loved him; and the lad stretch'd out
And babbled for the golden seal, that hung
From Allan's watch and sparkled by the fire.
Then they came in; but when the boy beheld
His mother, he cried out to come to her;
And Allan set him down, and Mary said:
   "O father!—if you let me call you so—
I never came a-begging for myself,
Or William, or this child; but now I come
For Dora; take her back, she loves you well. 140
O Sir, when William died, he died at peace
With all men; for I ask'd him, and he said,
He could not ever rue his marrying me—
I had been a patient wife; but, Sir, he said
That he was wrong to cross his father thus.
'God bless him!' he said, 'and may he never know
The troubles I have gone thro'!' Then he turn'd
His face and pass'd—unhappy that I am!
But now, Sir, let me have my boy, for you
Will make him hard, and he will learn to slight 150
His father's memory; and take Dora back,
And let all this be as it was before."
   So Mary said, and Dora hid her face
By Mary. There was silence in the room;
And all at once the old man burst in sobs:
   "I have been to blame—to blame. I have kill'd my son.
I have kill'd him—but I loved him—my dear son.
May God forgive me!—I have been to blame.
Kiss me, my children."
               Then they clung about
The old man's neck, and kiss'd him many times. 160
And all the man was broken with remorse;
And all his love came back a hundred-fold;
And for three hours he sobb'd o'er William's child
Thinking of William.
             So those four abode

Within one house together, and as years
Went forward Mary took another mate;
But Dora lived unmarried till her death.

[1835; publ. 1842]

THE PROGRESS OF SPRING

I

THE ground-flame of the crocus breaks the mould,
   Fair Spring slides hither o'er the Southern sea,
Wavers on her thin stem the snowdrop cold
   That trembles not to kisses of the bee.
Come, Spring, for now from all the dripping eaves
   The spear of ice has wept itself away,
And hour by hour unfolding woodbine leaves
   O'er his uncertain shadow droops the day.
She comes! The loosen'd rivulets run;
   The frost-bead melts upon her golden hair;   **10**
Her mantle, slowly greening in the Sun,
   Now wraps her close, now arching leaves her bare
   To breaths of balmier air;

II

Up leaps the lark, gone wild to welcome her,
   About her glance the tits, and shriek the jays,
Before her skims the jubilant woodpecker
   The linnet's bosom blushes at her gaze,
While round her brows a woodland culver flits,
   Watching her large light eyes and gracious looks,
And in her open palm a halcyon sits   **20**
   Patient—the secret splendor of the brooks.
Come, Spring! She comes on waste and wood,
   On farm and field; but enter also here,
Diffuse thyself at will thro' all my blood,
   And, tho' thy violet sicken into sere,
   Lodge with me all the year!

III

Once more a downy drift against the brakes,
   Self-darken'd in the sky, descending slow!
But gladly see I thro' the wavering flakes
   Yon blanching apricot like snow in snow.   **84**
These will thine eyes not brook in forest-paths,
   On their perpetual pine, nor round the beech;
They fuse themselves to little spicy baths,
   Solved in the tender blushes of the peach;
They lose themselves and die
   On that new life that gems the hawthorn line;
Thy gay lent-lilies wave and put them by,
   And out once more in varnish'd glory shine
   Thy stars of celandine.

IV

She floats across the hamlet. Heaven lours,   **40**
   But in the tearful splendor of her smiles
I see the slowly-thickening chestnut towers
   Fill out the spaces by the barren tiles.
Now past her feet the swallow circling flies,
   A clamorous cuckoo stoops to meet her hand;
Her light makes rainbows in my closing eyes,
   I hear a charm of song thro' all the land.
Come, Spring! She comes, and Earth is glad
   To roll her North below thy deepening dome,
But ere thy maiden birk be wholly clad,   **50**
   And these low bushes dip their twigs in foam,
   Make all true hearths thy home.

V

Across my garden! and the thicket stirs,
   The fountain pulses high in sunnier jets,
The blackcap warbles, and the turtle purrs,
   The starling claps his tiny castanets.
Still round her forehead wheels the woodland dove,
   And scatters on her throat the sparks of dew,
The kingcup fills her footprint, and above

Broaden the glowing isles of vernal blue.   60
Hail, ample presence of a Queen,
    Bountiful, beautiful, apparell'd gay,
Whose mantle, every shade of glancing green,
    Flies back in fragrant breezes to display
    A tunic white as May!

VI

She whispers, "From the South I bring you balm.
    For on a tropic mountain was I born,
While some dark dweller by the coco-palm
    Watch'd my far meadow zoned with airy morn;
From under rose a muffled moan of floods;   70
    I sat beneath a solitude of snow;
There no one came, the turf was fresh, the woods
    Plunged gulf on gulf thro' all their vales below.
I saw beyond their silent tops
    The steaming marshes of the scarlet cranes,
The slant seas leaning on the mangrove copse,
    And summer basking in the sultry plains
    About a land of canes.

VII

"Then from my vapor-girdle soaring forth
    I scaled the buoyant highway of the birds,   80
And drank the dews and drizzle of the North,
    That I might mix with men, and hear their words
On pathway'd plains; for—while my hand exults
    Within the bloodless heart of lowly flowers
To work old laws of Love to fresh results,
    Thro' manifold effect of simple powers—
I too would teach the man
    Beyond the darker hour to see the bright,
That his fresh life may close as it began,
    The still-fulfilling promise of a light   90
    Narrowing the bounds of night."

VIII

So wed thee with my soul, that I may mark
    The coming year's great good and varied ills,

And new developments, whatever spark
  Be struck from out the clash of warring wills;
Or whether, since our nature cannot rest,
  The smoke of war's volcano burst again
From hoary deeps that belt the changeful West,
  Old Empires, dwellings of the kings of men;
Or should those fail that hold the helm,   106
  While the long day of knowledge grows and warms,
And in the heart of this most ancient realm
  A hateful voice be utter'd, and alarms
  Sounding "To arms! to arms!"

IX

A simpler, saner lesson might he learn
  Who reads thy gradual process, Holy Spring.
Thy leaves possess the season in their turn,
  And in their time thy warblers rise on wing.
How surely glidest thou from March to May,
  And changest, breathing it, the sullen wind,   110
Thy scope of operation, day by day,
  Larger and fuller, like the human mind!
Thy warmths from bud to bud
  Accomplish that blind model in the seed,
And men have hopes, which race the restless blood,
  That after many changes may succeed
  Life which is Life indeed.

        [Before 1838; publ. 1889]

EARLY SPRING

I

ONCE more the Heavenly Power
  Makes all things new,
And domes the red-plow'd hills
  With loving blue;
The blackbirds have their wills,
  The throstles too.

II

Opens a door in heaven;
   From skies of glass
A Jacob's ladder falls
   On greening grass,
And o'er the mountain-walls
   Young angels pass.

10

III

Before them fleets the shower,
   And burst the buds,
And shine the level lands,
   And flash the floods;
The stars are from their hands
   Flung thro' the woods,

IV

The woods with living airs
   How softly fann'd,
Light airs from where the deep,
   All down the sand,
Is breathing in his sleep,
   Heard by the land.

20

V

O, follow, leaping blood,
   The season's lure!
O heart, look down and up
   Serene, secure,
Warm as the crocus cup,
   Like snowdrops, pure!

30

VI

Past, Future glimpse and fade
   Thro' some slight spell,
A gleam from yonder vale,

Some far blue fell,
And sympathies, how frail,
In sound and smell!

VII

Till at thy chuckled note,
Thou twinkling bird,
The fairy fancies range,
And, lightly stirr'd,   **40**
Ring little bells of change
From word to word.

VIII

For now the Heavenly Power
Makes all things new,
And thaws the cold, and fills
The flower with dew;
The blackbirds have their wills,
The poets too.
[An "early" poem; publ. 1883]

MOVE EASTWARD, HAPPY EARTH

Move eastward, happy earth, and leave
Yon orange sunset waning slow;
From fringes of the faded eve,
O happy planet, eastward go,
Till over thy dark shoulder glow
Thy silver sister-world, and rise
To glass herself in dewy eyes
That watch me from the glen below.

Ah, bear me with thee, smoothly borne,
Dip forward under starry light,   **10**
And move me to my marriage-morn,
And round again to happy night.
[1836?; publ. 1842]

A FAREWELL[1]

Flow down, cold rivulet, to the sea,
　　Thy tribute wave deliver;
No more by thee my steps shall be,
　　For ever and for ever.

Flow, softly flow, by lawn and lea,
　　A rivulet, then a river;
Nowhere by thee my steps shall be,
　　For ever and for ever.

But here will sigh thine alder-tree,
　　And here thine aspen shiver;　　　　　　10
And here by thee will hum the bee,
　　For ever and for ever.

A thousand suns will stream on thee,
　　A thousand moons will quiver;
But not by thee my steps shall be,
　　For ever and for ever.
　　　　　　　　　　[1837; publ. 1842]

LINES [2]

Here often, when a child I lay reclined,
　　I took delight in this locality.
Here stood the infant Ilion of the mind,
　　And here the Grecian ships did seem to be.
And here again I come, and only find
　　The drain-cut levels of the marshy lea,—
Gray sea-banks and pale sunsets,—dreary wind,
　　Dim shores, dense rains, and heavy-clouded sea!
　　　　　　　　　　[1837; publ. 1850]

[1] To the brook at Somersby.
[2] On Mablethorpe, on the Lincolnshire coast.

LOCKSLEY HALL

COMRADES, leave me here a little, while as yet 'tis early morn;
Leave me here, and when you want me, sound upon the bugle-
    horn.

'Tis the place, and all around it, as of old, the curlews call,
Dreary gleams about the moorland flying over Locksley Hall;

Locksley Hall, that in the distance overlooks the sandy tracts,
And the hollow ocean-ridges roaring into cataracts.

Many a night from yonder ivied casement, ere I went to rest,
Did I look on great Orion sloping slowly to the west.

Many a night I saw the Pleiads, rising thro' the mellow shade,
Glitter like a swarm of fireflies tangled in a silver braid.   10

Here about the beach I wander'd, nourishing a youth sublime
With the fairy tales of science, and the long result of time;

When the centuries behind me like a fruitful land reposed;
When I clung to all the present for the promise that it closed;

When I dipt into the future far as human eye could see,
Saw the vision of the world and all the wonder that would be.—

In the spring a fuller crimson comes upon the robin's breast;
In the spring the wanton lapwing gets himself another crest;

In the spring a livelier iris changes on the burnish'd dove;
In the spring a young man's fancy lightly turns to thoughts of
    love.   20

Then her cheek was pale and thinner than should be for one so
    young,
And her eyes on all my motions with a mute observance hung.

And I said, "My cousin Amy, speak, and speak the truth to me,
Trust me, cousin, all the current of my being sets to thee."

On her pallid cheek and forehead came a color and a light,
As I have seen the rosy red flushing in the northern night.

And she turn'd—her bosom shaken with a sudden storm of
    sighs—
All the spirit deeply dawning in the dark of hazel eyes—

Saying, "I have hid my feelings, fearing they should do me
    wrong;"
Saying, "Dost thou love me, cousin?" weeping, "I have loved
    thee long."   30

Love took up the glass of Time, and turn'd it in his glowing
    hands;
Every moment, lightly shaken, ran itself in golden sands.

Love took up the harp of Life, and smote on all the chords with
    might;
Smote the chord of Self, that, trembling, past in music out of
    sight.

Many a morning on the moorland did we hear the copses ring,
And her whisper throng'd my pulses with the fulness of the
    spring.

Many an evening by the waters did we watch the stately ships,
And our spirits rush'd together at the touching of the lips.

O my cousin, shallow-hearted! O my Amy, mine no more!
O the dreary, dreary moorland! O the barren, barren shore!   40

Falser than all fancy fathoms, falser than all songs have sung,
Puppet to a father's threat, and servile to a shrewish tongue!

Is it well to wish thee happy?—having known me—to decline
On a range of lower feelings and a narrower heart than mine!

Yet it shall be; thou shalt lower to his level day by day,
What is fine within thee growing coarse to sympathize with clay.

As the husband is, the wife is; thou art mated with a clown,
And the grossness of his nature will have weight to drag thee
    down.

He will hold thee, when his passion shall have spent its novel
    force,
Something better than his dog, a little dearer than his horse.   50

What is this? his eyes are heavy; think not they are glazed with
    wine.
Go to him, it is thy duty; kiss him, take his hand in thine.

It may be my lord is weary, that his brain is overwrought;
Soothe him with thy finer fancies, touch him with thy lighter
    thought.

He will answer to the purpose, easy things to understand—
Better thou wert dead before me, tho' I slew thee with my hand!

Better thou and I were lying, hidden from the heart's disgrace,
Roll'd in one another's arms, and silent in a last embrace.

Cursed be the social wants that sin against the strength of youth!
Cursed be the social lies that warp us from the living truth!   60

Cursed be the sickly forms that err from honest Nature's rule!
Cursed be the gold that gilds the straiten'd forehead of the fool!

Well—'t is well that I should bluster!—Hadst thou less unworthy
    proved—
Would to God—for I had loved thee more than ever wife was
    loved.

Am I mad, that I should cherish that which bears but bitter fruit?
I will pluck it from my bosom, tho' my heart be at the root.

Never, tho' my mortal summers to such length of years should
    come
As the many-winter'd crow that leads the clanging rookery home.

Where is comfort? in division of the records of the mind?
Can I part her from herself, and love her, as I knew her,
      kind?   70

I remember one that perish'd; sweetly did she speak and move;
Such a one do I remember, whom to look at was to love.

Can I think of her as dead, and love her for the love she bore?
No—she never loved me truly; love is love for evermore.

Comfort? comfort scorn'd of devils! this is truth the poet sings,
That a sorrow's crown of sorrow is remembering happier things.

Drug thy memories, lest thou learn it, lest thy heart be put to
      proof,
In the dead unhappy night, and when the rain is on the roof.

Like a dog, he hunts in dreams, and thou art staring at the wall,
Where the dying night-lamp flickers, and the shadows rise and
      fall.   80

Then a hand shall pass before thee, pointing to his drunken sleep,
To thy widow'd marriage-pillows, to the tears that thou wilt
      weep.

Thou shalt hear the "Never, never," whisper'd by the phantom
      years,
And a song from out the distance in the ringing of thine ears;

And an eye shall vex thee, looking ancient kindness on thy pain.
Turn thee, turn thee on thy pillow; get thee to thy rest again.

Nay, but Nature brings thee solace; for a tender voice will cry.
'Tis a purer life than thine, a lip to drain thy trouble dry.

Baby lips will laugh me down; my latest rival brings thee rest.
Baby fingers, waxen touches, press me from the mother's
      breast.   90

O, the child too clothes the father with a dearness not his due.
Half is thine and half is his; it will be worthy of the two.

O, I see thee old and formal, fitted to thy petty part,
With a little hoard of maxims preaching down a daughter's heart.

"They were dangerous guides the feelings—she herself was not
    exempt—
Truly, she herself had suffer'd"—Perish in thy self-contempt!

Overlive it—lower yet—be happy! wherefore should I care?
I myself must mix with action, lest I wither by despair.

What is that which I should turn to, lighting upon days like
    these?
Every door is barr'd with gold, and opens but to golden
    keys.   **100**

Every gate is throng'd with suitors, all the markets overflow.
I have but an angry fancy; what is that which I should do?

I had been content to perish, falling on the foeman's ground,
When the ranks are roll'd in vapor, and the winds are laid with
    sound.

But the jingling of the guinea helps the hurt that Honor feels,
And the nations do but murmur, snarling at each other's heels.

Can I but relive in sadness? I will turn that earlier page.
Hide me from my deep emotion, O thou wondrous Mother-Age!

Make me feel the wild pulsation that I felt before the strife,
When I heard my days before me, and the tumult of my
    life;   **110**

Yearning for the large excitement that the coming years would
    yield,
Eager-hearted as a boy when first he leaves his father's field,

And at night along the dusky highway near and nearer drawn,
Sees in heaven the light of London flaring like a dreary dawn;

And his spirit leaps within him to be gone before him then,
Underneath the light he looks at, in among the throngs of men;

Men, my brothers, men the workers, ever reaping something
    new;
That which they have done but earnest of the things that they
    shall do.

For I dipt into the future, far as human eye could see,
Saw the Vision of the world, and all the wonder that would
    be;   120

Saw the heavens fill with commerce, argosies of magic sails,
Pilots of the purple twilight, dropping down with costly bales;

Heard the heavens fill with shouting, and there rain'd a ghastly
    dew
From the nations' airy navies grappling in the central blue;

Far along the world-wide whisper of the south-wind rushing
    warm,
With the standards of the peoples plunging thro' the thunder-
    storm;

Till the war-drum throbb'd no longer, and the battle-flags were
    furl'd
In the Parliament of man, the Federation of the world.

There the common sense of most shall hold a fretful realm
    in awe,
And the kindly earth shall slumber, lapt in universal law.   130

So I triumph'd ere my passion sweeping thro' me left me dry,
Left me with the palsied heart, and left me with the jaundiced
    eye;

Eye, to which all order festers, all things here are out of joint.
Science moves, but slowly, slowly, creeping on from point to
    point;

Slowly comes a hungry people, as a lion, creeping nigher,
Glares at one that nods and winks behind a slowly-dying fire.

Yet I doubt not thro' the ages one increasing purpose runs,
And the thoughts of men are widen'd with the process of the
 suns.

What is that to him that reaps not harvest of his youthful joys,
Tho' the deep heart of existence beat for ever like a boy's? 140

Knowledge comes, but wisdom lingers, and I linger on the shore,
And the individual withers, and the world is more and more.

Knowledge comes, but wisdom lingers, and he bears a laden
 breast,
Full of sad experience, moving toward the stillness of his rest.

Hark, my merry comrades call me, sounding on the bugle-horn,
They to whom my foolish passion were a target for their scorn.

Shall it not be scorn to me to harp on such a moulder'd string?
I am shamed thro' all my nature to have loved so slight a thing.

Weakness to be wroth with weakness! woman's pleasure, woman's pain—
Nature made them blinder motions bounded in a shallower
 brain. 150

Woman is the lesser man, and all thy passions, match'd with
 mine,
Are as moonlight unto sunlight, and as water unto wine—

Here at least, where nature sickens, nothing. Ah, for some retreat
Deep in yonder shining Orient, where my life began to beat,

Where in wild Mahratta-battle fell my father evil-starr'd;—
I was left a trampled orphan, and a selfish uncle's ward.

Or to burst all links of habit—there to wander far away,
On from island unto island at the gateways of the day.

Larger constellations burning, mellow moons and happy skies,
Breadths of tropic shade and palms in cluster, knots of Paradise. 160

Never comes the trader, never floats an European flag,
Slides the bird o'er lustrous woodland, swings the trailer from
  the crag;

Droops the heavy-blossom'd bower, hangs the heavy-fruited
  tree—
Summer isles of Eden lying in dark-purple spheres of sea.

There methinks would be enjoyment more than in this march of
  mind,
In the steamship, in the railway, in the thoughts that shake mankind.

There the passions cramp'd no longer shall have scope and breathing space;
I will take some savage woman, she shall rear my dusky race.

Iron-jointed, supple-sinew'd, they shall dive, and they shall run,
Catch the wild goat by the hair, and hurl their lances in the
  sun;   170

Whistle back the parrot's call, and leap the rainbows of the
  brooks,
Not with blinded eyesight poring over miserable books—

Fool, again the dream, the fancy! but I *know* my words are wild,
But I count the gray barbarian lower than the Christian child.

I, to herd with narrow foreheads, vacant of our glorious gains,
Like a beast with lower pleasures, like a beast with lower pains!

Mated with a squalid savage—what to me were sun or clime?
I the heir of all the ages, in the foremost files of time—

I that rather held it better men should perish one by one,
Than that earth should stand at gaze like Joshua's moon in
  Ajalon!   180

Not in vain the distance beacons. Forward, forward let us range,
Let the great world spin for ever down the ringing grooves of
  change.

Thro' the shadow of the globe we sweep into the younger day;
Better fifty years of Europe than a cycle of Cathay.

Mother-Age,—for mine I knew not,—help me as when life begun;
Rift the hills, and roll the waters, flash the lightnings, weigh the
    sun.

O, I see the crescent promise of my spirit hath not set.
Ancient founts of inspiration well thro' all my fancy yet.

Howsoever these things be, a long farewell to Locksley Hall!
Now for me the woods may wither, now for me the roof-
    tree fall.   190

Comes a vapor from the margin, blackening over heath and holt,
Cramming all the blast before it, in its breast a thunderbolt.

Let it fall on Locksley Hall, with rain or hail, or fire or snow;
For the mighty wind arises, roaring seaward, and I go.
                       [1835–42; publ. 1842]

THE VISION OF SIN

I

I HAD a vision when the night was late;
A youth came riding toward a palace-gate.
He rode a horse with wings, that would have flown,
But that his heavy rider kept him down.
And from the palace came a child of sin,
And took him by the curls, and led him in,
Where sat a company with heated eyes,
Expecting when a fountain should arise.
A sleepy light upon their brows and lips—
As when the sun, a crescent of eclipse,   10
Dreams over lake and lawn, and isles and capes—
Suffused them, sitting, lying, languid shapes,
By heaps of gourds, and skins of wine, and piles of grapes.

II

Then methought I heard a mellow sound,
Gathering up from all the lower ground;
Narrowing in to where they sat assembled,
Low voluptuous music winding trembled,
Woven in circles. They that heard it sigh'd,
Panted hand-in-hand with faces pale,
Swung themselves, and in low tones replied;　　　　20
Till the fountain spouted, showering wide
Sleet of diamond-drift and pearly hail.
Then the music touch'd the gates and died,
Rose again from where it seem'd to fail,
Storm'd in orbs of song, a growing gale;
Till thronging in and in, to where they waited,
As 't were a hundred-throated nightingale,
The strong tempestuous treble throbb'd and palpitated;
Ran into its giddiest whirl of sound,
Caught the sparkles, and in circles,　　　　30
Purple gauzes, golden hazes, liquid mazes,
Flung the torrent rainbow round.
Then they started from their places,
Moved with violence, changed in hue,
Caught each other with wild grimaces,
Half-invisible to the view,
Wheeling with precipitate paces
To the melody, till they flew,
Hair and eyes and limbs and faces,
Twisted hard in fierce embraces,　　　　40
Like to Furies, like to Graces,
Dash'd together in blinding dew;
Till, kill'd with some luxurious agony,
The nerve-dissolving melody
Flutter'd headlong from the sky.

III

And then I look'd up toward a mountain-tract,
That girt the region with high cliff and lawn.
I saw that every morning, far withdrawn
Beyond the darkness and the cataract,

God made Himself an awful rose of dawn, 50
Unheeded; and detaching, fold by fold,
From those still heights, and, slowly drawing near,
A vapor heavy, hueless, formless, cold,
Came floating on for many a month and year,
Unheeded; and I thought I would have spoken,
And warn'd that madman ere it grew too late,
But, as in dreams, I could not. Mine was broken,
When that cold vapor touch'd the palace-gate,
And link'd again. I saw within my head
A gray and gap-tooth'd man as lean as death, 60
Who slowly rode across a wither'd heath,
And lighted at a ruin'd inn, and said:

IV

"Wrinkled ostler, grim and thin!
     Here is custom come your way;
Take my brute, and lead him in,
     Stuff his ribs with mouldy hay.

"Bitter barmaid, waning fast!
     See that sheets are on my bed.
What! the flower of life is past; 70
     It is long before you wed.

"Slip-shod waiter, lank and sour,
     At the Dragon on the heath!
Let us have a quiet hour,
     Let us hob-and-nob with Death.

"I am old, but let me drink;
     Bring me spices, bring me wine;
I remember, when I think,
     That my youth was half divine.

"Wine is good for shrivell'd lips,
     When a blanket wraps the day, 80
When the rotten woodland drips,
     And the leaf is stamp'd in clay.

"Sit thee down, and have no shame,
     Cheek by jowl, and knee by knee;

What care I for any name?
   What for order or degree?

"Let me screw thee up a peg;
   Let me loose thy tongue with wine;
Callest thou that thing a leg?
   Which is thinnest? thine or mine?   **90**

"Thou shalt not be saved by works,
   Thou hast been a sinner too;
Ruin'd trunks on wither'd forks,
   Empty scarecrows, I and you!

"Fill the cup and fill the can,
   Have a rouse before the morn:
Every moment dies a man,
   Every moment one is born.

"We are men of ruin'd blood;
   Therefore comes it we are wise.   **100**
Fish are we that love the mud,
   Rising to no fancy-flies.

"Name and fame! to fly sublime
   Thro' the courts, the camps, the schools,
Is to be the ball of Time,
   Bandied by the hands of fools.

"Friendship!—to be two in one—
   Let the canting liar pack!
Well I know, when I am gone,
   How she mouths behind my back.   **110**

"Virtue!—to be good and just—
   Every heart, when sifted well,
Is a clot of warmer dust,
   Mix'd with cunning sparks of hell.

"O, we two as well can look
   Whited thought and cleanly life
As the priest, above his book
   Leering at his neighbor's wife.

"Fill the cup and fill the can,
   Have a rouse before the morn: **120**
Every moment dies a man,
   Every moment one is born.

"Drink, and let the parties rave;
   They are fill'd with idle spleen,
Rising, falling, like a wave,
   For they know not what they mean.

"He that roars for liberty
   Faster binds a tyrant's power,
And the tyrant's cruel glee
   Forces on the freer hour. **130**

"Fill the can and fill the cup;
   All the windy ways of men
Are but dust that rises up,
   And is lightly laid again.

"Greet her with applausive breath,
   Freedom, gaily doth she tread;
In her right a civic wreath,
   In her left a human head.

"No, I love not what is new;
   She is of an ancient house, **140**
And I think we know the hue
   Of that cap upon her brows.

"Let her go! her thirst she slakes
   Where the bloody conduit runs,
Then her sweetest meal she makes
   On the first-born of her sons.

"Drink to lofty hopes that cool,—
   Visions of a perfect State;
Drink we, last, the public fool,
   Frantic love and frantic hate. **150**

"Chant me now some wicked stave,
   Till thy drooping courage rise,

And the glow-worm of the grave
　　Glimmer in thy rheumy eyes.

"Fear not thou to loose thy tongue,
　　Set thy hoary fancies free;
What is loathsome to the young
　　Savors well to thee and me.

"Change, reverting to the years,
　　When thy nerves could understand　　　　160
What there is in loving tears,
　　And the warmth of hand in hand.

"Tell me tales of thy first love—
　　April hopes, the fools of chance—
Till the graves begin to move,
　　And the dead begin to dance.

"Fill the can and fill the cup;
　　All the windy ways of men
Are but dust that rises up,
　　And is lightly laid again.　　　　170

"Trooping from their mouldy dens
　　The chap-fallen circle spreads—
Welcome, fellow-citizens,
　　Hollow hearts and empty heads!

"You are bones, and what of that?
　　Every face, however full,
Padded round with flesh and fat,
　　Is but modell'd on a skull.

"Death is king, and Vivat Rex!
　　Tread a measure on the stones,　　　　180
Madam—if I know your sex
　　From the fashion of your bones.

"No, I cannot praise the fire
　　In your eye—nor yet your lip;
All the more do I admire
　　Joints of cunning workmanship.

"Lo! God's likeness—the ground-plan—
    Neither modell'd, glazed, nor framed;
Buss me, thou rough sketch of man,
    Far too naked to be shamed!   190

"Drink to Fortune, drink to Chance,
    While we keep a little breath!
Drink to heavy Ignorance!
    Hob-and-nob with brother Death!

"Thou art mazed, the night is long,
    And the longer night is near—
What! I am not all as wrong
    As a bitter jest is dear.

"Youthful hopes, by scores, to all,
    When the locks are crisp and curl'd;   200
Unto me my maudlin gall
    And my mockeries of the world.

"Fill the cup and fill the can;
    Mingle madness, mingle scorn!
Dregs of life, and lees of man;
    Yet we will not die forlorn."

v

The voice grew faint; there came a further change;
Once more uprose the mystic mountain-range.
Below were men and horses pierced with worms,
And slowly quickening into lower forms;   210
By shards and scurf of salt, and scum of dross,
Old plash of rains, and refuse patch'd with moss.
Then some one spake: "Behold! it was a crime
Of sense avenged by sense that wore with time."
Another said: "The crime of sense became
The crime of malice, and is equal blame."
And one: "He had not wholly quench'd his power;
A little grain of conscience made him sour."
At last I heard a voice upon the slope
Cry to the summit, "Is there any hope?"   220

To which an answer peal'd from that high land,
But in a tongue no man could understand;
And on the glimmering limit far withdrawn
God made Himself an awful rose of dawn.

[publ. 1842]

THE NEW TIMON AND THE POETS [1]

WE KNOW him, out of Shakespeare's art,
    And those fine curses which he spoke;
The old Timon, with his noble heart,
    That, strongly loathing, greatly broke.

So died the Old: here comes the New.
    Regard him: a familiar face:
I thought we knew him: What, it's you,
    The padded man—that wears the stays—

Who killed the girls and thrilled the boys
    With dandy pathos when you wrote!   10
A Lion, you, that made a noise,
    And shook a mane *en papillotes*.

And once you tried the Muses too;
    You failed, Sir: therefore now you turn,
To fall on those who are to you
    As Captain is to Subaltern.

But men of long-enduring hopes,
    And careless what this hour may bring,
Can pardon little would-be POPES
    And BRUMMELLS, when they try to sting.   20

An Artist, Sir, should rest in Art,
    And waive a little of his claim;
To have the deep Poetic heart
    Is more than all poetic fame.

[1] In reply to lines in Bulwer-Lytton's *The New Timon*.

But you, Sir, you are hard to please;
   You never look but half content;
Nor like a gentleman at ease,
   With moral breadth of temperament.

And what with spites and what with fears,
   You cannot let a body be: 30
It's always ringing in your ears,
   "They call this man as good as *me*."

What profits now to understand
   The merits of a spotless shirt—
A dapper boot—a little hand—
   If half the little soul is dirt?

You talk of tinsel! why, we see
   The old mark of rouge upon your cheeks.
You prate of Nature! you are he
   That spilt his life about the cliques.   40

A TIMON you! Nay, nay, for shame:
   It looks too arrogant a jest—
The fierce old man—to take his name,
   You bandbox. Off, and let him rest.
                      [publ. 1846]

SONGS FROM *THE PRINCESS*

SWEET AND LOW

SWEET and low, sweet and low,
   Wind of the western sea,
Low, low, breathe and blow,
   Wind of the western sea!
Over the rolling waters go,
Come from the dying moon, and blow,
   Blow him again to me;
While my little one, while my pretty one, sleeps.

Sleep and rest, sleep and rest,
    Father will come to thee soon;   **10**
Rest, rest, on mother's breast,
    Father will come to thee soon;
Father will come to his babe in the nest,
Silver sails all out of the west
    Under the silver moon;
Sleep, my little one, sleep, my pretty one, sleep.
                [publ. 1850]

THE SPLENDOR FALLS

THE splendor falls on castle walls
    And snowy summits old in story;
The long light shakes across the lakes,
    And the wild cataract leaps in glory.
Blow, bugle, blow, set the wild echoes flying,
Blow, bugle; answer, echoes, dying, dying, dying.

O, hark, O, hear! how thin and clear,
    And thinner, clearer, farther going!
O, sweet and far from cliff and scar
    The horns of Elfland faintly blowing!   **10**
Blow, let us hear the purple glens replying,
Blow, bugle; answer, echoes, dying, dying, dying.

O love, they die in yon rich sky,
    They faint on hill or field or river;
Our echoes roll from soul to soul,
    And grow for ever and for ever.
Blow, bugle, blow, set the wild echoes flying,
And answer, echoes, answer, dying, dying, dying.
                [publ. 1850]

TEARS, IDLE TEARS

TEARS, idle tears, I know not what they mean,
Tears from the depth of some divine despair

Rise in the heart, and gather to the eyes,
In looking on the happy autumn-fields,
And thinking of the days that are no more.

Fresh as the first beam glittering on a sail,
That brings our friends up from the underworld,
Sad as the last which reddens over one
That sinks with all we love below the verge;
So sad, so fresh, the days that are no more.   10

Ah, sad and strange as in dark summer dawns
The earliest pipe of half-awaken'd birds
To dying ears, when unto dying eyes
The casement slowly grows a glimmering square;
So sad, so strange, the days that are no more.

Dear as remember'd kisses after death,
And sweet as those by hopeless fancy feign'd
On lips that are for others; deep as love,
Deep as first love, and wild with all regret;
O Death in Life, the days that are no more!   20
                              [publ. 1847]

O SWALLOW, SWALLOW

O Swallow, Swallow, flying, flying south,
Fly to her, and fall upon her gilded eaves,
And tell her, tell her, what I tell to thee.

O, tell her, Swallow, thou that knowest each,
That bright and fierce and fickle is the South,
And dark and true and tender is the North.

O Swallow, Swallow, if I could follow, and light
Upon her lattice, I would pipe and trill,
And cheep and twitter twenty million loves.

O, were I thou that she might take me in,   10
And lay me on her bosom, and her heart
Would rock the snowy cradle till I died!

Why lingereth she to clothe her heart with love,
Delaying as the tender ash delays
To clothe herself, when all the woods are green?

O, tell her, Swallow, that thy brood is flown;
Say to her, I do but wanton in the South,
But in the North long since my nest is made.

O, tell her, brief is life but love is long,   **20**
And brief the sun of summer in the North,
And brief the moon of beauty in the South.

O Swallow, flying from the golden woods,
Fly to her, and pipe and woo her, and make her mine,
And tell her, tell her, that I follow thee.
                                    [publ. 1847]

ASK ME NO MORE

ASK me no more: the moon may draw the sea;
    The cloud may stoop from heaven and take the shape,
    With fold to fold, of mountain or of cape;
But O too fond, when have I answer'd thee?
                        Ask me no more.

Ask me no more: what answer should I give?
    I love not hollow cheek or faded eye:
    Yet, O my friend, I will not have thee die!
Ask me no more, lest I should bid thee live;
                        Ask me no more.   **10**

Ask me no more: thy fate and mine are seal'd;
    I strove against the stream and all in vain:
    Let the great river take me to the main.
No more, dear love, for at a touch I yield;
                        Ask me no more.
                                    [publ. 1850]

NOW SLEEPS THE CRIMSON PETAL

Now sleeps the crimson petal, now the white;
Nor waves the cypress in the palace walk;
Nor winks the gold fin in the porphyry font.
The fire-fly wakens; waken thou with me.

Now droops the milk-white peacock like a ghost,
And like a ghost she glimmers on to me.

Now lies the Earth all Danaë to the stars,
And all thy heart lies open unto me.

Now slides the silent meteor on, and leaves
A shining furrow, as thy thoughts in me.   10

Now folds the lily all her sweetness up,
And slips into the bosom of the lake.
So fold thyself, my dearest, thou, and slip
Into my bosom and be lost in me.

                              [publ. 1847]

COME DOWN, O MAID

Come down, O maid, from yonder mountain height.
What pleasure lives in height (the shepherd sang),
In height and cold, the splendor of the hills?
But cease to move so near the heavens, and cease
To glide a sunbeam by the blasted pine,
To sit a star upon the sparkling spire;
And come, for Love is of the valley, come,
For Love is of the valley, come thou down
And find him; by the happy threshold, he,
Or hand in hand with Plenty in the maize,   10
Or red with spirted purple of the vats,
Or foxlike in the vine; nor cares to walk
With Death and Morning on the Silver Horns,

Nor wilt thou snare him in the white ravine,
Nor find him dropt upon the firths of ice,
That huddling slant in furrow-cloven falls
To roll the torrent out of dusky doors.
But follow; let the torrent dance thee down
To find him in the valley; let the wild
Lean-headed eagles yelp alone, and leave   20
The monstrous ledges there to slope, and spill
Their thousand wreaths of dangling water-smoke,
That like a broken purpose waste in air.
So waste not thou, but come; for all the vales
Await thee; azure pillars of the hearth
Arise to thee; the children call, and I
Thy shepherd pipe, and sweet is every sound,
Sweeter thy voice, but every sound is sweet;
Myriads of rivulets hurrying thro' the lawn,
The moan of doves in immemorial elms,   30
And murmuring of innumerable bees.

[publ. 1847]

THE EAGLE

FRAGMENT

HE CLASPS the crag with crooked hands;
Close to the sun in lonely lands,
Ring'd with the azure world, he stands.

The wrinkled sea beneath him crawls;
He watches from his mountain walls,
And like a thunderbolt he falls.

[1846–51?; publ. 1851]

COME NOT, WHEN I AM DEAD

COME not, when I am dead,
   To drop thy foolish tears upon my grave,
To trample round my fallen head,
   And vex the unhappy dust thou wouldst not save.

There let the wind sweep and the plover cry;
    But thou, go by.

Child, if it were thine error or thy crime
    I care no longer, being all unblest:
Wed whom thou wilt, but I am sick of time,
    And I desire to rest.   10
Pass on, weak heart, and leave me where I lie;
    Go by, go by.

             [1846–51?; publ. 1851]

IN MEMORIAM A.H.H.

OBIIT MDCCCXXXIII

STRONG Son of God, immortal Love,
    Whom we, that have not seen thy face,
    By faith, and faith alone, embrace,
Believing where we cannot prove;

Thine are these orbs of light and shade;
    Thou madest Life in man and brute;
    Thou madest Death; and lo, thy foot
Is on the skull which thou hast made.

Thou wilt not leave us in the dust:
    Thou madest man, he knows not why,   10
    He thinks he was not made to die;
And thou hast made him: thou art just.

Thou seemest human and divine,
    The highest, holiest manhood, thou.
    Our wills are ours, we know not how;
Our wills are ours, to make them thine.

Our little systems have their day;
    They have their day and cease to be;
    They are but broken lights of thee,
And thou, O Lord, art more than they.   20

We have but faith: we cannot know,
    For knowledge is of things we see;

And yet we trust it comes from thee,
A beam in darkness: let it grow.

Let knowledge grow from more to more,
But more of reverence in us dwell;
That mind and soul, according well,
May make one music as before,

But vaster. We are fools and slight;
We mock thee when we do not fear: 30
But help thy foolish ones to bear;
Help thy vain worlds to bear thy light.

Forgive what seem'd my sin in me,
What seem'd my worth since I began;
For merit lives from man to man,
And not from man, O Lord, to thee.

Forgive my grief for one removed,
Thy creature, whom I found so fair.
I trust he lives in thee, and there
I find him worthier to be loved.   40

Forgive these wild and wandering cries,
Confusions of a wasted youth;
Forgive them where they fail in truth,
And in thy wisdom make me wise.
    1849.

———————

I

I held it truth, with him who sings
To one clear harp in divers tones,
That men may rise on stepping-stones
Of their dead selves to higher things.

But who shall so forecast the years
And find in loss a gain to match?
Or reach a hand thro' time to catch
The far-off interest of tears?

Let Love clasp Grief lest both be drown'd,
  Let darkness keep her raven gloss.   10
  Ah, sweeter to be drunk with loss,
To dance with Death, to beat the ground,

Than that the victor Hours should scorn
  The long result of love, and boast,
  "Behold the man that loved and lost,
But all he was is overworn."

                   II

Old yew, which graspest at the stones
  That name the underlying dead,
  Thy fibres net the dreamless head,
Thy roots are wrapt about the bones.

The seasons bring the flower again,
  And bring the firstling to the flock;
  And in the dusk of thee the clock
Beats out the little lives of men.

O, not for thee the glow, the bloom,
  Who changest not in any gale,   10
  Nor branding summer suns avail
To touch thy thousand years of gloom;

And gazing on thee, sullen tree,
  Sick for thy stubborn hardihood,
  I seem to fail from out my blood
And grow incorporate into thee.

                  III

O Sorrow, cruel fellowship,
  O Priestess in the vaults of Death,
  O sweet and bitter in a breath,
What whispers from thy lying lip?

"The stars," she whispers, "blindly run;
  A web is woven across the sky;

From out waste places comes a cry,
And murmurs from the dying sun;

"And all the phantom, Nature, stands—
   With all the music in her tone,
   A hollow echo of my own,—
A hollow form with empty hands."   **10**

And shall I take a thing so blind,
   Embrace her as my natural good;
   Or crush her, like a vice of blood,
Upon the threshold of the mind?

IV

To Sleep I give my powers away;
   My will is bondsman to the dark;
   I sit within a helmless bark,
And with my heart I muse and say:

O heart, how fares it with thee now,
   That thou shouldst fail from thy desire,
   Who scarcely darest to inquire,
"What is it makes me beat so low?"

Something it is which thou hast lost,
   Some pleasure from thine early years.   **10**
   Break, thou deep vase of chilling tears,
That grief hath shaken into frost!

Such clouds of nameless trouble cross
   All night below the darken'd eyes;
   With morning wakes the will, and cries,
"Thou shalt not be the fool of loss."

V

I sometimes hold it half a sin
   To put in words the grief I feel;
   For words, like Nature, half reveal
And half conceal the Soul within.

But, for the unquiet heart and brain,
 A use in measured language lies;
 The sad mechanic exercise,
Like dull narcotics, numbing pain.

In words, like weeds, I'll wrap me o'er,
 Like coarsest clothes against the cold; 10
 But that large grief which these enfold
Is given in outline and no more.

VI

One writes, that "other friends remain,"
 That "loss is common to the race"—
 And common is the commonplace,
And vacant chaff well meant for grain.

That loss is common would not make
 My own less bitter, rather more.
 Too common! Never morning wore
To evening, but some heart did break.

O father, wheresoe'er thou be,
 Who pledgest now thy gallant son, **10**
 A shot, ere half thy draught be done,
Hath still'd the life that beat from thee.

O mother, praying God will save
 Thy sailor,—while thy head is bow'd,
 His heavy-shotted hammock-shroud
Drops in his vast and wandering grave.

Ye know no more than I who wrought
 At that last hour to please him well;
 Who mused on all I had to tell,
And something written, something thought; **20**

Expecting still his advent home;
 And ever met him on his way
 With wishes, thinking, "here to-day,"
Or "here to-morrow will he come."

O, somewhere, meek, unconscious dove,
  That sittest ranging golden hair;
  And glad to find thyself so fair,
Poor child, that waitest for thy love!

For now her father's chimney glows
  In expectation of a guest;   30
  And thinking "this will please him best,"
She takes a riband or a rose;

For he will see them on to-night;
  And with the thought her color burns;
  And, having left the glass, she turns
Once more to set a ringlet right;

And, even when she turn'd, the curse
  Had fallen, and her future lord
  Was drown'd in passing thro' the ford,   40
Or kill'd in falling from his horse.

O, what to her shall be the end?
  And what to me remains of good?
  To her perpetual maidenhood,
And unto me no second friend.

VII

Dark house, by which once more I stand
  Here in the long unlovely street,
  Doors, where my heart was used to beat
So quickly, waiting for a hand,

A hand that can be clasp'd no more—
  Behold me, for I cannot sleep,
  And like a guilty thing I creep
At earliest morning to the door.

He is not here; but far away
  The noise of life begins again,   10
  And ghastly thro' the drizzling rain
On the bald street breaks the blank day.

VIII

A happy lover who has come
    To look on her that loves him well,
    Who 'lights and rings the gateway bell,
And learns her gone and far from home;

He saddens, all the magic light
    Dies off at once from bower and hall,
    And all the place is dark, and all
The chambers emptied of delight:

So find I every pleasant spot
    In which we two were wont to meet,   10
    The field, the chamber, and the street,
For all is dark where thou art not.

Yet as that other, wandering there
    In those deserted walks, may find
    A flower beat with rain and wind,
Which once she foster'd up with care;

So seems it in my deep regret,
    O my forsaken heart, with thee
    And this poor flower of poesy
Which, little cared for, fades not yet.   20

But since it pleased a vanish'd eye,
    I go to plant it on his tomb,
    That if it can it there may bloom,
Or, dying, there at least may die.

IX

Fair ship, that from the Italian shore
    Sailest the placid ocean-plains
    With my lost Arthur's loved remains,
Spread thy full wings, and waft him o'er.

So draw him home to those that mourn
    In vain; a favorable speed

Ruffle thy mirror'd mast, and lead
Thro' prosperous floods his holy urn.

All night no ruder air perplex
   Thy sliding keel, till Phosphor, bright   **10**
   As our pure love, thro' early light
Shall glimmer on the dewy decks.

Sphere all your lights around, above;
   Sleep, gentle heavens, before the prow;
   Sleep, gentle winds, as he sleeps now,
My friend, the brother of my love;

My Arthur, whom I shall not see
   Till all my widow'd race be run;
   Dear as the mother to the son,
More than my brothers are to me.   **20**

x

I hear the noise about thy keel;
   I hear the bell struck in the night;
   I see the cabin-window bright;
I see the sailor at the wheel.

Thou bring'st the sailor to his wife,
   And travell'd men from foreign lands;
   And letters unto trembling hands;
And, thy dark freight, a vanish'd life.

So bring him; we have idle dreams;
   This look of quiet flatters thus   **10**
   Our home-bred fancies. O, to us,
The fools of habit, sweeter seems

To rest beneath the clover sod,
   That takes the sunshine and the rains,
   Or where the kneeling hamlet drains
The chalice of the grapes of God;

Than if with thee the roaring wells
   Should gulf him fathom-deep in brine,

And hands so often clasp'd in mine,
Should toss with tangle and with shells.   20

XI

Calm is the morn without a sound,
    Calm as to suit a calmer grief,
    And only thro' the faded leaf
The chestnut pattering to the ground;

Calm and deep peace on this high wold,
    And on these dews that drench the furze,
    And all the silvery gossamers
That twinkle into green and gold;

Calm and still light on yon great plain
    That sweeps with all its autumn bowers,   10
    And crowded farms and lessening towers,
To mingle with the bounding main;

Calm and deep peace in this wide air,
    These leaves that redden to the fall,
    And in my heart, if calm at all,
If any calm, a calm despair;

Calm on the seas, and silver sleep,
    And waves that sway themselves in rest,
    And dead calm in that noble breast
Which heaves but with the heaving deep.   20

XII

Lo, as a dove when up she springs
    To bear thro' heaven a tale of woe,
    Some dolorous message knit below
The wild pulsation of her wings;

Like her I go, I cannot stay;
    I leave this mortal ark behind,
    A weight of nerves without a mind,
And leave the cliffs, and haste away

O'er ocean-mirrors rounded large,
   And reach the glow of southern skies,
   And see the sails at distance rise,
And linger weeping on the marge,   10

And saying, "Comes he thus, my friend?
   Is this the end of all my care?"
   And circle moaning in the air,
"Is this the end? Is this the end?"

And forward dart again, and play
   About the prow, and back return
   To where the body sits, and learn
That I have been an hour away.   20

XIII

Tears of the widower, when he sees
   A late-lost form that sleep reveals,
   And moves his doubtful arms, and feels
Her place is empty, fall like these;

Which weep a loss for ever new,
   A void where heart on heart reposed;
   And, where warm hands have prest and closed,
Silence, till I be silent too;

Which weep the comrade of my choice,
   An awful thought, a life removed,   10
   The human-hearted man I loved,
A Spirit, not a breathing voice.

Come, Time, and teach me, many years,
   I do not suffer in a dream;
   For now so strange do these things seem,
Mine eyes have leisure for their tears,

My fancies time to rise on wing,
   And glance about the approaching sails,
   As tho' they brought but merchants' bales,
And not the burthen that they bring.   20

XIV

If one should bring me this report,
  That thou hadst touch'd the land to-day,
  And I went down unto the quay,
And found thee lying in the port;

And standing, muffled round with woe,
  Should see thy passengers in rank
  Come stepping lightly down the plank,
And beckoning unto those they know;

And if along with these should come
  The man I held as half-divine,
  Should strike a sudden hand in mine,
And ask a thousand things of home;   10

And I should tell him all my pain,
  And how my life had droop'd of late,
  And he should sorrow o'er my state
And marvel what possess'd my brain;

And I perceived no touch of change,
  No hint of death in all his frame,
  But found him all in all the same,
I should not feel it to be strange.   20

XV

To-night the winds begin to rise
  And roar from yonder dropping day;
  The last red leaf is whirl'd away,
The rooks are blown about the skies;

The forest crack'd, the waters curl'd,
  The cattle huddled on the lea;
  And wildly dash'd on tower and tree
The sunbeam strikes along the world:

And but for fancies, which aver
  That all thy motions gently pass   10

Athwart a plane of molten glass,
I scarce could brook the strain and stir

That makes the barren branches loud;
    And but for fear it is not so,
    The wild unrest that lives in woe
Would dote and pore on yonder cloud

That rises upward always higher,
    And onward drags a laboring breast,
    And topples round the dreary west,
A looming bastion fringed with fire.   20

XVI

What words are these have fallen from me?
    Can calm despair and wild unrest
    Be tenants of a single breast,
Or Sorrow such a changeling be?

Or doth she only seem to take
    The touch of change in calm or storm,
    But knows no more of transient form
In her deep self, than some dead lake

That holds the shadow of a lark
    Hung in the shadow of a heaven?   10
    Or has the shock, so harshly given,
Confused me like the unhappy bark

That strikes by night a craggy shelf,
    And staggers blindly ere she sink?
    And stunn'd me from my power to think
And all my knowledge of myself;

And made me that delirious man
    Whose fancy fuses old and new,
    And flashes into false and true,
And mingles all without a plan?   20

XVII

Thou comest, much wept for; such a breeze
   Compell'd thy canvas, and my prayer
   Was as the whisper of an air
To breathe thee over lonely seas.

For I in spirit saw thee move
   Thro' circles of the bounding sky,
   Week after week; the days go by;
Come quick, thou bringest all I love.

Henceforth, wherever thou mayst roam,
   My blessing, like a line of light,   10
   Is on the waters day and night,
And like a beacon guards thee home.

So may whatever tempest mars
   Mid-ocean spare thee, sacred bark,
   And balmy drops in summer dark
Slide from the bosom of the stars;

So kind an office hath been done,
   Such precious relics brought by thee,
   The dust of him I shall not see
Till all my widow'd race be run.   20

XVIII

'T is well; 't is something; we may stand
   Where he in English earth is laid,
   And from his ashes may be made
The violet of his native land.

'T is little; but it looks in truth
   As if the quiet bones were blest
   Among familiar names to rest
And in the places of his youth.

Come then, pure hands, and bear the head
   That sleeps or wears the mask of sleep,   10

And come, whatever loves to weep,
And hear the ritual of the dead.

Ah yet, even yet, if this might be,
   I, falling on his faithful heart,
   Would breathing thro' his lips impart
The life that almost dies in me;

That dies not, but endures with pain,
   And slowly forms the firmer mind,
   Treasuring the look it cannot find,
The words that are not heard again.   20

XIX

The Danube to the Severn gave
   The darken'd heart that beat no more;
   They laid him by the pleasant shore,
And in the hearing of the wave.

There twice a day the Severn fills;
   The salt sea-water passes by,
   And hushes half the babbling Wye,
And makes a silence in the hills.

The Wye is hush'd nor moved along,
   And hush'd my deepest grief of all,   10
   When fill'd with tears that cannot fall,
I brim with sorrow drowning song.

The tide flows down, the wave again
   Is vocal in its wooded walls;
   My deeper anguish also falls,
And I can speak a little then.

XX

The lesser griefs that may be said,
   'That breathe a thousand tender vows,
   Are but as servants in a house
Where lies the master newly dead;

Who speak their feeling as it is,
 And weep the fulness from the mind.
 "It will be hard," they say, "to find
Another service such as this."

My lighter moods are like to these,
 That out of words a comfort win; 10
 But there are other griefs within,
And tears that at their fountain freeze;

For by the hearth the children sit
 Cold in that atmosphere of death,
 And scarce endure to draw the breath,
Or like to noiseless phantoms flit;

But open converse is there none,
 So much the vital spirits sink
 To see the vacant chair, and think,
"How good! how kind! and he is gone." 20

XXI

I sing to him that rests below,
 And, since the grasses round me wave,
 I take the grasses of the grave,
And make them pipes whereon to blow.

The traveller hears me now and then,
 And sometimes harshly will he speak:
 "This fellow would make weakness weak,
And melt the waxen hearts of men."

Another answers: "Let him be,
 He loves to make parade of pain, 10
 That with his piping he may gain
The praise that comes to constancy."

A third is wroth: "Is this an hour
 For private sorrow's barren song,
 When more and more the people throng
The chairs and thrones of civil power?

"A time to sicken and to swoon,
  When Science reaches forth her arms
  To feel from world to world, and charms
Her secret from the latest moon?"   20

Behold, ye speak an idle thing;
  Ye never knew the sacred dust.
  I do but sing because I must,
And pipe but as the linnets sing;

And one is glad; her note is gay,
  For now her little ones have ranged;
  And one is sad; her note is changed,
Because her brood is stolen away.

XXII

The path by which we twain did go,
  Which led by tracts that pleased us well,
  Thro' four sweet years arose and fell,
From flower to flower, from snow to snow;

And we with singing cheer'd the way,
  And, crown'd with all the season lent,
  From April on to April went,
And glad at heart from May to May.

But where the path we walk'd began
  To slant the fifth autumnal slope,   10
  As we descended following Hope,
There sat the Shadow fear'd of man;

Who broke our fair companionship,
  And spread his mantle dark and cold,
  And wrapt thee formless in the fold,
And dull'd the murmur on thy lip,

And bore thee where I could not see
  Nor follow, tho' I walk in haste,
  And think that somewhere in the waste
The Shadow sits and waits for me.   20

XXIII

Now, sometimes in my sorrow shut,
  Or breaking into song by fits,
  Alone, alone, to where he sits,
The Shadow cloak'd from head to foot,

Who keeps the keys of all the creeds,
  I wander, often falling lame,
  And looking back to whence I came,
Or on to where the pathway leads;

And crying, How changed from where it ran
  Thro' lands where not a leaf was dumb,   10
  But all the lavish hills would hum
The murmur of a happy Pan;

When each by turns was guide to each,
  And Fancy light from Fancy caught,
  And Thought leapt out to wed with Thought
Ere Thought could wed itself with Speech;

And all we met was fair and good,
  And all was good that Time could bring,
  And all the secret of the Spring
Moved in the chambers of the blood;   20

And many an old philosophy
  On Argive heights divinely sang,
  And round us all the thicket rang
To many a flute of Arcady.

XXIV

And was the day of my delight
  As pure and perfect as I say?
  The very source and fount of day
Is dash'd with wandering isles of night.

If all was good and fair we met,
  This earth had been the Paradise

It never look'd to human eyes
Since our first sun arose and set.

And is it that the haze of grief
   Makes former gladness loom so great?   **10**
   The lowness of the present state,
That sets the past in this relief?

Or that the past will always win
   A glory from its being far,
   And orb into the perfect star
We saw not when we moved therein?

XXV

i know that this was Life,—the track
   Whereon with equal feet we fared;
   And then, as now, the day prepared
The daily burden for the back.

But this it was that made me move
   As light as carrier-birds in air;
   I loved the weight I had to bear,
Because it needed help of Love;

Nor could I weary, heart or limb,
   When mighty Love would cleave in twain   **10**
   The lading of a single pain,
And part it, giving half to him.

XXVI

Still onward winds the dreary way;
   I with it, for I long to prove
   No lapse of moons can canker Love,
Whatever fickle tongues may say.

And if that eye which watches guilt
   And goodness, and hath power to see
   Within the green the moulder'd tree,
And towers fallen as soon as built—

O, if indeed that eye foresee
   Or see—in Him is no before—   **10**
   In more of life true life no more
And Love the indifference to be,

Then might I find, ere yet the morn
   Breaks hither over Indian seas,
   That Shadow waiting with the keys,
To shroud me from my proper scorn.

XXVII

I envy not in any moods
   The captive void of noble rage,
   The linnet born within the cage,
That never knew the summer woods;

I envy not the beast that takes
   His license in the field of time,
   Unfetter'd by the sense of crime,
To whom a conscience never wakes;

Nor, what may count itself as blest,
   The heart that never plighted troth   **10**
   But stagnates in the weeds of sloth;
Nor any want-begotten rest.

I hold it true, whate'er befall;
   I feel it, when I sorrow most;
   'Tis better to have loved and lost
Than never to have loved at all.

XXVIII

The time draws near the birth of Christ.
   The moon is hid, the night is still;
   The Christmas bells from hill to hill
Answer each other in the mist.

Four voices of four hamlets round,
   From far and near, on mead and moor,

Swell out and fail, as if a door
Were shut between me and the sound;

Each voice four changes on the wind,
   That now dilate, and now decrease,
   Peace and goodwill, goodwill and peace,
Peace and goodwill, to all mankind.   **10**

This year I slept and woke with pain,
   I almost wish'd no more to wake,
   And that my hold on life would break
Before I heard those bells again;

But they my troubled spirit rule,
   For they controll'd me when a boy;
   They bring me sorrow touch'd with joy,
The merry, merry bells of Yule.   **20**

XXIX

With such compelling cause to grieve
   As daily vexes household peace,
   And chains regret to his decease,
How dare we keep our Christmas-eve,

Which brings no more a welcome guest
   To enrich the threshold of the night
   With shower'd largess of delight
In dance and song and game and jest?

Yet go, and while the holly boughs
   Entwine the cold baptismal font,   **10**
   Make one wreath more for Use and Wont,
That guard the portals of the house;

Old sisters of a day gone by,
   Gray nurses, loving nothing new—
   Why should they miss their yearly due
Before their time? They too will die.

XXX

With trembling fingers did we weave
   The holly round the Chrismas hearth;
   A rainy cloud possess'd the earth,
And sadly fell our Christmas-eve.

At our old pastimes in the hall
   We gamboll'd, making vain pretence
   Of gladness, with an awful sense
Of one mute Shadow watching all.

We paused: the winds were in the beech;
   We heard them sweep the winter land;   10
   And in a circle hand-in-hand
Sat silent, looking each at each.

Then echo-like our voices rang;
   We sung, tho' every eye was dim,
   A merry song we sang with him
Last year; impetuously we sang.

We ceased; a gentler feeling crept
   Upon us: surely rest is meet.
   "They rest," we said, "their sleep is sweet,"
And silence follow'd, and we wept.   20

Our voices took a higher range;
   Once more we sang: "They do not die
   Nor lose their mortal sympathy,
Nor change to us, although they change;

"Rapt from the fickle and the frail
   With gather'd power, yet the same,
   Pierces the keen seraphic flame
From orb to orb, from veil to veil."

Rise, happy morn, rise, holy morn,
   Draw forth the cheerful day from night: 30
   O Father, touch the east, and light
The light that shone when Hope was born.

XXXI

When Lazarus left his charnel-cave,
 And home to Mary's house return'd,
 Was this demanded—if he yearn'd
To hear her weeping by his grave?

"Where wert thou, brother, those four days?"
 There lives no record of reply,
 Which telling what it is to die
Had surely added praise to praise.

From every house the neighbors met,
 The streets were fill'd with joyful sound,   10
 A solemn gladness even crown'd
The purple brows of Olivet.

Behold a man raised up by Christ!
 The rest remaineth unreveal'd;
 He told it not, or something seal'd
The lips of that Evangelist.

XXXII

Her eyes are homes of silent prayer,
 Nor other thought her mind admits
 But, he was dead, and there he sits,
And he that brought him back is there.

Then one deep love doth supersede
 All other, when her ardent gaze
 Roves from the living brother's face,
And rests upon the Life indeed.

All subtle thought, all curious fears,
 Borne down by gladness so complete,   10
 She bows, she bathes the Saviour's feet
With costly spikenard and with tears.

Thrice blest whose lives are faithful prayers,
 Whose loves in higher love endure;

What souls possess themselves so pure,
Or is there blessedness like theirs?

XXXIII

O thou that after toil and storm
      Mayst seem to have reach'd a purer air,
      Whose faith has centre everywhere,
Nor cares to fix itself to form,

Leave thou thy sister when she prays
      Her early heaven, her happy views;
      Nor thou with shadow'd hint confuse
A life that leads melodious days.

Her faith thro' form is pure as thine,
      Her hands are quicker unto good.   10
      O, sacred be the flesh and blood
To which she links a truth divine!

See thou, that countest reason ripe
      In holding by the law within,
      Thou fail not in a world of sin,
And even for want of such a type.

XXXIV

My own dim life should teach me this,
      That life shall live for evermore,
      Else earth is darkness at the core,
And dust and ashes all that is;

This round of green, this orb of flame,
      Fantastic beauty; such as lurks
      In some wild poet, when he works
Without a conscience or an aim.

What then were God to such as I?
      'T were hardly worth my while to choose   10
      Of things all mortal, or to use
A little patience ere I die;

'T were best at once to sink to peace,
　　Like birds the charming serpent draws
　　To drop head-foremost in the jaws
Of vacant darkness and to cease.

XXXV

Yet if some voice that man could trust
　　Should murmur from the narrow house,
　　"The cheeks drop in, the body bows;
Man dies, nor is there hope in dust;"

Might I not say? "Yet even here,
　　But for one hour, O Love, I strive
　　To keep so sweet a thing alive."
But I should turn mine ears and hear

The moanings of the homeless sea,
　　The sound of streams that swift or slow　　　　10
　　Draw down Æonian hills, and sow
The dust of continents to be;

And Love would answer with a sigh,
　　"The sound of that forgetful shore
　　Will change my sweetness more and more,
Half-dead to know that I shall die."

O me, what profits it to put
　　An idle case? If Death were seen
　　At first as Death, Love had not been,
Or been in narrowest working shut,　　　　　　20

Mere fellowship of sluggish moods,
　　Or in his coarsest Satyr-shape
　　Had bruised the herb and crush'd the grape,
And bask'd and batten'd in the woods.

XXXVI

Tho' truths in manhood darkly join,
　　Deep-seated in our mystic frame,

We yield all blessing to the name
Of Him that made them current coin;

For Wisdom dealt with mortal powers,
    Where truth in closest words shall fail,
    When truth embodied in a tale
Shall enter in at lowly doors.

And so the Word had breath, and wrought
    With human hands the creed of creeds   10
    In loveliness of perfect deeds,
More strong than all poetic thought;

Which he may read that binds the sheaf,
    Or builds the house, or digs the grave,
    And those wild eyes that watch the wave
In roarings round the coral reef.

XXXVII

Urania speaks with darken'd brow:
    "Thou pratest here where thou art least;
    This faith has many a purer priest,
And many an abler voice than thou.

"Go down beside thy native rill,
    On thy Parnassus set thy feet,
    And hear thy laurel whisper sweet
About the ledges of the hill."

And my Melpomene replies,
    A touch of shame upon her cheek: 10
    "I am not worthy even to speak
Of thy prevailing mysteries;

"For I am but an earthly Muse,
    And owning but a little art
    To lull with song an aching heart,
And render human love his dues;

"But brooding on the dear one dead,
    And all he said of things divine,—

And dear to me as sacred wine
To dying lips is all he said,—   20

"I murmur'd, as I came along,
  Of comfort clasp'd in truth reveal'd,
  And loiter'd in the master's field,
And darken'd sanctities with song."

XXXVIII

With weary steps I loiter on,
  Tho' always under alter'd skies
  The purple from the distance dies,
My prospect and horizon gone.

No joy the blowing season gives,
  The herald melodies of spring,
  But in the songs I love to sing
A doubtful gleam of solace lives.

If any care for what is here
  Survive in spirits render'd free,   10
  Then are these songs I sing of thee
Not all ungrateful to thine ear.

XXXIX

Old warder of these buried bones,
  And answering now my random stroke
  With fruitful cloud and living smoke,
Dark yew, that graspest at the stones

And dippest toward the dreamless head,
  To thee too comes the golden hour
  When flower is feeling after flower;
But Sorrow,—fixt upon the dead,

And darkening the dark graves of men,—
  What whisper'd from her lying lips?   10
  Thy gloom is kindled at the tips,
And passes into gloom again.

XL

Could we forget the widow'd hour
    And look on Spirits breathed away,
    As on a maiden in the day
When first she wears her orange-flower!

When crown'd with blessing she doth rise
    To take her latest leave of home,
    And hopes and light regrets that come
Make April of her tender eyes;

And doubtful joys the father move,
    And tears are on the mother's face,   10
    As parting with a long embrace
She enters other realms of love;

Her office there to rear, to teach,
    Becoming as is meet and fit
    A link among the days, to knit
The generations each with each;

And, doubtless, unto thee is given
    A life that bears immortal fruit
    In those great offices that suit
The full-grown energies of heaven.   20

Ay me, the difference I discern!
    How often shall her old fireside
    Be cheer'd with tidings of the bride,
How often she herself return,

And tell them all they would have told,
    And bring her babe, and make her boast,
    Till even those that miss'd her most
Shall count new things as dear as old;

But thou and I have shaken hands,
    Till growing winters lay me low;   30
    My paths are in the fields I know,
And thine in undiscover'd lands.

XLI

Thy spirit ere our fatal loss
   Did ever rise from high to higher,
   As mounts the heavenward altar-fire,
As flies the lighter thro' the gross.

But thou art turn'd to something strange,
   And I have lost the links that bound
   Thy changes; here upon the ground,
No more partaker of thy change.

Deep folly! yet that this could be—
   That I could wing my will with might   **10**
   To leap the grades of life and light,
And flash at once, my friend, to thee!

For tho' my nature rarely yields
   To that vague fear implied in death,
   Nor shudders at the gulfs beneath,
The howlings from forgotten fields;

Yet oft when sundown skirts the moor
   An inner trouble I behold,
   A spectral doubt which makes me cold,
That I shall be thy mate no more,   **20**

Tho' following with an upward mind
   The wonders that have come to thee,
   Thro' all the secular to-be,
But evermore a life behind.

XLII

I vex my heart with fancies dim.
   He still outstript me in the race;
   It was but unity of place
That made me dream I rank'd with him.

And so may Place retain us still,
   And he the much-beloved again.

A lord of large experience, train
To riper growth the mind and will;

And what delights can equal those
    That stir the spirit's inner deeps,
    When one that loves, but knows not, reaps
A truth from one that loves and knows?   **10**

XLIII

If Sleep and Death be truly one,
    And every spirit's folded bloom
    Thro' all its intervital gloom
In some long trance should slumber on;

Unconscious of the sliding hour,
    Bare of the body, might it last,
    And silent traces of the past
Be all the color of the flower:

So then were nothing lost to man;
    So that still garden of the souls   **10**
    In many a figured leaf enrolls
The total world since life began;

And love will last as pure and whole
    As when he loved me here in Time,
    And at the spiritual prime
Rewaken with the dawning soul.

XLIV

How fares it with the happy dead?
    For here the man is more and more;
    But he forgets the days before
God shut the doorways of his head.

The days have vanish'd, tone and tint,
    And yet perhaps the hoarding sense
    Gives out at times—he knows not whence—
A little flash, a mystic hint;

And in the long harmonious years—
   If Death so taste Lethean springs—
   May some dim touch of earthly things
Surprise thee ranging with thy peers.

10

If such a dreamy touch should fall,
   O, turn thee round, resolve the doubt;
   My guardian angel will speak out
In that high place, and tell thee all.

XLV

The baby new to earth and sky,
   What time his tender palm is prest
   Against the circle of the breast,
Has never thought that "this is I;"

But as he grows he gathers much,
   And learns the use of "I" and "me,"
   And finds "I am not what I see,
And other than the things I touch."

So rounds he to a separate mind
   From whence clear memory may begin,
   As thro' the frame that binds him in
His isolation grows defined.

10

This use may lie in blood and breath,
   Which else were fruitless of their due,
   Had man to learn himself anew
Beyond the second birth of death.

XLVI

We ranging down this lower track,
   The path we came by, thorn and flower,
   Is shadow'd by the growing hour,
Lest life should fail in looking back.

So be it: there no shade can last
   In that deep dawn behind the tomb,

But clear from marge to marge shall bloom
The eternal landscape of the past;

A lifelong tract of time reveal'd,
 The fruitful hours of still increase; 10
 Days order'd in a wealthy peace,
And those five years its richest field.

O Love, thy province were not large,
 A bounded field, nor stretching far;
 Look also, Love, a brooding star,
A rosy warmth from marge to marge.

XLVII

That each, who seems a separate whole,
 Should move his rounds, and fusing all
 The skirts of self again, should fall
Remerging in the general Soul,

Is faith as vague as all unsweet.
 Eternal form shall still divide
 The eternal soul from all beside;
And I shall know him when we meet;

And we shall sit at endless feast,
 Enjoying each the other's good. 10
 What vaster dream can hit the mood
Of Love on earth? He seeks at least

Upon the last and sharpest height,
 Before the spirits fade away,
 Some landing-place, to clasp and say,
"Farewell! We lose ourselves in light."

XLVIII

If these brief lays, of Sorrow born,
 Were taken to be such as closed
 Grave doubts and answers here proposed,
Then these were such as men might scorn.

Her care is not to part and prove;
    She takes, when harsher moods remit,
    What slender shade of doubt may flit,
And makes it vassal unto love;

And hence, indeed, she sports with words,
    But better serves a wholesome law,   10
    And holds it sin and shame to draw
The deepest measure from the chords;

Nor dare she trust a larger lay,
    But rather loosens from the lip
    Short swallow-flights of song, that dip
Their wings in tears, and skim away.

XLIX

From art, from nature, from the schools,
    Let random influences glance,
    Like light in many a shiver'd lance
That breaks about the dappled pools.

The lightest wave of thought shall lisp,
    The fancy's tenderest eddy wreathe,
    The slightest air of song shall breathe
To make the sullen surface crisp.

And look thy look, and go thy way,
    But blame not thou the winds that make   10
    The seeming-wanton ripple break,
The tender-pencill'd shadow play.

Beneath all fancied hopes and fears
    Ay me, the sorrow deepens down,
    Whose muffled motions blindly drown
The bases of my life in tears.

L

Be near me when my light is low,
    When the blood creeps, and the nerves prick

And tingle; and the heart is sick,
And all the wheels of being slow.

Be near me when the sensuous frame
  Is rack'd with pangs that conquer trust;
  And Time, a maniac scattering dust,
And Life, a Fury slinging flame.

Be near me when my faith is dry,
  And men the flies of latter spring,   10
  That lay their eggs, and sting and sing
And weave their petty cells and die.

Be near me when I fade away,
  To point the term of human strife,
  And on the low dark verge of life
The twilight of eternal day.

LI

Do we indeed desire the dead
  Should still be near us at our side?
  Is there no baseness we would hide?
No inner vileness that we dread?

Shall he for whose applause I strove,
  I had such reverence for his blame,
  See with clear eye some hidden shame
And I be lessen'd in his love?

I wrong the grave with fears untrue.
  Shall love be blamed for want of faith?   10
  There must be wisdom with great Death;
The dead shall look me thro' and thro'.

Be near us when we climb or fall;
  Ye watch, like God, the rolling hours
  With larger other eyes than ours,
To make allowance for us all.

LII

I cannot love thee as I ought,
　　For love reflects the thing beloved;
　　My words are only words, and moved
Upon the topmost froth of thought.

"Yet blame not thou thy plaintive song,"
　　The Spirit of true love replied;
　　"Thou canst not move me from thy side,
Nor human frailty do me wrong.

"What keeps a spirit wholly true
　　To that ideal which he bears?
　　What record? not the sinless years   **10**
That breathed beneath the Syrian blue;

"So fret not, like an idle girl,
　　That life is dash'd with flecks of sin.
　　Abide; thy wealth is gather'd in,
When Time hath sunder'd shell from pearl."

LIII

How many a father have I seen,
　　A sober man, among his boys,
　　Whose youth was full of foolish noise,
Who wears his manhood hale and green;

And dare we to this fancy give,
　　That had the wild oat not been sown,
　　The soil, left barren, scarce had grown
The grain by which a man may live?

Or, if we held the doctrine sound
　　For life outliving heats of youth,   **10**
　　Yet who would preach it as a truth
To those that eddy round and round?

Hold thou the good, define it well;
　　For fear divine Philosophy

Should push beyond her mark, and be
Procuress to the Lords of Hell.

LIV

O, yet we trust that somehow good
 Will be the final goal of ill,
 To pangs of nature, sins of will,
Defects of doubt, and taints of blood;

That nothing walks with aimless feet;
 That not one life shall be destroy'd,
 Or cast as rubbish to the void,
When God hath made the pile complete;

That not a worm is cloven in vain;
 That not a moth with vain desire   10
 Is shrivell'd in a fruitless fire,
Or but subserves another's gain.

Behold, we know not anything;
 I can but trust that good shall fall
 At last—far off—at last, to all,
And every winter change to spring.

So runs my dream; but what am I?
 An infant crying in the night;
 An infant crying for the light,
And with no language but a cry.   20

LV

The wish, that of the living whole
 No life may fail beyond the grave,
 Derives it not from what we have
The likest God within the soul?

Are God and Nature then at strife,
 That Nature lends such evil dreams?
 So careful of the type she seems,
So careless of the single life,

That I, considering everywhere
  Her secret meaning in her deeds,   10
  And finding that of fifty seeds
She often brings but one to bear,

I falter where I firmly trod,
  And falling with my weight of cares
  Upon the great world's altar-stairs
That slope thro' darkness up to God,

I stretch lame hands of faith, and grope,
  And gather dust and chaff, and call
  To what I feel is Lord of all,
And faintly trust the larger hope.   20

LVI

"So careful of the type?" but no.
  From scarped cliff and quarried stone
  She cries, "A thousand types are gone;
I care for nothing, all shall go.

"Thou makest thine appeal to me:
  I bring to life, I bring to death;
  The spirit does but mean the breath:
I know no more." And he, shall he,

Man, her last work, who seem'd so fair,
  Such splendid purpose in his eyes,   10
  Who roll'd the psalm to wintry skies,
Who built him fanes of fruitless prayer,

Who trusted God was love indeed
  And love Creation's final law—
  Tho' Nature, red in tooth and claw
With ravine, shriek'd against his creed—

Who loved, who suffer'd countless ills,
  Who battled for the True, the Just,
  Be blown about the desert dust,
Or seal'd within the iron hills?   20

No more? A monster then, a dream,
   A discord. Dragons of the prime,
   That tare each other in their slime,
Were mellow music match'd with him.

O life as futile, then, as frail!
   O for thy voice to soothe and bless!
   What hope of answer, or redress?
Behind the veil, behind the veil.

LVII

Peace; come away: the song of woe
   Is after all an earthly song.
   Peace; come away: we do him wrong
To sing so wildly: let us go.

Come; let us go: your cheeks are pale;
   But half my life I leave behind.
   Methinks my friend is richly shrined;
But I shall pass, my work will fail.

Yet in these ears, till hearing dies,
   One set slow bell will seem to toll
   The passing of the sweetest soul
That ever look'd with human eyes.

10

I hear it now, and o'er and o'er,
   Eternal greetings to the dead;
   And "Ave, Ave, Ave," said,
"Adieu, adieu," for evermore.

LVIII

In those sad words I took farewell.
   Like echoes in sepulchral halls,
   As drop by drop the water falls
In vaults and catacombs, they fell;

And, falling, idly broke the peace
   Of hearts that beat from day to day,

Half-conscious of their dying clay,
And those cold crypts where they shall cease.

The high Muse answer'd: "Wherefore grieve
  Thy brethren with a fruitless 'tear?   10
  Abide a little longer here,
And thou shalt take a nobler leave."

LIX

O Sorrow, wilt thou live with me
  No casual mistress, but a wife,
  My bosom-friend and half of life;
As I confess it needs must be?

O Sorrow, wilt thou rule my blood,
  Be sometimes lovely like a bride,
  And put thy harsher moods aside,
If thou wilt have me wise and good?

My centred passion cannot move,
  Nor will it lessen from to-day;   10
  But I'll have leave at times to play
As with the creature of my love;

And set thee forth, for thou art mine,
  With so much hope for years to come,
  That, howsoe'er I know thee, some
Could hardly tell what name were thine.

LX

He past, a soul of nobler tone;
  My spirit loved and loves him yet,
  Like some poor girl whose heart is set
On one whose rank exceeds her own.

He mixing with his proper sphere,
  She finds the baseness of her lot,
  Half jealous of she knows not what,
And envying all that meet him there.

The little village looks forlorn;
    She sighs amid her narrow days,
    Moving about the household ways,
In that dark house where she was born.

The foolish neighbors come and go,
    And tease her till the day draws by;
    At night she weeps, "How vain am I!
How should he love a thing so low?"

LXI

If, in thy second state sublime,
    Thy ransom'd reason change replies
    With all the circle of the wise,
The perfect flower of human time;

And if thou cast thine eyes below,
    How dimly character'd and slight,
    How dwarf'd a growth of cold and night,
How blanch'd with darkness must I grow!

Yet turn thee to the doubtful shore,
    Where thy first form was made a man;
    I loved thee, Spirit, and love, nor can
The soul of Shakespeare love thee more.

10

LXII

Tho' if an eye that's downward cast
    Could make thee somewhat blench or fail,
    Then be my love an idle tale
And fading legend of the past;

And thou, as one that once declined,
    When he was little more than boy,
    On some unworthy heart with joy,
But lives to wed an equal mind,

And breathes a novel world, the while
    His other passion wholly dies,

10

Or in the light of deeper eyes
Is matter for a flying smile.

LXIII

Yet pity for a horse o'er-driven,
    And love in which my hound has part,
    Can hang no weight upon my heart
In its assumptions up to heaven;

And I am so much more than these,
    As thou, perchance, art more than I,
    And yet I spare them sympathy,
And I would set their pains at ease.

So mayst thou watch me where I weep,
    As, unto vaster motions bound,
    The circuits of thine orbit round
A higher height, a deeper deep.

LXIV

Dost thou look back on what hath been,
    As some divinely gifted man,
    Whose life in low estate began
And on a simple village green;

Who breaks his birth's invidious bar,
    And grasps the skirts of happy chance,
    And breasts the blows of circumstance,
And grapples with his evil star;

Who makes by force his merit known
    And lives to clutch the golden keys,
    To mould a mighty state's decrees,
And shape the whisper of the throne;

And moving up from high to higher,
    Becomes on Fortune's crowning slope
    The pillar of a people's hope,
The centre of a world's desire;

Yet feels, as in a pensive dream,
  When all his active powers are still,
  A distant dearness in the hill,
A secret sweetness in the stream,   20

The limit of his narrower fate,
  While yet beside its vocal springs
  He play'd at counsellors and kings,
With one that was his earliest mate;

Who ploughs with pain his native lea
  And reaps the labor of his hands,
  Or in the furrow musing stands:
"Does my old friend remember me?"

LXV

Sweet soul, do with me as thou wilt;
  I lull a fancy trouble-tost
  With "Love's too precious to be lost,
A little grain shall not be spilt."

And in that solace can I sing,
  Till out of painful phases wrought
  There flutters up a happy thought,
Self-balanced on a lightsome wing;

Since we deserved the name of friends,
  And thine effect so lives in me,   10
  A part of mine may live in thee
And move thee on to noble ends.

LXVI

You thought my heart too far diseased;
  You wonder when my fancies play
  To find me gay among the gay,
Like one with any trifle pleased.

The shade by which my life was crost,
  Which makes a desert in the mind,

Has made me kindly with my kind,
And like to him whose sight is lost;

Whose feet are guided thro' the land,
 Whose jest among his friends is free,
 Who takes the children on his knee,
And winds their curls about his hand.

He plays with threads, he beats his chair
 For pastime, dreaming of the sky;
 His inner day can never die,
His night of loss is always there.

LXVII

When on my bed the moonlight falls,
 I know that in thy place of rest
 By that broad water of the west
There comes a glory on the walls:

Thy marble bright in dark appears,
 As slowly steals a silver flame
 Along the letters of thy name,
And o'er the number of thy years.

The mystic glory swims away,
 From off my bed the moonlight dies;
 And closing eaves of wearied eyes
I sleep till dusk is dipt in gray;

And then I know the mist is drawn
 A lucid veil from coast to coast,
 And in the dark church like a ghost
Thy tablet glimmers to the dawn.

LXVIII

When in the down I sink my head,
 Sleep, Death's twin-brother, times my breath;
 Sleep, Death's twin-brother, knows not Death,
Nor can I dream of thee as dead.

I walk as ere I walk'd forlorn,
   When all our path was fresh with dew,
   And all the bugle breezes blew
Reveillée to the breaking morn.

But what is this? I turn about,
   I find a trouble in thine eye,   10
   Which makes me sad I know not why,
Nor can my dream resolve the doubt;

But ere the lark hath left the lea
   I wake, and I discern the truth;
   It is the trouble of my youth
That foolish sleep transfers to thee.

LXIX

I dream'd there would be Spring no more,
   That Nature's ancient power was lost;
   The streets were black with smoke and frost,
They chatter'd trifles at the door;

I wander'd from the noisy town,
   I found a wood with thorny boughs;
   I took the thorns to bind my brows,
I wore them like a civic crown;

I met with scoffs, I met with scorns
   From youth and babe and hoary hairs: 10
   They call'd me in the public squares
The fool that wears a crown of thorns.

They call'd me fool, they call'd me child:
   I found an angel of the night;
   The voice was low, the look was bright;
He look'd upon my crown and smiled.

He reach'd the glory of a hand,
   That seem'd to touch it into leaf;
   The voice was not the voice of grief,
The words were hard to understand.   20

LXX

I cannot see the features right,
　　When on the gloom I strive to paint
　　The face I know; the hues are faint
And mix with hollow masks of night;

Cloud-towers by ghostly masons wrought,
　　A gulf that ever shuts and gapes,
　　A hand that points, and palled shapes
In shadowy thoroughfares of thought;

And crowds that stream from yawning doors,
　　And shoals of pucker'd faces drive;   10
　　Dark bulks that tumble half alive,
And lazy lengths on boundless shores;

Till all at once beyond the will
　　I hear a wizard music roll,
　　And thro' a lattice on the soul
Looks thy fair face and makes it still.

LXXI

Sleep, kinsman thou to death and trance
　　And madness, thou hast forged at last
　　A night-long present of the past
In which we went thro' summer France.

Hadst thou such credit with the soul?
　　Then bring an opiate trebly strong,
　　Drug down the blindfold sense of wrong,
That so my pleasure may be whole;

While now we talk as once we talk'd
　　Of men and minds, the dust of change,   10
　　The days that grow to something strange,
In walking as of old we walk'd

Beside the river's wooded reach,
　　The fortress, and the mountain ridge,

The cataract flashing from the bridge,
The breaker breaking on the beach.

LXXII

Risest thou thus, dim dawn, again,
     And howlest, issuing out of night,
     With blasts that blow the poplar white,
And lash with storm the streaming pane?

Day, when my crown'd estate begun
     To pine in that reverse of doom,
     Which sicken'd every living bloom,
And blurr'd the splendor of the sun;

Who usherest in the dolorous hour
     With thy quick tears that make the rose   10
     Pull sideways, and the daisy close
Her crimson fringes to the shower;

Who mightst have heaved a windless flame
     Up the deep East, or, whispering, play'd
     A chequer-work of beam and shade
Along the hills, yet look'd the same,

As wan, as chill, as wild as now;
     Day, mark'd as with some hideous crime,
     When the dark hand struck down thro' time,
And cancell'd nature's best: but thou,   20

Lift as thou mayst thy burthen'd brows
     Thro' clouds that drench the morning star,
     And whirl the ungarner'd sheaf afar,
And sow the sky with flying boughs,

And up thy vault with roaring sound
     Climb thy thick noon, disastrous day;
     Touch thy dull goal of joyless gray,
And hide thy shame beneath the ground.

LXXIII

So many worlds, so much to do,
　　So little done, such things to be,
　　How know I what had need of thee,
For thou wert strong as thou wert true?

The fame is quench'd that I foresaw,
　　The head hath miss'd an earthly wreath:
　　I curse not Nature, no, nor Death;
For nothing is that errs from law.

We pass; the path that each man trod
　　Is dim, or will be dim, with weeds.　　　　**10**
　　What fame is left for human deeds
In endless age? It rests with God.

O hollow wraith of dying fame,
　　Fade wholly, while the soul exults,
　　And self-infolds the large results
Of force that would have forged a name.

LXXIV

As sometimes in a dead man's face,
　　To those that watch it more and more,
　　A likeness, hardly seen before,
Comes out—to some one of his race;

So, dearest, now thy brows are cold,
　　I see thee what thou art, and know
　　Thy likeness to the wise below,
Thy kindred with the great of old.

But there is more than I can see,
　　And what I see I leave unsaid,　　　　**10**
　　Nor speak it, knowing Death has made
His darkness beautiful with thee.

LXXV

I leave thy praises unexpress'd
   In verse that brings myself relief,
   And by the measure of my grief
I leave thy greatness to be guess'd.

What practice howsoe'er expert
   In fitting aptest words to things,
   Or voice the richest-toned that sings,
Hath power to give thee as thou wert?

I care not in these fading days
   To raise a cry that lasts not long,   **10**
   And round thee with the breeze of song
To stir a little dust of praise.

Thy leaf has perish'd in the green,
   And, while we breathe beneath the sun,
   The world which credits what is done
Is cold to all that might have been.

So here shall silence guard thy fame;
   But somewhere, out of human view,
   Whate'er thy hands are set to do
Is wrought with tumult of acclaim.   **20**

LXXVI

Take wings of fancy, and ascend,
   And in a moment set thy face
   Where all the starry heavens of space
Are sharpen'd to a needle's end;

Take wings of foresight; lighten thro'
   The secular abyss to come,
   And lo, thy deepest lays are dumb
Before the mouldering of a yew;

And if the matin songs, that woke
   The darkness of our planet, last,   **10**

Thine own shall wither in the vast,
Ere half the lifetime of an oak.

Ere these have clothed their branchy bowers
    With fifty Mays, thy songs are vain;
    And what are they when these remain
The ruin'd shells of hollow towers?

LXXVII

What hope is here for modern rhyme
    To him who turns a musing eye
    On songs, and deeds, and lives, that lie
Foreshorten'd in the tract of time?

These mortal lullabies of pain
    May bind a book, may line a box,
    May serve to curl a maiden's locks;
Or when a thousand moons shall wane

A man upon a stall may find,
    And, passing, turn the page that tells   **10**
    A grief, then changed to something else,
Sung by a long-forgotten mind.

But what of that? My darken'd ways
    Shall ring with music all the same;
    To breathe my loss is more than fame,
To utter love more sweet than praise.

LXXVIII

Again at Christmas did we weave
    The holly round the Christmas hearth;
    The silent snow possess'd the earth,
And calmly fell our Christmas-eve.

The yule-clog sparkled keen with frost,
    No wing of wind the region swept,
    But over all things brooding slept
The quiet sense of something lost.

As in the winters left behind,
    Again our ancient games had place,   10
    The mimic picture's breathing grace,
And dance and song and hoodman-blind.

Who show'd a token of distress?
    No single tear, no mark of pain—
    O sorrow, then can sorrow wane?
O grief, can grief be changed to less?

O last regret, regret can die!
    No—mixt with all this mystic frame,
    Her deep relations are the same,
But with long use her tears are dry.   20

LXXIX

"More than my brothers are to me,"—
    Let this not vex thee, noble heart!
    I know thee of what force thou art
To hold the costliest love in fee.

But thou and I are one in kind,
    As moulded like in Nature's mint;
    And hill and wood and field did print
The same sweet forms in either mind.

For us the same cold streamlet curl'd
    Thro' all his eddying coves, the same   10
    All winds that roam the twilight came
In whispers of the beauteous world.

At one dear knee we proffer'd vows,
    One lesson from one book we learn'd,
    Ere childhood's flaxen ringlet turn'd
To black and brown on kindred brows.

And so my wealth resembles thine,
    But he was rich where I was poor,
    And he supplied my want the more
As his unlikeness fitted mine.   20

LXXX

If any vague desire should rise,
  That holy Death ere Arthur died
  Had moved me kindly from his side,
And dropt the dust on tearless eyes;

Then fancy shapes, as fancy can,
  The grief my loss in him had wrought,
  A grief as deep as life or thought,
But stay'd in peace with God and man.

I make a picture in the brain;
  I hear the sentence that he speaks;   **10**
  He bears the burthen of the weeks,
But turns his burthen into gain.

His credit thus shall set me free;
  And, influence-rich to soothe and save,
  Unused example from the grave
Reach out dead hands to comfort me.

LXXXI

Could I have said while he was here,
  "My love shall now no further range;
  There cannot come a mellower change,
For now is love mature in ear"?

Love, then, had hope of richer store:
  What end is here to my complaint?
  This haunting whisper makes me faint,
"More years had made me love thee more."

But Death returns an answer sweet:
  "My sudden frost was sudden gain,   **10**
  And gave all ripeness to the grain
It might have drawn from after-heat."

LXXXII

I wage not any feud with Death
　　For changes wrought on form and face;
　　No lower life that earth's embrace
May breed with him can fright my faith.

Eternal process moving on,
　　From state to state the spirit walks;
　　And these are but the shatter'd stalks,
Or ruin'd chrysalis of one.

Nor blame I Death, because he bare
　　The use of virtue out of earth;
　　I know transplanted human worth
Will bloom to profit, otherwhere.

For this alone on Death I wreak
　　The wrath that garners in my heart:
　　He put our lives so far apart
We cannot hear each other speak.

LXXXIII

Dip down upon the northern shore,
　　O sweet new-year delaying long;
　　Thou doest expectant Nature wrong;
Delaying long, delay no more.

What stays thee from the clouded noons,
　　Thy sweetness from its proper place?
　　Can trouble live with April days,
Or sadness in the summer moons?

Bring orchis, bring the foxglove spire,
　　The little speedwell's darling blue,
　　Deep tulips dash'd with fiery dew,
Laburnums, dropping-wells of fire.

O thou, new-year, delaying long,
　　Delayest the sorrow in my blood,

That longs to burst a frozen bud
And flood a fresher throat with song.

LXXXIV

When I contemplate all alone
 The life that had been thine below,
 And fix my thoughts on all the glow
To which thy crescent would have grown,

I see thee sitting crown'd with good,
 A central warmth diffusing bliss
 In glance and smile, and clasp and kiss,
On all the branches of thy blood;

Thy blood, my friend, and partly mine;
 For now the day was drawing on,   10
 When thou shouldst link thy life with one
Of mine own house, and boys of thine

Had babbled "Uncle" on my knee;
 But that remorseless iron hour
 Made cypress of her orange flower,
Despair of hope, and earth of thee.

I seem to meet their least desire,
 To clap their cheeks, to call them mine.
 I see their unborn faces shine
Beside the never-lighted fire.   20

I see myself an honor'd guest,
 Thy partner in the flowery walk
 Of letters, genial table-talk,
Or deep dispute, and graceful jest;

While now thy prosperous labor fills
 The lips of men with honest praise,
 And sun by sun the happy days
Descend below the golden hills

With promise of a morn as fair;
 And all the train of bounteous hours   30

Conduct, by paths of growing powers,
To reverence and the silver hair;

Till slowly worn her earthly robe,
  Her lavish mission richly wrought,
  Leaving great legacies of thought,
Thy spirit should fail from off the globe;

What time mine own might also flee,
  As link'd with thine in love and fate,
  And, hovering o'er the dolorous strait
To the other shore, involved in thee,   40

Arrive at last the blessed goal,
  And He that died in Holy Land
  Would reach us out the shining hand,
And take us as a single soul.

What reed was that on which I leant?
  Ah, backward fancy, wherefore wake
  The old bitterness again, and break
The low beginnings of content?

LXXXV

This truth came borne with bier and pall,
  I felt it, when I sorrow'd most,
  'Tis better to have loved and lost,
Than never to have loved at all—

O true in word, and tried in deed,
  Demanding, so to bring relief
  To this which is our common grief,
What kind of life is that I lead;

And whether trust in things above
  Be dimm'd of sorrow, or sustain'd;   10
  And whether love for him have drain'd
My capabilities of love;

Your words have virtue such as draws
  A faithful answer from the breast,

Thro' light reproaches, half exprest,
And loyal unto kindly laws.

My blood an even tenor kept,
   Till on mine ear this message falls,
   That in Vienna's fatal walls
God's finger touch'd him, and he slept.   20

The great Intelligences fair
   That range above our mortal state,
   In circle round the blessed gate,
Received and gave him welcome there;

And led him thro' the blissful climes,
   And show'd him in the fountain fresh
   All knowledge that the sons of flesh
Shall gather in the cycled times.

But I remain'd, whose hopes were dim,
   Whose life, whose thoughts were little worth,   30
   To wander on a darken'd earth,
Where all things round me breathed of him.

O friendship, equal-poised control,
   O heart, with kindliest motion warm,
   O sacred essence, other form,
O solemn ghost, O crowned soul!

Yet none could better know than I,
   How much of act at human hands
   The sense of human will demands
By which we dare to live or die.   40

Whatever way my days decline,
   I felt and feel, tho' left alone,
   His being working in mine own,
The footsteps of his life in mine;

A life that all the Muses deck'd
   With gifts of grace, that might express
   All-comprehensive tenderness,
All-subtilizing intellect:

And so my passion hath not swerved
    To works of weakness, but I find   50
    An image comforting the mind,
And in my grief a strength reserved.

Likewise the imaginative woe,
    That loved to handle spiritual strife,
    Diffused the shock thro' all my life,
But in the present broke the blow.

My pulses therefore beat again
    For other friends that once I met;
    Nor can it suit me to forget
The mighty hopes that make us men.   60

I woo your love: I count it crime
    To mourn for any overmuch;
    I, the divided half of such
A friendship as had master'd Time;

Which masters Time indeed, and is
    Eternal, separate from fears.
    The all-assuming months and years
Can take no part away from this;

But Summer on the steaming floods,
    And Spring that swells the narrow brooks.   70
    And Autumn, with a noise of rooks,
That gather in the waning woods,

And every pulse of wind and wave
    Recalls, in change of light or gloom,
    My old affection of the tomb,
And my prime passion in the grave.

My old affection of the tomb,
    A part of stillness, yearns to speak:
    "Arise, and get thee forth and seek
A friendship for the years to come.   80

"I watch thee from the quiet shore;
    Thy spirit up to mine can reach;

But in dear words of human speech
We two communicate no more."

And I, "Can clouds of nature stain
    The starry clearness of the free?
    How is it? Canst thou feel for me
Some painless sympathy with pain?"

And lightly does the whisper fall:
    " 'T is hard for thee to fathom this;   90
    I triumph in conclusive bliss,
And that serene result of all."

So hold I commerce with the dead;
    Or so methinks the dead would say;
    Or so shall grief with symbols play
And pining life be fancy-fed.

Now looking to some settled end,
    That these things pass, and I shall prove
    A meeting somewhere, love with love,
I crave your pardon, O my friend;   100

If not so fresh, with love as true,
    I, clasping brother-hands, aver
    I could not, if I would, transfer
The whole I felt for him to you.

For which be they that hold apart
    The promise of the golden hours?
    First love, first friendship, equal powers,
That marry with the virgin heart.

Still mine, that cannot but deplore,
    That beats within a lonely place,   110
    That yet remembers his embrace,
But at his footstep leaps no more,

My heart, tho' widow'd, may not rest
    Quite in the love of what is gone,
    But seeks to beat in time with one
That warms another living breast.

Ah, take the imperfect gift I bring,
   Knowing the primrose yet is dear,
   The primrose of the later year,
As not unlike to that of Spring.   120

LXXXVI

Sweet after showers, ambrosial air,
   That rollest from the gorgeous gloom
   Of evening over brake and bloom
And meadow, slowly breathing bare

The round of space, and rapt below
   Thro' all the dewy-tassell'd wood,
   And shadowing down the horned flood
In ripples, fan my brows and blow

The fever from my cheek, and sigh
   The full new life that feeds thy breath   10
   Throughout my frame, till Doubt and Death,
Ill brethren, let the fancy fly

From belt to belt of crimson seas
   On leagues of odor streaming far,
   To where in yonder orient star
A hundred spirits whisper "Peace."

LXXXVII

I past beside the reverend walls
   In which of old I wore the gown;
   I roved at random thro' the town,
And saw the tumult of the halls;

And heard once more in college fanes
   The storm their high-built organs make,
   And thunder-music, rolling, shake
The prophet blazon'd on the panes;

And caught once more the distant shout,
   The measured pulse of racing oars   10
   Among the willows; paced the shores
And many a bridge, and all about

The same gray flats again, and felt
   The same, but not the same; and last
   Up that long walk of limes I past
To see the rooms in which he dwelt.

Another name was on the door.
   I linger'd; all within was noise
   Of songs, and clapping hands, and boys
That crash'd the glass and beat the floor;   20

Where once we held debate, a band
   Of youthful friends, on mind and art,
   And labor, and the changing mart,
And all the framework of the land;

When one would aim an arrow fair,
   But send it slackly from the string;
   And one would pierce an outer ring,
And one an inner, here and there;

And last the master-bowman, he,
   Would cleave the mark. A willing ear   30
   We lent him. Who but hung to hear
The rapt oration flowing free

From point to point, with power and grace
   And music in the bounds of law,
   To those conclusions when we saw
The God within him light his face,

And seem to lift the form, and glow
   In azure orbits heavenly-wise;
   And over those ethereal eyes
The bar of Michael Angelo?   40

LXXXVIII

Wild bird, whose warble, liquid sweet,
   Rings Eden thro' the budded quicks,
   O, tell me where the senses mix,
O, tell me where the passions meet,

Whence radiate: fierce extremes employ
   Thy spirits in the darkening leaf,
   And in the midmost heart of grief
Thy passion clasps a secret joy;

And I—my harp would prelude woe—
   I cannot all command the strings;   **10**
   The glory of the sum of things
Will flash along the chords and go.

LXXXIX

Witch-elms that counterchange the floor
   Of this flat lawn with dusk and bright;
   And thou, with all thy breadth and height
Of foliage, towering sycamore;

How often, hither wandering down,
   My Arthur found your shadows fair,
   And shook to all the liberal air
The dust and din and steam of town!

He brought an eye for all he saw;
   He mixt in all our simple sports;   **10**
   They pleased him, fresh from brawling courts
And dusty purlieus of the law.

O joy to him in this retreat,
   Inmantled in ambrosial dark,
   To drink the cooler air, and mark
The landscape winking thro' the heat!

O sound to rout the brood of cares,
   The sweep of scythe in morning dew,
   The gust that round the garden flew,
And tumbled half the mellowing pears!   **20**

O bliss, when all in circle drawn
   About him, heart and ear were fed
   To hear him, as he lay and read
The Tuscan poets on the lawn!

Or in the all-golden afternoon
 A guest, or happy sister, sung,
 Or here she brought the harp and flung
A ballad to the brightening moon.

Nor less it pleased in livelier moods,   **30**
 Beyond the bounding hill to stray,
 And break the livelong summer day
With banquet in the distant woods;

Whereat we glanced from theme to theme,
 Discuss'd the books to love or hate,
 Or touch'd the changes of the state,
Or threaded some Socratic dream;

But if I praised the busy town,
 He loved to rail against it still,
 For "ground in yonder social mill
We rub each other's angles down,   **40**

"And merge," he said, "in form and gloss
 The picturesque of man and man."
 We talk'd: the stream beneath us ran,
The wine-flask lying couch'd in moss,

Or cool'd within the glooming wave;
 And last, returning from afar,
 Before the crimson-circled star
Had fallen into her father's grave,

And brushing ankle-deep in flowers,   **50**
 We heard behind the woodbine veil
 The milk that bubbled in the pail,
And buzzings of the honeyed hours.

XC

He tasted love with half his mind,
 Nor ever drank the inviolate spring
 Where nighest heaven, who first could **fling**
This bitter seed among mankind·

That could the dead, whose dying eyes
   Were closed with wail, resume their life,
   They would but find in child and wife
An iron welcome when they rise.

'T was well, indeed, when warm with wine,
   To pledge them with a kindly tear,   **10**
   To talk them o'er, to wish them here,
To count their memories half divine;

But if they came who past away,
   Behold their brides in other hands;
   The hard heir strides about their lands,
And will not yield them for a day.

Yea, tho' their sons were none of these,
   Not less the yet-loved sire would make
   Confusion worse than death, and shake
The pillars of domestic peace.   **20**

Ah, dear, but come thou back to me!
   Whatever change the years have wrought,
   I find not yet one lonely thought
That cries against my wish for thee.

XCI

When rosy plumelets tuft the larch,
   And rarely pipes the mounted thrush,
   Or underneath the barren bush
Flits by the sea-blue bird of March;

Come, wear the form by which I know
   Thy spirit in time among thy peers;
   The hope of unaccomplish'd years
Be large and lucid round thy brow.

When summer's hourly-mellowing change
   May breathe, with many roses sweet,   **10**
   Upon the thousand waves of wheat
That ripple round the lowly grange,

Come; not in watches of the night,
    But where the sunbeam broodeth warm,
    Come, beauteous in thine after form,
And like a finer light in light.

XCII

If any vision should reveal
    Thy likeness, I might count it vain
    As but the canker of the brain;
Yea, tho' it spake and made appeal

To chances where our lots were cast
    Together in the days behind,
    I might but say, I hear a wind
Of memory murmuring the past.

Yea, tho' it spake and bared to view
    A fact within the coming year;   10
    And tho' the months, revolving near,
Should prove the phantom-warning true,

They might not seem thy prophecies,
    But spiritual presentiments,
    And such refraction of events
As often rises ere they rise.

XCIII

I shall not see thee. Dare I say
    No spirit ever brake the band
    That stays him from the native land
Where first he walk'd when claspt in clay?

No visual shade of some one lost,
    But he, the Spirit himself, may come
    Where all the nerve of sense is numb,
Spirit to Spirit, Ghost to Ghost.

O, therefore from thy sightless range
    With gods in unconjectured bliss,   10

O, from the distance of the abyss
Of tenfold-complicated change,

Descend, and touch, and enter; hear
   The wish too strong for words to name,
   That in this blindness of the frame
My Ghost may feel that thine is near.

XCIV

How pure at heart and sound in head,
   With what divine affections bold
   Should be the man whose thought would hold
An hour's communion with the dead.

In vain shalt thou, or any, call
   The spirits from their golden day,
   Except, like them, thou too canst say,
My spirit is at peace with all.

They haunt the silence of the breast,
   Imaginations calm and fair,   **10**
   The memory like a cloudless air,
The conscience as a sea at rest;

But when the heart is full of din,
   And doubt beside the portal waits,
   They can but listen at the gates,
And hear the household jar within.

XCV

By night we linger'd on the lawn,
   For underfoot the herb was dry;
   And genial warmth; and o'er the sky
The silvery haze of summer drawn;

And calm that let the tapers burn
   Unwavering: not a cricket chirr'd;
   The brook alone far-off was heard,
And on the board the fluttering urn.

And bats went round in fragrant skies,
   And wheel'd or lit the filmy shapes   **10**
   That haunt the dusk, with ermine capes
And woolly breasts and beaded eyes;

While now we sang old songs that peal'd
   From knoll to knoll, where, couch'd at ease,
   The white kine glimmer'd, and the trees
Laid their dark arms about the field.

But when those others, one by one,
   Withdrew themselves from me and night,
   And in the house light after light
Went out, and I was all alone,   **20**

A hunger seized my heart; I read
   Of that glad year which once had been,
   In those fallen leaves which kept their green,
The noble letters of the dead.

And strangely on the silence broke
   The silent-speaking words, and strange
   Was love's dumb cry defying change
To test his worth; and strangely spoke

The faith, the vigor, bold to dwell
   On doubts that drive the coward back,   **30**
   And keen thro' wordy snares to track
Suggestion to her inmost cell.

So word by word, and line by line,
   The dead man touch'd me from the past,
   And all at once it seem'd at last
The living soul was flash'd on mine,

And mine in this was wound, and whirl'd
   About empyreal heights of thought,
   And came on that which is, and caught
The deep pulsations of the world,   **40**

Æonian music measuring out
   The steps of Time—the shocks of Chance—

The blows of Death. At length my trance
Was cancell'd, stricken thro' with doubt.

Vague words! but ah, how hard to frame
   In matter-moulded forms of speech,
   Or even for intellect to reach
Thro' memory that which I became;

Till now the doubtful dusk reveal'd
   The knolls once more where, couch'd at ease,   **50**
   The white kine glimmer'd, and the trees
Laid their dark arms about the field;

And suck'd from out the distant gloom
   A breeze began to tremble o'er
   The large leaves of the sycamore,
And fluctuate all the still perfume,

And gathering freshlier overhead
   Rock'd the full-foliaged elms, and swung
   The heavy-folded rose, and flung
The lilies to and fro, and said,   **60**

"The dawn, the dawn," and died away;
   And East and West, without a breath,
   Mixt their dim lights, like life and death,
To broaden into boundless day.

XCVI

You say, but with no touch of scorn,
   Sweet-hearted, you, whose light-blue eyes
   Are tender over drowning flies,
You tell me, doubt is Devil-born.

I know not: one indeed I knew
   In many a subtle question versed,
   Who touch'd a jarring lyre at first,
But ever strove to make it true;

Perplext in faith, but pure in deeds,
   At last he beat his music out.   **10**

There lives more faith in honest doubt,
Believe me, than in half the creeds.

He fought his doubts and gather'd strength,
   He would not make his judgment blind,
   He faced the spectres of the mind
And laid them; thus he came at length

To find a stronger faith his own,
   And Power was with him in the night,
   Which makes the darkness and the light,
And dwells not in the light alone,   20

But in the darkness and the cloud,
   As over Sinaï's peaks of old,
   While Israel made their gods of gold,
Altho' the trumpet blew so loud.

XCVII

My love has talk'd with rocks and trees;
   He finds on misty mountain-ground
   His own vast shadow glory-crown'd;
He sees himself in all he sees.

Two partners of a married life—
   I look'd on these and thought of thee
   In vastness and in mystery,
And of my spirit as of a wife.

These two—they dwelt with eye on eye,
   Their hearts of old have beat in tune,
   Their meetings made December June,
Their every parting was to die.   10

Their love has never past away;
   The days she never can forget
   Are earnest that he loves her yet,
Whate'er the faithless people say.

Her life is lone, he sits apart;
   He loves her yet, she will not weep,

Tho' rapt in matters dark and deep
He seems to slight her simple heart.   20

He thrids the labyrinth of the mind,
    He reads the secret of the star,
    He seems so near and yet so far,
He looks so cold: she thinks him kind.

She keeps the gift of years before,
    A wither'd violet is her bliss;
    She knows not what his greatness is,
For that, for all, she loves him more.

For him she plays, to him she sings
    Of early faith and plighted vows;   30
    She knows but matters of the house,
And he, he knows a thousand things.

Her faith is fixt and cannot move,
    She darkly feels him great and wise,
    She dwells on him with faithful eyes,
"I cannot understand; I love."

XCVIII

You leave us: you will see the Rhine,
    And those fair hills I sail'd below,
    When I was there with him; and go
By summer belts of wheat and vine

To where he breathed his latest breath,
    That city. All her splendor seems
    No livelier than the wisp that gleams
On Lethe in the eyes of Death.

Let her great Danube rolling fair
    Enwind her isles, unmark'd of me;   10
    I have not seen, I will not see
Vienna; rather dream that there,

A treble darkness, Evil haunts
    The birth, the bridal; friend from friend

Is oftener parted, fathers bend
Above more graves, a thousand wants

Gnarr at the heels of men, and prey
   By each cold hearth, and sadness flings
   Her shadow on the blaze of kings.
And yet myself have heard him say,   **20**

That not in any mother town
   With statelier progress to and fro
   The double tides of chariots flow
By park and suburb under brown

Of lustier leaves; nor more content,
   He told me, lives in any crowd,
   When all is gay with lamps, and loud
With sport and song, in booth and tent,

Imperial halls, or open plain;
   And wheels the circled dance, and breaks   **30**
   The rocket molten into flakes
Of crimson or in emerald rain.

XCIX

Risest thou thus, dim dawn, again,
   So loud with voices of the birds,
   So thick with lowings of the herds,
Day, when I lost the flower of men;

Who tremblest thro' thy darkling red
   On yon swollen brook that bubbles fast
   By meadows breathing of the past,
And woodlands holy to the dead;

Who murmurest in the foliaged eaves
   A song that slights the coming care,   **10**
   And Autumn laying here and there
A fiery finger on the leaves;

Who wakenest with thy balmy breath
   To myriads on the genial earth,

Memories of bridal, or of birth,
And unto myriads more, of death.

O, wheresoever those may be,
  Betwixt the slumber of the poles,
  To-day they count as kindred souls;
They know me not, but mourn with me.   **20**

C

I climb the hill: from end to end
  Of all the landscape underneath,
  I find no place that does not breathe
Some gracious memory of my friend;

No gray old grange, or lonely fold,
  Or low morass and whispering reed,
  Or simple stile from mead to mead,
Or sheepwalk up the windy wold;

Nor hoary knoll of ash and haw
  That hears the latest linnet trill,   **10**
  Nor quarry trench'd along the hill
And haunted by the wrangling daw;

Nor runlet tinkling from the rock;
  Nor pastoral rivulet that swerves
  To left and right thro' meadowy curves,
That feed the mothers of the flock;

But each has pleased a kindred eye,
  And each reflects a kindlier day;
  And, leaving these, to pass away,
I think once more he seems to die.   **20**

CI

Unwatch'd, the garden bough shall sway,
  The tender blossom flutter down,
  Unloved, that beech will gather brown,
This maple burn itself away;

Unloved, the sunflower, shining fair,
    Ray round with flames her disk of seed,
    And many a rose-carnation feed
With summer spice the humming air;

Unloved, by many a sandy bar,
    The brook shall babble down the plain,
    At noon or when the Lesser Wain
Is twisting round the polar star;   10

Uncared for, gird the windy grove,
    And flood the haunts of hern and crake,
    Or into silver arrows break
The sailing moon in creek and cove;

Till from the garden and the wild
    A fresh association blow,
    And year by year the landscape grow
Familiar to the stranger's child;   20

As year by year the laborer tills
    His wonted glebe, or lops the glades,
    And year by year our memory fades
From all the circle of the hills.

CII

We leave the well-beloved place
    Where first we gazed upon the sky;
    The roofs that heard our earliest cry
Will shelter one of stranger race.

We go, but ere we go from home,
    As down the garden-walks I move,
    Two spirits of a diverse love
Contend for loving masterdom.

One whispers, "Here thy boyhood sung
    Long since its matin song, and heard   10
    The low love-language of the bird
In native hazels tassel-hung."

The other answers, "Yea, but here
    Thy feet have stray'd in after hours
    With thy lost friend among the bowers,
And this hath made them trebly dear."

These two have striven half the day,
    And each prefers his separate claim,
    Poor rivals in a losing game,
That will not yield each other way.   20

I turn to go; my feet are set
    To leave the pleasant fields and farms;
    They mix in one another's arms
To one pure image of regret.

CIII

On that last night before we went
    From out the doors where I was bred,
    I dream'd a vision of the dead,
Which left my after-morn content.

Methought I dwelt within a hall,
    And maidens with me; distant hills
    From hidden summits fed with rills
A river sliding by the wall.

The hall with harp and carol rang.
    They sang of what is wise and good   10
    And graceful. In the centre stood
A statue veil'd, to which they sang;

And which, tho' veil'd, was known to me,
    The shape of him I loved, and love
    For ever. Then flew in a dove
And brought a summons from the sea;

And when they learnt that I must go,
    They wept and wail'd, but led the way
    To where a little shallop lay
At anchor in the flood below;   20

And on by many a level mead,
   And shadowing bluff that made the banks,
   We glided winding under ranks
Of iris and the golden reed;

And still as vaster grew the shore
   And roll'd the floods in grander space,
   The maidens gather'd strength and grace
And presence, lordlier than before;

And I myself, who sat apart
   And watch'd them, wax'd in every limb;   30
   I felt the thews of Anakim,
The pulses of a Titan's heart;

As one would sing the death of war,
   And one would chant the history
   Of that great race which is to be,
And one the shaping of a star;

Until the forward-creeping tides
   Began to foam, and we to draw
   From deep to deep, to where we saw
A great ship lift her shining sides.   40

The man we loved was there on deck,
   But thrice as large as man he bent
   To greet us. Up the side I went,
And fell in silence on his neck;

Whereat those maidens with one mind
   Bewail'd their lot; I did them wrong:
   "We served thee here," they said, "so long,
And wilt thou leave us now behind?"

So rapt I was, they could not win
   An answer from my lips, but he   50
   Replying, "Enter likewise ye
And go with us:" they enter'd in.

And while the wind began to sweep
   A music out of sheet and shroud,

We steer'd her toward a crimson cloud
That landlike slept along the deep.

CIV

The time draws near the birth of Christ;
　　The moon is hid, the night is still;
　　A single church below the hill
Is pealing, folded in the mist.

A single peal of bells below,
　　That wakens at this hour of rest
　　A single murmur in the breast,
That these are not the bells I know.

Like strangers' voices here they sound,
　　In lands where not a memory strays,   10
　　Nor landmark breathes of other days,
But all is new unhallow'd ground.

CV

To-night ungather'd let us leave
　　This laurel, let this holly stand:
　　We live within the stranger's land,
And strangely falls our Christmas-eve.

Our father's dust is left alone
　　And silent under other snows:
　　There in due time the woodbine blows,
The violet comes, but we are gone.

No more shall wayward grief abuse
　　The genial hour with mask and mime;   10
　　For change of place, like growth of time,
Has broke the bond of dying use.

Let cares that petty shadows cast,
　　By which our lives are chiefly proved,
　　A little spare the night I loved,
And hold it solemn to the past.

But let no footstep beat the floor,
   Nor bowl of wassail mantle warm;
   For who would keep an ancient form
Thro' which the spirit breathes no more? **20**

Be neither song, nor game, nor feast;
   Nor harp be touch'd, nor flute be blown;
   No dance, no motion, save alone
What lightens in the lucid East

Of rising worlds by yonder wood.
   Long sleeps the summer in the seed;
   Run out your measured arcs, and lead
The closing cycle rich in good.

CVI

Ring out, wild bells, to the wild sky,
   The flying cloud, the frosty light:
   The year is dying in the night;
Ring out, wild bells, and let him die.

Ring out the old, ring in the new,
   Ring, happy bells, across the snow:
   The year is going, let him go;
Ring out the false, ring in the true.

Ring out the grief that saps the mind,
   For those that here we see no more; **10**
   Ring out the feud of rich and poor,
Ring in redress to all mankind.

Ring out a slowly dying cause,
   And ancient forms of party strife;
   Ring in the nobler modes of life,
With sweeter manners, purer laws.

Ring out the want, the care, the sin,
   The faithless coldness of the times;
   Ring out, ring out my mournful rhymes,
But ring the fuller minstrel in. **20**

Ring out false pride in place and blood,
　　The civic slander and the spite;
　　Ring in the love of truth and right,
Ring in the common love of good.

Ring out old shapes of foul disease;
　　Ring out the narrowing lust of gold;
　　Ring out the thousand wars of old,
Ring in the thousand years of peace.

Ring in the valiant man and free,
　　The larger heart, the kindlier hand;　　　　30
　　Ring out the darkness of the land,
Ring in the Christ that is to be.

CVII

It is the day when he was born,
　　A bitter day that early sank
　　Behind a purple-frosty bank
Of vapor, leaving night forlorn.

The time admits not flowers or leaves
　　To deck the banquet. Fiercely flies
　　The blast of North and East, and ice
Makes daggers at the sharpen'd eaves,

And bristles all the brakes and thorns
　　To yon hard crescent, as she hangs　　　　10
　　Above the wood which grides and clangs
Its leafless ribs and iron horns

Together, in the drifts that pass
　　To darken on the rolling brine
　　That breaks the coast. But fetch the wine,
Arrange the board and brim the glass;

Bring in great logs and let them lie,
　　To make a solid core of heat;
　　Be cheerful-minded, talk and treat
Of all things even as he were by;　　　　20

We keep the day. With festal cheer,
   With books and music, surely we
   Will drink to him, whate'er he be,
And sing the songs he loved to hear.

CVIII

I will not shut me from my kind,
   And, lest I stiffen into stone,
   I will not eat my heart alone,
Nor feed with sighs a passing wind:

What profit lies in barren faith,
   And vacant yearning, tho' with might
   To scale the heaven's highest height,
Or dive below the wells of death?

What find I in the highest place,
   But mine own phantom chanting hymns?   **10**
   And on the depths of death there swims
The reflex of a human face.

I'll rather take what fruit may be
   Of sorrow under human skies:
   'T is held that sorrow makes us wise,
Whatever wisdom sleep with thee.

CIX

Heart-affluence in discursive talk
   From household fountains never dry;
   The critic clearness of an eye
That saw thro' all the Muses' walk;

Seraphic intellect and force
   To seize and throw the doubts of man;
   Impassion'd logic, which outran
The hearer in its fiery course;

High nature amorous of the good,
   But touch'd with no ascetic gloom;   **10**
   And passion pure in snowy bloom
Thro' all the years of April blood;

A love of freedom rarely felt,
  Of freedom in her regal seat
  Of England; not the schoolboy heat,
The blind hysterics of the Celt;

And manhood fused with female grace
  In such a sort, the child would twine
  A trustful hand, unask'd, in thine,
And find his comfort in thy face;   **20**

All these have been, and thee mine eyes
  Have look'd on: if they look'd in vain,
  My shame is greater who remain,
Nor let thy wisdom make me wise.

CX

Thy converse drew us with delight,
  The men of rathe and riper years;
  The feeble soul, a haunt of fears,
Forgot his weakness in thy sight.

On thee the loyal-hearted hung,
  The proud was half disarm'd of pride,
  Nor cared the serpent at thy side
To flicker with his double tongue.

The stern were mild when thou wert by,
  The flippant put himself to school   **10**
  And heard thee, and the brazen fool
Was soften'd, and he knew not why;

While I, thy nearest, sat apart,
  And felt thy triumph was as mine;
  And loved them more, that they were thine,
The graceful tact, the Christian art;

Nor mine the sweetness or the skill,
  But mine the love that will not tire,
  And, born of love, the vague desire
That spurs an imitative will.   **20**

CXI

The churl in spirit, up or down
   Along the scale of ranks, thro' all,
   To him who grasps a golden ball,
By blood a king, at heart a clown,—

The churl in spirit, howe'er he veil
   His want in forms for fashion's sake,
   Will let his coltish nature break
At seasons thro' the gilded pale;

For who can always act? but he,
   To whom a thousand memories call,   10
   Not being less but more than all
The gentleness he seem'd to be,

Best seem'd the thing he was, and join'd
   Each office of the social hour
   To noble manners, as the flower
And native growth of noble mind;

Nor ever narrowness or spite,
   Or villain fancy fleeting by,
   Drew in the expression of an eye
Where God and Nature met in light;   20

And thus he bore without abuse
   The grand old name of gentleman,
   Defamed by every charlatan,
And soil'd with all ignoble use.

CXII

High wisdom holds my wisdom less,
   That I, who gaze with temperate eyes
   On glorious insufficiencies,
Set light by narrower perfectness.

But thou, that fillest all the room
   Of all my love, art reason why

I seem to cast a careless eye
On souls, the lesser lords of doom.

For what wert thou? some novel power
   Sprang up for ever at a touch,
   And hope could never hope too much,
In watching thee from hour to hour,

Large elements in order brought,
   And tracts of calm from tempest made,
   And world-wide fluctuation sway'd
In vassal tides that follow'd thought.

CXIII

'T is held that sorrow makes us wise;
   Yet how much wisdom sleeps with thee
   Which not alone had guided me,
But served the seasons that may rise;

For can I doubt, who knew thee keen
   In intellect, with force and skill
   To strive, to fashion, to fulfil—
I doubt not what thou wouldst have been:

A life in civic action warm,
   A soul on highest mission sent,
   A potent voice of Parliament,
A pillar steadfast in the storm,

Should licensed boldness gather force,
   Becoming, when the time has birth,
   A lever to uplift the earth
And roll it in another course,

With thousand shocks that come and go,
   With agonies, with energies,
   With overthrowings, and with cries,
And undulations to and fro.

CXIV

Who loves not Knowledge? Who shall **rail**
   Against her beauty? May she mix
   With men and prosper! Who shall **fix**
Her pillars? Let her work prevail.

But on her forehead sits a fire;
   She sets her forward countenance
   And leaps into the future chance,
Submitting all things to desire.

Half-grown as yet, a child, and vain—
   She cannot fight the fear of death.   **10**
   What is she, cut from love and faith,
But some wild Pallas from the brain

Of demons? fiery-hot to burst
   All barriers in her onward race
   For power. Let her know her place;
She is the second, not the first.

A higher hand must make her mild,
   If all be not in vain, and guide
   Her footsteps, moving side by side
With Wisdom, like the younger child;   **20**

For she is earthly of the mind,
   But Wisdom heavenly of the soul.
   O friend, who camest to thy goal
So early, leaving me behind,

I would the great world grew like thee,
   Who grewest not alone in power
   And knowledge, but by year and **hour**
In reverence and in charity.

CXV

Now fades the last long streak of snow,
   Now burgeons every maze of quick

About the flowering squares, and thick
By ashen roots the violets blow.

Now rings the woodland loud and long,
   The distance takes a lovelier hue,
   And drown'd in yonder living blue
The lark becomes a sightless song.

Now dance the lights on lawn and lea,
   The flocks are whiter down the vale,   **10**
   And milkier every milky sail
On winding stream or distant sea;

Where now the seamew pipes, or dives
   In yonder greening gleam, and fly
   The happy birds, that change their sky
To build and brood, that live their lives

From land to land; and in my breast
   Spring wakens too, and my regret
   Becomes an April violet,
And buds and blossoms like the rest.   **20**

CXVI

Is it, then, regret for buried time
   That keenlier in sweet April wakes,
   And meets the year, and gives and takes
The colors of the crescent prime?

Not all: the songs, the stirring air,
   The life re-orient out of dust,
   Cry thro' the sense to hearten trust
In that which made the world so fair.

Not all regret: the face will shine
   Upon me, while I muse alone,   **10**
   And that dear voice, I once have known,
Still speak to me of me and mine.

Yet less of sorrow lives in me
   For days of happy commune dead,

    Less yearning for the friendship fled
Than some strong bond which is to be.

CXVII

O days and hours, your work is this,
    To hold me from my proper place,
    A little while from his embrace,
For fuller gain of after bliss;

That out of distance might ensue
    Desire of nearness doubly sweet,
    And unto meeting, when we meet,
Delight a hundredfold accrue,

For every grain of sand that runs,
    And every span of shade that steals,   10
    And every kiss of toothed wheels,
And all the courses of the suns.

CXVIII

Contemplate all this work of Time,
    The giant laboring in his youth;
    Nor dream of human love and truth,
As dying Nature's earth and lime;

But trust that those we call the dead
    Are breathers of an ampler day
    For ever nobler ends. They say,
The solid earth whereon we tread

In tracts of fluent heat began,
    And grew to seeming-random forms,   10
    The seeming prey of cyclic storms,
Till at the last arose the man;

Who throve and branch'd from clime to clime,
    The herald of a higher race,
    And of himself in higher place,
If so he type this work of time

Within himself, from more to more;
   Or, crown'd with attributes of woe
   Like glories, move his course, and show
That life is not as idle ore,   20

But iron dug from central gloom,
   And heated hot with burning fears,
   And dipt in baths of hissing tears,
And batter'd with the shocks of doom

To shape and use. Arise and fly
   The reeling Faun, the sensual feast;
   Move upward, working out the beast,
And let the ape and tiger die.

CXIX

Doors, where my heart was used to beat
   So quickly, not as one that weeps
   I come once more; the city sleeps;
I smell the meadow in the street;

I hear a chirp of birds; I see
   Betwixt the black fronts long-withdrawn
   A light-blue lane of early dawn,
And think of early days and thee,

And bless thee, for thy lips are bland,
   And bright the friendship of thine eye;   10
   And in my thoughts with scarce a sigh
I take the pressure of thine hand.

CXX

I trust I have not wasted breath:
   I think we are not wholly brain,
   Magnetic mockeries; not in vain,
Like Paul with beasts, I fought with Death;

Not only cunning casts in clay:
   Let Science prove we are, and then

What matters Science unto men,
At least to me? I would not stay.

Let him, the wiser man who springs
   Hereafter, up from childhood shape
   His action like the greater ape,
But I was *born* to other things.

CXXI

Sad Hesper o'er the buried sun
   And ready, thou, to die with him,
   Thou watchest all things ever dim
And dimmer, and a glory done.

The team is loosen'd from the wain,
   The boat is drawn upon the shore;
   Thou listenest to the closing door,
And life is darken'd in the brain.

Bright Phosphor, fresher for the night,
   By thee the world's great work is heard
   Beginning, and the wakeful bird;
Behind thee comes the greater light.

The market boat is on the stream,
   And voices hail it from the brink;
   Thou hear'st the village hammer clink,
And see'st the moving of the team.

Sweet Hesper-Phosphor, double name
   For what is one, the first, the last,
   Thou, like my present and my past,
Thy place is changed; thou art the same.

CXXII

O, wast thou with me, dearest, then,
   While I rose up against my doom,
   And yearn'd to burst the folded gloom,
To bare the eternal heavens again,

To feel once more, in placid awe,
   The strong imagination roll
   A sphere of stars about my soul,
In all her motion one with law?

If thou wert with me, and the grave
   Divide us not, be with me now,   10
   And enter in at breast and brow,
Till all my blood, a fuller wave,

Be quicken'd with a livelier breath,
   And like an inconsiderate boy,
   As in the former flash of joy,
I slip the thoughts of life and death;

And all the breeze of Fancy blows,
   And every dewdrop paints a bow,
   The wizard lightnings deeply glow,
And every thought breaks out a rose.   20

CXXIII

There rolls the deep where grew the tree.
   O earth, what changes hast thou seen!
   There where the long street roars hath been
The stillness of the central sea.

The hills are shadows, and they flow
   From form to form, and nothing stands;
   They melt like mist, the solid lands,
Like clouds they shape themselves and go.

But in my spirit will I dwell,
   And dream my dream, and hold it true;   10
   For tho' my lips may breathe adieu,
I cannot think the thing farewell.

CXXIV

That which we dare invoke to bless;
   Our dearest faith; our ghastliest doubt;

He, They, One, All; within, without;
The Power in darkness whom we guess,—

I found Him not in world or sun,
   Or eagle's wing, or insect's eye,
   Nor thro' the questions men may try,
The petty cobwebs we have spun.

If e'er when faith had fallen asleep,
   I heard a voice, "believe no more,"   **10**
   And heard an ever-breaking shore
That tumbled in the Godless deep,

A warmth within the breast would melt
   The freezing reason's colder part,
   And like a man in wrath the heart
Stood up and answer'd, "I have felt."

No, like a child in doubt and fear:
   But that blind clamor made me wise;
   Then was I as a child that cries,
But, crying, knows his father near;   **20**

And what I am beheld again
   What is, and no man understands;
   And out of darkness came the hands
That reach thro' nature, moulding men.

CXXV

Whatever I have said or sung,
   Some bitter notes my harp would give,
   Yea, tho' there often seem'd to live
A contradiction on the tongue,

Yet Hope had never lost her youth,
   She did but look through dimmer eyes;
   Or Love but play'd with gracious lies,
Because he felt so fix'd in truth;

And if the song were full of care,
   He breathed the spirit of the song;   **10**

And if the words were sweet and strong
He set his royal signet there;

Abiding with me till I sail
   To seek thee on the mystic deeps,
   And this electric force, that keeps
A thousand pulses dancing, fail.

CXXVI

Love is and was my lord and king,
   And in his presence I attend
   To hear the tidings of my friend,
Which every hour his couriers bring.

Love is and was my king and lord,
   And will be, tho' as yet I keep
   Within his court on earth, and sleep
Encompass'd by his faithful guard,

And hear at times a sentinel
   Who moves about from place to place,   10
   And whispers to the worlds of space,
In the deep night, that all is well.

CXXVII

And all is well, tho' faith and form
   Be sunder'd in the night of fear;
   Well roars the storm to those that hear
A deeper voice across the storm,

Proclaiming social truth shall spread,
   And justice, even tho' thrice again
   The red fool-fury of the Seine
Should pile her barricades with dead.

But ill for him that wears a crown,
   And him, the lazar, in his rags!   10
   They tremble, the sustaining crags;
The spires of ice are toppled down,

And molten up, and roar in flood;
  The fortress crashes from on high,
  The brute earth lightens to the sky,
And the great Æon sinks in blood,

And compass'd by the fires of hell;
  While thou, dear spirit, happy star,
  O'erlook'st the tumult from afar,
And smilest, knowing all is well.   20

CXXVIII

The love that rose on stronger wings,
  Unpalsied when he met with Death,
  Is comrade of the lesser faith
That sees the course of human things.

No doubt vast eddies in the flood
  Of onward time shall yet be made,
  And throned races may degrade;
Yet, O ye mysteries of good,

Wild Hours that fly with Hope and Fear,
  If all your office had to do   10
  With old results that look like new—
If this were all your mission here,

To draw, to sheathe a useless sword,
  To fool the crowd with glorious lies,
  To cleave a creed in sects and cries,
To change the bearing of a word,

To shift an arbitrary power,
  To cramp the student at his desk,
  To make old bareness picturesque
And tuft with grass a feudal tower,   20

Why, then my scorn might well descend
  On you and yours. I see in part
  That all, as in some piece of art,
Is toil coöperant to an end.

CXXIX

Dear friend, far off, my lost desire,
　　So far, so near in woe and weal,
　　O loved the most, when most I feel
There is a lower and a higher;

Known and unknown, human, divine;
　　Sweet human hand and lips and eye;
　　Dear heavenly friend that canst not die,
Mine, mine, for ever, ever mine;

Strange friend, past, present, and to be;
　　Loved deeplier, darklier understood;　　　　10
　　Behold, I dream a dream of good,
And mingle all the world with thee.

CXXX

Thy voice is on the rolling air;
　　I hear thee where the waters run;
　　Thou standest in the rising sun,
And in the setting thou art fair.

What art thou then? I cannot guess;
　　But tho' I seem in star and flower
　　To feel thee some diffusive power,
I do not therefore love thee less.

My love involves the love before;
　　My love is vaster passion now;　　　　10
　　Tho' mix'd with God and Nature thou,
I seem to love thee more and more.

Far off thou art, but ever nigh;
　　I have thee still, and I rejoice;
　　I prosper, circled with thy voice;
I shall not lose thee tho' I die.

CXXXI

O living will that shalt endure
   When all that seems shall suffer shock,
   Rise in the spiritual rock,
Flow thro' our deeds and make them pure,

That we may lift from out of dust
   A voice as unto him that hears,
   A cry above the conquer'd years
To one that with us works, and trust,

With faith that comes of self-control,
   The truths that never can be proved   10
   Until we close with all we loved,
And all we flow from, soul in soul.

———

O true and tried, so well and long,
   Demand not thou a marriage lay;
   In that it is thy marriage day
Is music more than any song.

Nor have I felt so much of bliss
   Since first he told me that he loved
   A daughter of our house, nor proved
Since that dark day a day like this;   20

Tho' I since then have number'd o'er
   Some thrice three years; they went and came,
   Remade the blood and changed the frame,
And yet is love not less, but more;

No longer caring to embalm
   In dying songs a dead regret,
   But like a statue solid-set,
And moulded in colossal calm.

Regret is dead, but love is more
   Than in the summers that are flown.   30

For I myself with these have grown
To something greater than before;

Which makes appear the songs I made
   As echoes out of weaker times,
   As half but idle brawling rhymes,
The sport of random sun and shade.

But where is she, the bridal flower,
   That must be made a wife ere noon?
   She enters, glowing like the moon
Of Eden on its bridal bower.   **40**

On me she bends her blissful eyes
   And then on thee; they meet thy look
   And brighten like the star that shook
Betwixt the palms of Paradise.

O, when her life was yet in bud,
   He too foretold the perfect rose.
   For thee she grew, for thee she grows
For ever, and as fair as good.

And thou art worthy, full of power;
   As gentle; liberal-minded, great,
   Consistent; wearing all that weight   **50**
Of learning lightly like a flower.

But now set out: the noon is near,
   And I must give away the bride;
   She fears not, or with thee beside
And me behind her, will not fear.

For I that danced her on my knee,
   That watch'd her on her nurse's arm,
   That shielded all her life from harm,
At last must part with her to thee;   **60**

Now waiting to be made a wife,
   Her feet, my darling, on the dead;
   Their pensive tablets round her head
And the most living words of life

Breathed in her ear. The ring is on,
    The "Wilt thou?" answer'd, and again
    The "Wilt thou?" ask'd, till out of twain
Her sweet "I will" has made you one.

Now sign your names, which shall be read,
    Mute symbols of a joyful morn,   70
    By village eyes as yet unborn.
The names are sign'd, and overhead

Begins the clash and clang that tells
    The joy to every wandering breeze;
    The blind wall rocks, and on the trees
The dead leaf trembles to the bells.

O happy hour, and happier hours
    Await them. Many a merry face
    Salutes them—maidens of the place,
That pelt us in the porch with flowers.   80

O happy hour, behold the bride
    With him to whom her hand I gave.
    They leave the porch, they pass the grave
That has to-day its sunny side.

To-day the grave is bright for me,
    For them the light of life increased,
    Who stay to share the morning feast,
Who rest to-night beside the sea.

Let all my genial spirits advance
    To meet and greet a whiter sun;   90
    My drooping memory will not shun
The foaming grape of eastern France.

It circles round, and fancy plays,
    And hearts are warm'd and faces bloom,
    As drinking health to bride and groom
We wish them store of happy days.

Nor count me all to blame if I
    Conjecture of a stiller guest,

Perchance, perchance, among the rest,
And, tho' in silence, wishing joy.   100

But they must go, the time draws on,
  And those white-favor'd horses wait;
  They rise, but linger; it is late;
Farewell, we kiss, and they are gone.

A shade falls on us like the dark
  From little cloudlets on the grass,
  But sweeps away as out we pass
To range the woods, to roam the park,

Discussing how their courtship grew,
  And talk of others that are wed,   110
  And how she look'd, and what he said,
And back we come at fall of dew.

Again the feast, the speech, the glee,
  The shade of passing thought, the wealth
  Of words and wit, the double health,
The crowning cup, the three-times-three,

And last the dance;—till I retire.
  Dumb is that tower which spake so loud,
  And high in heaven the streaming cloud,
And on the downs a rising fire: 120

And rise, O moon, from yonder down,
  Till over down and over dale
  All night the shining vapor sail
And pass the silent-lighted town,

The white-faced halls, the glancing rills,
  And catch at every mountain head,
  And o'er the friths that branch and spread
Their sleeping silver thro' the hills;

And touch with shade the bridal doors,
  With tender gloom the roof, the wall;   130
  And breaking let the splendor fall
To spangle all the happy shores

By which they rest, and ocean sounds,
   And, star and system rolling past,
   A soul shall draw from out the vast
And strike his being into bounds,

And, moved thro' life of lower phase,
   Result in man, be born and think,
   And act and love, a closer link
Betwixt us and the crowning race   140

Of those that, eye to eye, shall look
   On knowledge; under whose command
   Is Earth and Earth's, and in their hand
Is Nature like an open book;

No longer half-akin to brute,
   For all we thought and loved and did,
   And hoped, and suffer'd, is but seed
Of what in them is flower and fruit;

Whereof the man that with me trod
   This planet was a noble type   150
   Appearing ere the times were ripe,
That friend of mine who lives in God,

That God, which ever lives and loves,
   One God, one law, one element,
   And one far-off divine event,
To which the whole creation moves.
                    [1833–50; publ. 1850]

ODE ON THE DEATH OF THE DUKE OF WELLINGTON

I

BURY the Great Duke
   With an empire's lamentation;
Let us bury the Great Duke
   To the noise of the mourning of a mighty nation:
Mourning when their leaders fall,

Warriors carry the warrior's pall,
And sorrow darkens hamlet and hall.

II

Where shall we lay the man whom we deplore?
Here, in streaming London's central roar.
Let the sound of those he wrought for,   10
And the feet of those he fought for,
Echo round his bones for evermore.

III

Lead out the pageant: sad and slow,
As fits an universal woe,
Let the long, long procession go,
And let the sorrowing crowd about it grow,
And let the mournful martial music blow;
The last great Englishman is low.

IV

Mourn, for to us he seems the last,
Remembering all his greatness in the past.   20
No more in soldier fashion will he greet
With lifted hand the gazer in the street.
O friends, our chief state-oracle is mute!
Mourn for the man of long-enduring blood,
The statesman-warrior, moderate, resolute,
Whole in himself, a common good.
Mourn for the man of amplest influence,
Yet clearest of ambitious crime,
Our greatest yet with least pretence,
Great in council and great in war,   30
Foremost captain of his time,
Rich in saving common-sense,
And, as the greatest only are,
In his simplicity sublime.
O good gray head which all men knew,
O voice from which their omens all men drew,
O iron nerve to true occasion true,
O fallen at length that tower of strength

Which stood four-square to all the winds that blew!
Such was he whom we deplore.   40
The long self-sacrifice of life is o'er.
The great World-victor's victor will be seen no more.

V

All is over and done.
Render thanks to the Giver,
England, for thy son.
Let the bell be toll'd.
Render thanks to the Giver,
And render him to the mould.
Under the cross of gold
That shines over city and river,   50
There he shall rest for ever
Among the wise and the bold.
Let the bell be toll'd,
And a reverent people behold
The towering car, the sable steeds.
Bright let it be with its blazon'd deeds,
Dark in its funeral fold.
Let the bell be toll'd,
And a deeper knell in the heart be knoll'd;
And the sound of the sorrowing anthem roll'd   60
Thro' the dome of the golden cross;
And the volleying cannon thunder his loss;
He knew their voices of old.
For many a time in many a clime
His captain's-ear has heard them boom
Bellowing victory, bellowing doom.
When he with those deep voices wrought,
Guarding realms and kings from shame,
With those deep voices our dead captain taught
The tyrant, and asserts his claim   70
In that dread sound to the great name
Which he has worn so pure of blame,
In praise and in dispraise the same,
A man of well-attemper'd frame.
O civic muse, to such a name,
To such a name for ages long,
To such a name,

Preserve a broad approach of fame,
And ever-echoing avenues of song!

VI

"Who is he that cometh, like an honor'd guest,   80
With banner and with music, with soldier and with priest,
With a nation weeping, and breaking on my rest?"—
Mighty Seaman, this is he
Was great by land as thou by sea.
Thine island loves thee well, thou famous man,
The greatest sailor since our world began.
Now, to the roll of muffled drums,
To thee the greatest soldier comes;
For this is he
Was great by land as thou by sea.   90
His foes were thine; he kept us free;
O, give him welcome, this is he
Worthy of our gorgeous rites,
And worthy to be laid by thee;
For this is England's greatest son,
He that gain'd a hundred fights,
Nor ever lost an English gun;
This is he that far away
Against the myriads of Assaye
Clash'd with his fiery few and won;   100
And underneath another sun,
Warring on a later day,
Round affrighted Lisbon drew
The treble works, the vast designs
Of his labor'd rampart-lines,
Where he greatly stood at bay,
Whence he issued forth anew,
And ever great and greater grew,
Beating from the wasted vines
Back to France her banded swarms,   110
Back to France with countless blows,
Till o'er the hills her eagles flew
Beyond the Pyrenean pines,
Follow'd up in valley and glen
With blare of bugle, clamor of men,
Roll of cannon and clash of arms,

And England pouring on her foes.
Such a war had such a close.
Again their ravening eagle rose
In anger, wheel'd on Europe-shadowing wings,   120
And barking for the thrones of kings;
Till one that sought but Duty's iron crown
On that loud Sabbath shook the spoiler down;
A day of onsets of despair!
Dash'd on every rocky square,
Their surging charges foam'd themselves away,
Last, the Prussian trumpet blew;
Thro' the long-tormented air
Heaven flash'd a sudden jubilant ray,
And down we swept and charged and overthrew.   130
So great a soldier taught us there
What long-enduring hearts could do
In that world-earthquake, Waterloo!
Mighty Seaman, tender and true,
And pure as he from taint of craven guile,
O saviour of the silver-coasted isle,
O shaker of the Baltic and the Nile,
If aught of things that here befall
Touch a spirit among things divine,
If love of country move thee there at all,   140
Be glad, because his bones are laid by thine!
And thro' the centuries let a people's voice
In full acclaim,
A people's voice,
The proof and echo of all human fame,
A people's voice, when they rejoice
At civic revel and pomp and game,
Attest their great commander's claim
With honor, honor, honor, honor to him,
Eternal honor to his name.   150

VII

A people's voice! we are a people yet.
Tho' all men else their nobler dreams forget,
Confused by brainless mobs and lawless Powers,
Thank Him who isled us here, and roughly set
His Briton in blown seas and storming showers,

We have a voice with which to pay the debt
Of boundless love and reverence and regret
To those great men who fought, and kept it ours.
And keep it ours, O God, from brute control!
O Statesmen, guard us, guard the eye, the soul   160
Of Europe, keep our noble England whole,
And save the one true seed of freedom sown
Betwixt a people and their ancient throne,
That sober freedom out of which there springs
Our loyal passion for our temperate kings!
For, saving that, ye help to save mankind
Till public wrong be crumbled into dust,
And drill the raw world for the march of mind,
Till crowds at length be sane and crowns be just.
But wink no more in slothful overtrust.   170
Remember him who led your hosts;
He bade you guard the sacred coasts.
Your cannons moulder on the seaward wall;
His voice is silent in your council-hall
For ever; and whatever tempests lour
For ever silent; even if they broke
In thunder, silent; yet remember all
He spoke among you, and the Man who spoke;
Who never sold the truth to serve the hour,
Nor palter'd with Eternal God for power;   180
Who let the turbid streams of rumor flow
Thro' either babbling world of high and low;
Whose life was work, whose language rife
With rugged maxims hewn from life;
Who never spoke against a foe;
Whose eighty winters freeze with one rebuke
All great self-seekers trampling on the right.
Truth-teller was our England's Alfred named;
Truth-lover was our English Duke;
Whatever record leap to light   190
He never shall be shamed.

VIII

Lo! the leader in these glorious wars
Now to glorious burial slowly borne,
Follow'd by the brave of other lands,

He, on whom from both her open hands
Lavish Honor shower'd all her stars,
And affluent Fortune emptied all her horn.
Yea, let all good things await
Him who cares not to be great
But as he saves or serves the state.   200
Not once or twice in our rough island-story
The path of duty was the way to glory.
He that walks it, only thirsting
For the right, and learns to deaden
Love of self, before his journey closes,
He shall find the stubborn thistle bursting
Into glossy purples, which outredden
All voluptuous garden-roses.
Not once or twice in our fair island-story
The path of duty was the way to glory.   210
He, that ever following her commands,
On with toil of heart and knees and hands,
Thro' the long gorge to the far light has won
His path upward, and prevail'd,
Shall find the toppling crags of Duty scaled
Are close upon the shining table-lands
To which our God Himself is moon and sun.
Such was he: his work is done.
But while the races of mankind endure
Let his great example stand   220
Colossal, seen of every land,
And keep the soldier firm, the statesman pure;
Till in all lands and thro' all human story
The path of duty be the way to glory.
And let the land whose hearths he saved from shame
For many and many an age proclaim
At civic revel and pomp and game,
And when the long-illumined cities flame,
Their ever-loyal iron leader's fame,
With honor, honor, honor, honor to him,   230
Eternal honor to his name.

IX

Peace, his triumph will be sung
By some yet unmoulded tongue

Far on in summers that we shall not see.
Peace, it is a day of pain
For one about whose patriarchal knee
Late the little children clung.
O peace, it is a day of pain
For one upon whose hand and heart and brain
Once the weight and fate of Europe hung.   240
Ours the pain, be his the gain!
More than is of man's degree
Must be with us, watching here
At this, our great solemnity.
Whom we see not we revere;
We revere, and we refrain
From talk of battles loud and vain,
And brawling memories all too free
For such a wise humility
As befits a solemn fane: 250
We revere, and while we hear
The tides of Music's golden sea
Setting toward eternity,
Uplifted high in heart and hope are we,
Until we doubt not that for one so true
There must be other nobler work to do
Than when he fought at Waterloo,
And Victor he must ever be.
For tho' the Giant Ages heave the hill
And break the shore, and evermore   260
Make and break, and work their will,
Tho' world on world in myriad myriads roll
Round us, each with different powers,
And other forms of life than ours,
What know we greater than the soul?
On God and Godlike men we build our trust.
Hush, the Dead March wails in the people's ears;
The dark crowd moves, and there are sobs and tears;
The black earth yawns; the mortal disappears;
Ashes to ashes, dust to dust;   270
He is gone who seem'd so great.—
Gone, but nothing can bereave him
Of the force he made his own
Being here, and we believe him
Something far advanced in State.

And that he wears a truer crown
Than any wreath that man can weave him.
Speak no more of his renown,
Lay your earthly fancies down,
And in the vast cathedral leave him,   **280**
God accept him, Christ receive him!

[publ. 1852, 1853, 1855]

TO E.L., ON HIS TRAVELS IN GREECE [1]

ILLYRIAN woodlands, echoing falls
    Of water, sheets of summer glass,
    The long divine Peneïan pass,
The vast Akrokeraunian walls,

Tomohrit, Athos, all things fair,
    With such a pencil, such a pen,
    You shadow forth to distant men,
I read and felt that I was there.

And trust me while I turn'd the page,
    And track'd you still on classic ground,   **10**
    I grew in gladness till I found
My spirits in the golden age.

For me the torrent ever pour'd
    And glisten'd—here and there alone
    The broad-limb'd Gods at random thrown
By fountain-urns;—and Naiads oar'd

A glimmering shoulder under gloom
    Of cavern pillars; on the swell
    The silver lily heaved and fell;
And many a slope was rich in bloom,   **20**

From him that on the mountain lea
    By dancing rivulets fed his flocks
    To him who sat upon the rocks
And fluted to the morning sea.

[publ. 1853]

[1] Edward Lear, artist and author.

THE DAISY

WRITTEN AT EDINBURGH

O LOVE, what hours were thine and mine,
In lands of palm and southern pine;
   In lands of palm, or orange-blossom,
Of olive, aloe, and maize and vine!

What Roman strength Turbìa show'd
In ruin, by the mountain road;
   How like a gem, beneath, the city
Of little Monaco, basking, glow'd!

How richly down the rocky dell
The torrent vineyard streaming fell   **10**
   To meet the sun and sunny waters,
That only heaved with a summer swell!

What slender campanili grew
By bays, the peacock's neck in hue;
   Where, here and there, on sandy beaches
A milky-bell'd amaryllis blew!

How young Columbus seem'd to rove,
Yet present in his natal grove,
   Now watching high on mountain cornice,
And steering, now, from a purple cove,   **20**

Now pacing mute by ocean's rim;
Till, in a narrow street and dim,
   I stay'd the wheels at Cogoletto,
And drank, and loyally drank to him!

Nor knew we well what pleased us most;
Not the clipt palm of which they boast,
   But distant color, happy hamlet,
A moulder'd citadel on the coast,

Or tower, or high hill-convent, seen
A light amid its olives green;   **30**

Or olive-hoary cape in ocean;
Or rosy blossom in hot ravine,

Where oleanders flush'd the bed
Of silent torrents, gravel-spread;
    And, crossing, oft we saw the glisten
Of ice, far up on a mountain head.

We loved that hall, tho' white and cold,
Those niched shapes of noble mould,
    A princely people's awful princes,
The grave, severe Genovese of old.   40

At Florence too what golden hours,
In those long galleries, were ours;
    What drives about the fresh Cascinè,
Or walks in Boboli's ducal bowers!

In bright vignettes, and each complete,
Of tower or duomo, sunny-sweet,
    Or palace, how the city glitter'd,
Thro' cypress avenues, at our feet!

But when we crost the Lombard plain
Remember what a plague of rain;   50
    Of rain at Reggio, rain at Parma,
At Lodi rain, Piacenza rain.

And stern and sad—so rare the smiles
Of sunlight—look'd the Lombard piles;
    Porch-pillars on the lion resting,
And sombre, old, colonnaded aisles.

O Milan, O the chanting quires,
The giant windows' blazon'd fires,
    The height, the space, the gloom, the glory!
A mount of marble, a hundred spires!   60

I climb'd the roofs at break of day;
Sun-smitten Alps before me lay.
    I stood among the silent statues,
And statued pinnacles, mute as they.

How faintly-flush'd, how phantom-fair,
Was Monte Rosa, hanging there
   A thousand shadowy-pencill'd valleys
And snowy dells in a golden air!

Remember how we came at last
To Como; shower and storm and blast   70
   Had blown the lake beyond his limit,
And all was flooded; and how we past

From Como, when the light was gray,
And in my head, for half the day,
   The rich Virgilian rustic measure
Of "Lari Maxume," all the way,

Like ballad-burthen music, kept,
As on the Lariano crept,
   To that fair port below the castle
Of Queen Theodolind, where we slept;   80

Or hardly slept, but watch'd awake
A cypress in the moonlight shake,
   The moonlight touching o'er a terrace
One tall agavè above the lake.

What more? we took our last adieu,
And up the snowy Splügen drew;
   But ere we reach'd the highest summit
I pluck'd a daisy, I gave it you.

It told of England then to me,
And now it tells of Italy.   90
   O love, we two shall go no longer
To lands of summer across the sea,

So dear a life your arms enfold
Whose crying is a cry for gold;
   Yet here to-night in this dark city,
When ill and weary, alone and cold,

I found, tho' crush'd to hard and dry,
This nursling of another sky

Still in the little book you lent me,
And where you tenderly laid it by;   100

And I forgot the clouded Forth,
The gloom that saddens heaven and earth,
    The bitter east, the misty summer
And gray metropolis of the North.

Perchance to lull the throbs of pain,
Perchance to charm a vacant brain,
    Perchance to dream you still beside me,
My fancy fled to the South again.
                    [1853; publ. 1855]

TO THE REV. F. D. MAURICE

COME, when no graver cares employ,
Godfather, come and see your boy;
    Your presence will be sun in winter,
Making the little one leap for joy.

For, being of that honest few
Who give the Fiend himself his due,
    Should eighty thousand college-councils
Thunder "Anathema," friend, at you,

Should all our churchmen foam in spite
At you, so careful of the right,   10
    Yet one lay-hearth would give you welcome—
Take it and come—to the Isle of Wight;

Where, far from noise and smoke of town,
I watch the twilight falling brown
    All round a careless-order'd garden
Close to the ridge of a noble down.

You'll have no scandal while you dine,
But honest talk and wholesome wine,
    And only hear the magpie gossip
Garrulous under a roof of pine;   20

For groves of pine on either hand,
To break the blast of winter, stand,
   And further on, the hoary Channel
Tumbles a billow on chalk and sand;

Where, if below the milky steep
Some ship of battle slowly creep,
   And on thro' zones of light and shadow
Glimmer away to the lonely deep,

We migh⸀ discuss the Northern sin
Which made a selfish war begin,   36
   Dispute the claims, arrange the chances,—
Emperor, Ottoman, which shall win;

Or whether war's avenging rod
Shall lash all Europe into blood;
   Till you should turn to dearer matters,
Dear to the man that is dear to God,—

How best to help the slender store,
How mend the dwellings, of the poor,
   How gain in life, as life advances,
Valor and charity more and more.   40

Come, Maurice, come; the lawn as yet
Is hoar with rime or spongy-wet,
   But when the wreath of March has blossom'd,—
Crocus, anemone, violet,—

Or later, pay one visit here,
For those are few we hold as dear;
   Nor pay but one, but come for many,
Many and many a happy year.
               [1854; publ. 1855]

THE CHARGE OF THE LIGHT BRIGADE

I

Half a league, half a league,
Half a league onward.

All in the valley of Death
  Rode the six hundred.
"Forward the Light Brigade!
Charge fc the guns!" he said.
Into the valley of Death
  Rode the six hundred.

II

"Forward, the Light Brigade!"
Was there a man dismay'd?   **10**
Not tho' the soldier knew
  Some one had blunder'd.
Theirs not to make reply,
Theirs not to reason why,
Theirs but to do and die.
Into the valley of Death
  Rode the six hundred.

III

Cannon to right of them,
Cannon to left of them,
Cannon in front of them   **20**
  Volley'd and thunder'd;
Storm'd at with shot and shell,
Boldly they rode and well,
Into the jaws of Death,
Into the mouth of hell
  Rode the six hundred.

IV

Flash'd all their sabres bare,
Flash'd as they turn'd in air
Sabring the gunners there,
Charging an army, while   **30**
  All the world wonder'd.
Plunged in the battery-smoke
Right thro' the line they broke;
Cossack and Russian
Reel'd from the sabre-stroke
  Shatter'd and sunder'd.

Then they rode back, but not,
Not the six hundred.

V

Cannon to right of them,
Cannon to left of them,   40
Cannon behind them
    Volley'd and thunder'd;
Storm'd at with shot and shell,
While horse and hero fell,
They that had fought so well
Came thro' the jaws of Death,
Back from the mouth of hell,
All that was left of them,
    Left of six hundred.

VI

When can their glory fade?   50
O the wild charge they made!
    All the world wonder'd.
Honor the charge they made!
Honor the Light Brigade,
    Noble six hundred!
        [1854; publ. 1854]

MAUD; A MONODRAMA

PART I

I

I

I HATE the dreadful hollow behind the little wood;
Its lips in the field above are dabbled with blood-red heath,
The red-ribb'd ledges drip with a silent horror of blood,
And Echo there, whatever is ask'd her, answers "Death."

II

For there in the ghastly pit long since a body was found,
His who had given me life—O father! O God! was it well?—
Mangled, and flatten'd, and crush'd, and dinted into the ground;
There yet lies the rock that fell with him when he fell.

III

Did he fling himself down? who knows? for a vast speculation
     had fail'd,
And ever he mutter'd and madden'd, and ever wann'd with
     despair,   10
And out he walk'd when the wind like a broken worldling wail'd,
And the flying gold of the ruin'd woodlands drove thro' the air.

IV

I remember the time, for the roots of my hair were stirr'd
By a shuffled step, by a dead weight trail'd, by a whisper'd
     fright,
And my pulses closed their gates with a shock on my heart as
     I heard
The shrill-edged shriek of a mother divide the shuddering night.

V

Villainy somewhere! whose? One says, we are villains all.
Not he; his honest fame should at least by me be maintained;
But that old man, now lord of the broad estate and the Hall,
Dropt off gorged from a scheme that had left us flaccid and
     drain'd.   20

VI

Why do they prate of the blessings of peace? we have made them
     a curse,
Pickpockets, each hand lusting for all that is not its own;
And lust of gain, in the spirit of Cain, is it better or worse
Than the heart of the citizen hissing in war on his own hearth-
     stone?

VII

But these are the days of advance, the works of the men of mind,
When who but a fool would have faith in a tradesman's ware or
    his word?
Is it peace or war? Civil war, as I think, and that of a kind
The viler, as underhand, not openly bearing the sword.

VIII

Sooner or later I too may passively take the print
Of the golden age—why not? I have neither hope nor trust;   30
May make my heart as a millstone, set my face as a flint.
Cheat and be cheated, and die—who knows? we are ashes and
    dust.

IX

Peace sitting under her olive, and slurring the days gone by,
When the poor are hovell'd and hustled together, each sex, like
    swine,
When only the ledger lives, and when only not all men lie;
Peace in her vineyard—yes!—but a company forges the wine.

X

And the vitriol madness flushes up in the ruffian's head,
Till the filthy by-lane rings to the yell of the trampled wife,
And chalk and alum and plaster are sold to the poor for bread,
And the spirit of murder works in the very means of life,   40

XI

And Sleep must lie down arm'd, for the villainous centre-bits
Grind on the wakeful ear in the hush of the moonless nights,
While another is cheating the sick of a few last gasps, as he sits
To pestle a poison'd poison behind his crimson lights.

XII

When a Mammonite mother kills her babe for a burial fee,
And Timour-Mammon grins on a pile of children's bones,

Is it peace or war? better, war! loud war by land and by sea,
War with a thousand battles, and shaking a hundred thrones!

XIII

For I trust if an enemy's fleet came yonder round by the hill,
And the rushing battle-bolt sang from the three-decker out of
    the foam,   50
That the smooth-faced, snub-nosed rogue would leap from his
    counter and till,
And strike, if he could, were it but with his cheating yardwand,
    home.—

XIV

What! am I raging alone as my father raged in his mood?
Must *I* too creep to the hollow and dash myself down and die
Rather than hold by the law that I made, nevermore to brood
On a horror of shatter'd limbs and a wretched swindler's lie?

XV

Would there be sorrow for *me*? there was *love* in the passionate
    shriek,
Love for the silent thing that had made false haste to the grave—
Wrapt in a cloak, as I saw him, and thought he would rise and
    speak
And rave at the lie and the liar, ah God, as he used to rave.   60

XVI

I am sick of the Hall and the hill, I am sick of the moor and the
    main.
Why should I stay? can a sweeter chance ever come to me here?
O, having the nerves of motion as well as the nerves of pain,
Were it not wise if I fled from the place and the pit and the fear?

XVII

Workmen up at the Hall!—they are coming back from abroad;
The dark old place will be gilt by the touch of a millionaire.

I have heard, I know not whence, of the singular beauty of
    Maud;
I play'd with the girl when a child; she promised then to be fair.

XVIII

Maud, with her venturous climbings and tumbles and childish
    escapes,
Maud, the delight of the village, the ringing joy of the Hall,   70
Maud, with her sweet purse-mouth when my father dangled the
    grapes,
Maud, the beloved of my mother, the moon-faced darling of
    all,—

XIX

What is she now? My dreams are bad. She may bring me a curse.
No, there is fatter game on the moor; she will let me alone.
Thanks; for the fiend best knows whether woman or man be the
    worse.
I will bury myself in myself, and the Devil may pipe to his own.

II

Long have I sigh'd for a calm; God grant I may find it at last!
It will never be broken by Maud; she has neither savor nor salt.
But a cold and clear-cut face, as I found when her carriage past,
Perfectly beautiful; let it be granted her; where is the fault?   80
All that I saw—for her eyes were downcast, not to be seen—
Faultily faultless, icily regular, splendidly null,
Dead perfection, no more; nothing more, if it had not been
For a chance of travel, a paleness, an hour's defect of the rose,
Or an underlip, you may call it a little too ripe, too full,
Or the least little delicate aquiline curve in a sensitive nose,
From which I escaped heart-free, with the least little touch of
    spleen.

III

Cold and clear-cut face, why come you so cruelly meek,
Breaking a slumber in which all spleenful folly was drown'd?
Pale with the golden beam of an eyelash dead on the cheek,   90
Passionless, pale, cold face, star-sweet on a gloom profound;
Womanlike, taking revenge too deep for a transient wrong

Done but in thought to your beauty, and ever as pale as before
Growing and fading and growing upon me without a sound,
Luminous, gemlike, ghostlike, deathlike, half the night long
Growing and fading and growing, till I could bear it no more,
But arose, and all by myself in my own dark garden ground,
Listening now to the tide in its broad-flung shipwrecking roar,
Now to the scream of a madden'd beach dragg'd down by the
    wave,
Walk'd in a wintry wind by a ghastly glimmer, and found   100
The shining daffodil dead, and Orion low in his grave.

IV

I

A million emeralds break from the ruby-budded lime
In the little grove where I sit—ah, wherefore cannot I be
Like things of the season gay, like the bountiful season bland,
When the far-off sail is blown by the breeze of a softer clime,
Half-lost in the liquid azure bloom of a crescent of sea,
The silent sapphire-spangled marriage ring of the land?

II

Below me, there, is the village, and looks how quiet and small!
And yet bubbles o'er like a city, with gossip, scandal, and spite;
And Jack on his ale-house bench has as many lies as a Czar;   110
And here on the landward side, by a red rock, glimmers the Hall;
And up in the high Hall-garden I see her pass like a light;
But sorrow seize me if ever that light be my leading star!

III

When have I bow'd to her father, the wrinkled head of the race?
I met her to-day with her brother, but not to her brother I bow'd;
I bow'd to his lady-sister as she rode by on the moor,
But the fire of a foolish pride flash'd over her beautiful face.
O child, you wrong your beauty, believe it, in being so proud;
Your father has wealth well-gotten, and I am nameless and poor.

IV

I keep but a man and a maid, ever ready to slander and
    steal; 120
I know it, and smile a hard-set smile, like a stoic, or like
A wiser epicurean, and let the world have its way.
For nature is one with rapine, a harm no preacher can heal;
The Mayfly is torn by the swallow, the sparrow spear'd by the
    shrike,
And the whole little wood where I sit is a world of plunder and
    prey.

V

We are puppets, Man in his pride, and Beauty fair in her flower;
Do we move ourselves, or are moved by an unseen hand at a
    game
That pushes us off from the board, and others ever succeed?
Ah yet, we cannot be kind to each other here for an hour;
We whisper, and hint, and chuckle, and grin at a brother's
    shame; 130
However we brave it out, we men are a little breed.

VI

A monstrous eft was of old the lord and master of earth,
For him did his high sun flame, and his river billowing ran,
And he felt himself in his force to be Nature's crowning race.
As nine months go to the shaping an infant ripe for his birth,
So many a million of ages have gone to the making of man:
He now is first, but is he the last? is he not too base?

VII

The man of science himself is fonder of glory, and vain,
An eye well-practised in nature, a spirit bounded and poor;
The passionate heart of the poet is whirl'd into folly and
    vice. 140
I would not marvel at either, but keep a temperate brain;
For not to desire or admire, if a man could learn it, were more
Than to walk all day like the sultan of old in a garden of spice

VIII

For the drift of the Maker is dark, an Isis hid by the veil.
Who knows the ways of the world, how God will bring them
about?
Our planet is one, the suns are many, the world is wide.
Shall I weep if a Poland fall? shall I shriek if a Hungary fail?
Or an infant civilization be ruled with rod or with knout?
I have not made the world, and He that made it will guide.

IX

Be mine a philosopher's life in the quiet woodland ways,   150
Where if I cannot be gay let a passionless peace be my lot,
Far-off from the clamor of liars belied in the hubbub of lies;
From the long-neck'd geese of the world that are ever hissing
dispraise
Because their natures are little, and, whether he heed it or not,
Where each man walks with his head in a cloud of poisonous
flies.

X

And most of all would I flee from the cruel madness of love
The honey of poison-flowers and all the measureless ill.
Ah, Maud, you milk-white fawn, you are all unmeet for a wife.
Your mother is mute in her grave as her image in marble above;
Your father is ever in London, you wander about at your
will;   160
You have but fed on the roses and lain in the lilies of life.

V

I

A voice by the cedar tree
In the meadow under the Hall!
She is singing an air that is known to me,
A passionate ballad gallant and gay,
A martial song like a trumpet's call!
Singing alone in the morning of life,

In the happy morning of life and of May,
Singing of men that in battle array,
Ready in heart and ready in hand,   170
March with banner and bugle and fife
To the death, for their native land.

II

Maud with her exquisite face,
And wild voice pealing up to the sunny sky,
And feet like sunny gems on an English green,
Maud in the light of her youth and her grace,
Singing of Death, and of Honor that cannot die,
Till I well could weep for a time so sordid and mean,
And myself so languid and base.

III

Silence, beautiful voice!   180
Be still, for you only trouble the mind
With a joy in which I cannot rejoice,
A glory I shall not find.
Still! I will hear you no more,
For your sweetness hardly leaves me a choice
But to move to the meadow and fall before
Her feet on the meadow grass, and adore,
Not her, who is neither courtly nor kind,
Not her, not her, but a voice.

VI

I

Morning arises stormy and pale,   190
No sun, but a wannish glare
In fold upon fold of hueless cloud;
And the budded peaks of the wood are bow'd,
Caught, and cuff'd by the gale:
I had fancied it would be fair.

II

Whom but Maud should I meet
Last night, when the sunset burn'd
On the blossom'd gable-ends
At the head of the village street,
Whom but Maud should I meet?   200
And she touch'd my hand with a smile so sweet,
She made me divine amends
For a courtesy not return'd.

III

And thus a delicate spark
Of glowing and growing light
Thro' the livelong hours of the dark
Kept itself warm in the heart of my dreams,
Ready to burst in a color'd flame;
Till at last, when the morning came
In a cloud, it faded, and seems   210
But an ashen-gray delight.

IV

What if with her sunny hair,
And smile as sunny as cold,
She meant to weave me a snare
Of some coquettish deceit,
Cleopatra-like as of old
To entangle me when we met,
To have her lion roll in a silken net
And fawn at a victor's feet.

V

Ah, what shall I be at fifty   220
Should Nature keep me alive,
If I find the world so bitter
When I am but twenty-five?
Yet, if she were not a cheat,
If Maud were all that she seem'd,

And her smile were all that I dream'd,
Then the world were not so bitter
But a smile could make it sweet.

VI

What if, tho' her eye seem'd full
Of a kind intent to me, 230
What if that dandy-despot, he,
That jewell'd mass of millinery,
That oil'd and curl'd Assyrian bull
Smelling of musk and of insolence,
Her brother, from whom I keep aloof,
Who wants the finer politic sense
To mask, tho' but in his own behoof,
With a glassy smile his brutal scorn—
What if he had told her yestermorn
How prettily for his own sweet sake 240
A face of tenderness might be feign'd,
And a moist mirage in desert eyes,
That so, when the rotten hustings shake
In another month to his brazen lies,
A wretched vote may be gain'd?

VII

For a raven ever croaks, at my side,
Keep watch and ward, keep watch and ward,
Or thou wilt prove their tool.
Yea, too, myself from myself I guard,
For often a man's own angry pride 250
Is cap and bells for a fool.

VIII

Perhaps the smile and tender tone
Came out of her pitying womanhood,
For am I not, am I not, here alone
So many a summer since she died,
My mother, who was so gentle and good?
Living alone in an empty house,
Here half-hid in the gleaming wood,

Where I hear the dead at midday moan,
And the shrieking rush of the wainscot mouse,　266
And my own sad name in corners cried,
When the shiver of dancing leaves is thrown
About its echoing chambers wide,
Till a morbid hate and horror have grown
Of a world in which I have hardly mixt,
And a morbid eating lichen fixt
On a heart half-turn'd to stone.

IX

O heart of stone, are you flesh, and caught
By that you swore to withstand?
For what was it else within me wrought　270
But, I fear, the new strong wine of love,
That made my tongue so stammer and trip
When I saw the treasured splendor, her hand,
Come sliding out of her sacred glove,
And the sunlight broke from her lip?

X

I have play'd with her when a child;
She remembers it now we meet.
Ah, well, well, well, I *may* be beguiled
By some coquettish deceit.
Yet, if she were not a cheat,　280
If Maud were all that she seem'd,
And her smile had all that I dream'd,
Then the world were not so bitter
But a smile could make it sweet.

VII

I

Did I hear it half in a doze
　Long since, I know not where?
Did I dream it an hour ago,
　When asleep in this arm-chair

II

Men were drinking together,
  Drinking and talking of me:
"Well, if it prove a girl, the boy
  Will have plenty; so let it be."   290

III

Is it an echo of something
  Read with a boy's delight,
Viziers nodding together
  In some Arabian night?

IV

Strange, that I hear two men,
  Somewhere, talking of me:
"Well, if it prove a girl, my boy
  Will have plenty; so let it be."   300

VIII

She came to the village church,
And sat by a pillar alone;
An angel watching an urn
Wept over her, carved in stone;
And once, but once, she lifted her eyes,
And suddenly, sweetly, strangely blush'd
To find they were met by my own;
And suddenly, sweetly, my heart beat stronger
And thicker, until I heard no longer
The snowy-banded, dilettante,   310
Delicate-handed priest intone;
And thought, is it pride? and mused and sigh'd,
 No surely, now it cannot be pride."

IX

  1 was walking a mile,
  More than a mile from the shore,

The sun look'd out with a smile
Betwixt the cloud and the moor;
And riding at set of day
Over the dark moor land,
Rapidly riding far away,   320
She waved to me with her hand.
There were two at her side,
Something flash'd in the sun,
Down by the hill I saw them ride,
In a moment they were gone;
Like a sudden spark
Struck vainly in the night,
Then returns the dark
With no more hope of light.

X

I

Sick, am I sick of a jealous dread?   330
Was not one of the two at her side
This new-made lord, whose splendor plucks
The slavish hat from the villager's head?
Whose old grandfather has lately died,
Gone to a blacker pit, for whom
Grimy nakedness dragging his trucks
And laying his trams in a poison'd gloom
Wrought, till he crept from a gutted mine
Master of half a servile shire,
And left his coal all turn'd into gold   340
To a grandson, first of his noble line,
Rich in the grace all women desire,
Strong in the power that all men adore,
And simper and set their voices lower,
And soften as if to a girl, and hold
Awe-stricken breaths at a work divine,
Seeing his gewgaw castle shine,
New as his title, built last year,
There amid perky larches and pine,
And over the sullen-purple moor—   350
Look at it—pricking a cockney ear.

II

What, has he found my jewel out?
For one of the two that rode at her side
Bound for the Hall, I am sure was he;
Bound for the Hall, and I think for a bride.
Blithe would her brother's acceptance be.
Maud could be gracious too, no doubt,
To a lord, a captain, a padded shape,
A bought commission, a waxen face,
A rabbit mouth that is ever agape—   360
Bought? what is it he cannot buy?
And therefore splenetic, personal, base,
A wounded thing with a rancorous cry,
At war with myself and a wretched race,
Sick, sick to the heart of life, am I.

III

Last week came one to the county town,
To preach our poor little army down,
And play the game of the despot kings,
Tho' the state has done it and thrice as well.
This broad-brimm'd hawker of holy things,   370
Whose ear is cramm'd with his cotton, and rings
Even in dreams to the chink of his pence,
This huckster put down war! can he tell
Whether war be a cause or a consequence?
Put down the passions that make earth hell!
Down with ambition, avarice, pride,
Jealousy, down! cut off from the mind
The bitter springs of anger and fear!
Down too, down at your own fireside,   380
With the evil tongue and the evil ear,
For each is at war with mankind!

IV

I wish I could hear again
The chivalrous battle-song
That she warbled alone in her joy!

I might persuade myself then
She would not do herself this great wrong,
To take a wanton dissolute boy
For a man and leader of men.

V

Ah God, for a man with heart, head, hand,
Like some of the simple great ones gone   390
For ever and ever by,
One still strong man in a blatant land,
Whatever they call him—what care I?—
Aristocrat, democrat, autocrat—one
Who can rule and dare not lie!

VI

And ah for a man to arise in me,
That the man I am may cease to be!

XI

I

O, let the solid ground
    Not fail beneath my feet
Before my life has found   400
    What some have found so sweet!
Then let come what come may,
What matter if I go mad,
I shall have had my day.

II

Let the sweet heavens endure,
    Not close and darken above me
Before I am quite quite sure
    That there is one to love me!
Then let come what come may
To a life that has been so sad,   410
I shall have had my day.

XII

I

Birds in the high Hall-garden
  When twilight was falling,
Maud, Maud, Maud, Maud,
  They were crying and calling.

II

Where was Maud? in our wood;
  And I—who else?—was with her,
Gathering woodland lilies,
  Myriads blow together.

III

Birds in our wood sang   **420**
  Ringing thro' the valleys,
Maud is here, here, here
  In among the lilies.

IV

I kiss'd her slender hand,
  She took the kiss sedately;
Maud is not seventeen,
  But she is tall and stately.

V

I to cry out on pride
  Who have won her favor!
O, Maud were sure of heaven   **430**
  If lowliness could save her!

VI

I know the way she went
  Home with her maiden posy,

For her feet have touch'd the meadows
   And left the daisies rosy.

VII

Birds in the high Hall-garden
   Were crying and calling to her,
Where is Maud, Maud, Maud?
   One is come to woo her.

VIII

Look, a horse at the door,   **440**
   And little King Charley snarling!
Go back, my lord, across the moor,
   You are not her darling.

XIII

I

Scorn'd, to be scorn'd by one that I scorn,
Is that a matter to make me fret?
That a calamity hard to be borne?
Well, he may live to hate me yet.
Fool that I am to be vext with his pride!
I past him, I was crossing his lands;
He stood on the path a little aside;   **450**
His face, as I grant, in spite of spite,
Has a broad-blown comeliness, red and white,
And six feet two, as I think, he stands;
But his essences turn'd the live air sick,
And barbarous opulence jewel-thick
Sunn'd itself on his breast and his hands.

II

Who shall call me ungentle, unfair?
I long'd so heartily then and there
To give him the grasp of fellowship;
But while I past he was humming an air,   **460**

Stopt, and then with a riding-whip
Leisurely tapping a glossy boot,
And curving a contumelious lip,
Gorgonized me from head to foot
With a stony British stare.

III

Why sits he here in his father's chair?
That old man never comes to his place;
Shall I believe him ashamed to be seen?
For only once, in the village street,
Last year, I caught a glimpse of his face,   470
A gray old wolf and a lean.
Scarcely, now, would I call him a cheat;
For then, perhaps, as a child of deceit,
She might by a true descent be untrue;
And Maud is as true as Maud is sweet,
Tho' I fancy her sweetness only due
To the sweeter blood by the other side;
Her mother has been a thing complete,
However she came to be so allied.
And fair without, faithful within,   480
Maud to him is nothing akin.
Some peculiar mystic grace
Made her only the child of her mother,
And heap'd the whole inherited sin
On that huge scapegoat of the race,
All, all upon the brother.

IV

Peace, angry spirit, and let him be!
Has not his sister smiled on me?

XIV

I

Maud has a garden of roses
And lilies fair on a lawn;   490

There she walks in her state
And tends upon bed and bower,
And thither I climb'd at dawn
And stood by her garden-gate.
A lion ramps at the top,
He is claspt by a passion-flower.

II

Maud's own little oak-room—
Which Maud, like a precious stone
Set in the heart of the carven gloom,
Lights with herself, when alone   500
She sits by her music and books
And her brother lingers late
With a roystering company—looks
Upon Maud's own garden-gate;
And I thought as I stood, if a hand, as white
As ocean-foam in the moon, were laid
On the hasp of the window, and my Delight
Had a sudden desire, like a glorious ghost, to glide,
Like a beam of the seventh heaven, down to my side,
There were but a step to be made.   510

III

The fancy flatter'd my mind,
And again seem'd overbold;
Now I thought that she cared for me,
Now I thought she was kind
Only because she was cold.

IV

I heard no sound where I stood
But the rivulet on from the lawn
Running down to my own dark wood,
Or the voice of the long sea-wave as it swell'd
Now and then in the dim-gray dawn;   520
But I look'd, and round, all round the house I beheld
The death-white curtain drawn,
Felt a horror over me creep,

Prickle my skin and catch my breath,
Knew that the death-white curtain meant but sleep,
Yet I shudder'd and thought like a fool of the sleep of death.

XV

So dark a mind within me dwells,
   And I make myself such evil cheer,
That if *I* be dear to some one else,
   Then some one else may have much to fear;   530
But if *I* be dear to some one else,
   Then I should be to myself more dear.
Shall I not take care of all that I think,
Yea, even of wretched meat and drink,
If I be dear,
If I be dear to some one else?

XVI

I

This lump of earth has left his estate
The lighter by the loss of his weight;
And so that he find what he went to seek,
And fulsome pleasure clog him, and drown   540
His heart in the gross mud-honey of town,
He may stay for a year who has gone for a week.
But this is the day when I must speak,
And I see my Oread coming down,
O, this is the day!
O beautiful creature, what am I
That I dare to look her way?
Think I may hold dominion sweet,
Lord of the pulse that is lord of her breast,
And dream of her beauty with tender dread,   550
From the delicate Arab arch of her feet
To the grace that, bright and light as the crest
Of a peacock, sits on her shining head,
And she knows it not—O, if she knew it,
To know her beauty might half undo it!
I know it the one bright thing to save

My yet young life in the wilds of Time,
Perhaps from madness, perhaps from crime,
Perhaps from a selfish grave.

II

What, if she be fasten'd to this fool lord,   560
Dare I bid her abide by her word?
Should I love her so well if she
Had given her word to a thing so low?
Shall I love her as well if she
Can break her word were it even for me?
I trust that it is not so.

III

Catch not my breath, O clamorous heart,
Let not my tongue be a thrall to my eye,
For I must tell her before we part,
I must tell her, or die.   570

XVII

Go not, happy day,
    From the shining fields,
Go not, happy day,
    Till the maiden yields.
Rosy is the West,
    Rosy is the South,
Roses are her cheeks,
    And a rose her mouth.
When the happy Yes
    Falters from her lips,   580
Pass and blush the news
    Over glowing ships;
Over blowing seas,
    Over seas at rest,
Pass the happy news,
    Blush it thro the West;
Till the red man dance
    By his red cedar-tree,
And the red man's babe
    Leap, beyond the sea.   590

Blush from West to East,
  Blush from East to West,
Till the West is East,
  Blush it thro' the West.
Rosy is the West,
  Rosy is the South,
Roses are her cheeks,
  And a rose her mouth.

XVIII

I

I have led her home, my love, my only friend.
There is none like her, none.   600
And never yet so warmly ran my blood
And sweetly, on and on
Calming itself to the long-wish'd-for end,
Full to the banks, close on the promised good.

II

None like her, none.
Just now the dry-tongued laurels' pattering talk
Seem'd her light foot along the garden walk,
And shook my heart to think she comes once more.
But even then I heard her close the door;
The gates of heaven are closed, and she is gone.   610

III

There is none like her, none,
Nor will be when our summers have deceased.
O, art thou sighing for Lebanon
In the long breeze that streams to thy delicious East,
Sighing for Lebanon,
Dark cedar, tho' thy limbs have here increased,
Upon a pastoral slope as fair,
And looking to the South and fed
With honey'd rain and delicate air,
And haunted by the starry head   620
Of her whose gentle will has changed my fate,

And made my life a perfumed altar-flame;
And over whom thy darkness must have spread
With such delight as theirs of old, thy great
Forefathers of the thornless garden, there
Shadowing the snow-limb'd Eve from whom she came?

IV

Here will I lie, while these long branches sway,
And you fair stars that crown a happy day
Go in and out as if at merry play,
Who am no more so all forlorn   630
As when it seem'd far better to be born
To labor and the mattock-harden'd hand
Than nursed at ease and brought to understand
A sad astrology, the boundless plan
That makes you tyrants in your iron skies,
Innumerable, pitiless, passionless eyes,
Cold fires, yet with power to burn and brand
His nothingness into man.

V

But now shine on, and what care I,
Who in this stormy gulf have found a pearl   640
The countercharm of space and hollow sky,
And do accept my madness, and would die
To save from some slight shame one simple girl?—

VI

Would die, for sullen-seeming Death may give
More life to Love than is or ever was
In our low world, where yet 'tis sweet to live.
Let no one ask me how it came to pass;
It seems that I am happy, that to me
A livelier emerald twinkles in the grass,
A purer sapphire melts into the sea.   650

VII

Not die, but live a life of truest breath,
And teach true life to fight with mortal wrongs.

O, why should Love, like men in drinking-songs,
Spice his fair banquet with the dust of death?
Make answer, Maud my bliss,
Maud made my Maud by that long loving kiss,
Life of my life, wilt thou not answer this?
"The dusky strand of Death inwoven here
With dear Love's tie, makes Love himself more dear."

VIII

Is that enchanted moan only the swell   **660**
Of the long waves that roll in yonder bay?
And hark the clock within, the silver knell
Of twelve sweet hours that past in bridal white,
And died to live, long as my pulses play;
But now by this my love has closed her sight
And given false death her hand, and stolen away
To dreamful wastes where footless fancies dwell
Among the fragments of the golden day.
May nothing there her maiden grace affright!
Dear heart, I feel with thee the drowsy spell.   **670**
My bride to be, my evermore delight,
My own heart's heart, my ownest own, farewell;
It is but for a little space I go.
And ye meanwhile far over moor and fell
Beat to the noiseless music of the night!
Has our whole earth gone nearer to the glow
Of your soft splendors that you look so bright?
I have climb'd nearer out of lonely hell.
Beat, happy stars, timing with things below,
Beat with my heart more blest than heart can tell,   **680**
Blest, but for some dark undercurrent woe
That seems to draw—but it shall not be so;
Let all be well, be well.

XIX

I

Her brother is coming back to-night,
Breaking up my dream of delight.

II

My dream? do I dream of bliss?
I have walk'd awake with Truth.
O, when did a morning shine
So rich in atonement as this
For my dark-dawning youth,   690
Darken'd watching a mother decline
And that dead man at her heart and mine;
For who was left to watch her but I?
Yet so did I let my freshness die.

III

I trust that I did not talk
To gentle Maud in our walk—
For often in lonely wanderings
I have cursed him even to lifeless things—
But I trust that I did not talk,
Not touch on her father's sin.   700
I am sure I did but speak
Of my mother's faded cheek
When it slowly grew so thin
That I felt she was slowly dying
Vext with lawyers and harass'd with debt;
For how often I caught her with eyes all wet,
Shaking her head at her son and sighing
A world of trouble within!

IV

And Maud too, Maud was moved
To speak of the mother she loved   710
As one scarce less forlorn,
Dying abroad and it seems apart
From him who had ceased to share her heart,
And ever mourning over the feud,
The household Fury sprinkled with blood
By which our houses are torn.
How strange was what she said,
When only Maud and the brother

Hung over her dying bed—
That Maud's dark father and mine   720
Had bound us one to the other,
Betrothed us over their wine,
On the day when Maud was born;
Seal'd her mine from her first sweet breath!
Mine, mine by a right, from birth till death!
Mine, mine—our fathers have sworn!

V

But the true blood spilt had in it a heat
To dissolve the precious seal on a bond,
That, if left uncancell'd, had been so sweet;
And none of us thought of a something beyond,   730
A desire that awoke in the heart of the child,
As it were a duty done to the tomb,
To be friends for her sake, to be reconciled;
And I was cursing them and my doom,
And letting a dangerous thought run wild
While often abroad in the fragrant gloom
Of foreign churches—I see her there,
Bright English lily, breathing a prayer
To be friends, to be reconciled!

VI

But then what a flint is he!   746
Abroad, at Florence, at Rome,
I find whenever she touch'd on me
This brother had laugh'd her down,
And at last, when each came home,
He had darken'd into a frown,
Chid her, and forbid her to speak
To me, her friend of the years before;
And this was what had redden'd her cheek
When I bow'd to her on the moor.

VII

Yet Maud, altho' not blind   750
To the faults of his heart and mind,

I see she cannot but love him,
And says he is rough but kind,
And wishes me to approve him,
And tells me, when she lay
Sick once, with a fear of worse,
That he left his wine and horses and play,
Sat with her, read to her, night and day,
And tended her like a nurse.

VIII

Kind? but the death-bed desire   760
Spurn'd by this heir of the liar—
Rough but kind? yet I know
He has plotted against me in this,
That he plots against me still.
Kind to Maud? that were not amiss.
Well, rough but kind; why, let it be so,
For shall not Maud have her will?

IX

For, Maud, so tender and true,
As long as my life endures
I feel I shall owe you a debt   770
That I never can hope to pay;
And if ever I should forget
That I owe this debt to you
And for your sweet sake to yours,
O, then, what then shall I say?—
If ever I *should* forget,
May God make me more wretched
Than ever I have been yet!

X

So now I have sworn to bury
All this dead body of hate,   780
I feel so free and so clear
By the loss of that dead weight,
That I should grow light-headed, I fear,
Fantastically merry,

But that her brother comes, like a blight
On my fresh hope, to the Hall to-night.

XX

I

Strange, that I felt so gay,
Strange, that *I* tried to-day
To beguile her melancholy;
The Sultan, as we name him—   790
She did not wish to blame him—
But he vext her and perplext her
With his worldly talk and folly.
Was it gentle to reprove her
For stealing out of view
From a little lazy lover
Who but claims her as his due?
Or for chilling his caresses
By the coldness of her manners,
Nay, the plainness of her dresses?   800
Now I know her but in two,
Nor can pronounce upon it
If one should ask me whether
The habit, hat, and feather,
Or the frock and gipsy bonnet
Be the neater and completer;
For nothing can be sweeter
Than maiden Maud in either.

II

But to-morrow, if we live,
Our ponderous squire will give   810
A grand political dinner
To half the squirelings near;
And Maud will wear her jewels,
And the bird of prey will hover,
And the titmouse hope to win her
With his chirrup at her ear.

III

A grand political dinner
To the men of many acres,
A gathering of the Tory,
A dinner and then a dance   820
For the maids and marriage-makers,
And every eye but mine will glance
At Maud in all her glory.

IV

For I am not invited,
But, with the Sultan's pardon,
I am all as well delighted,
For I know her own rose-garden,
And mean to linger in it
Till the dancing will be over;
And then, O, then, come out to me   830
For a minute, but for a minute,
Come out to your own true lover,
That your true lover may see
Your glory also, and render
All homage to his own darling,
Queen Maud in all her splendor.

XXI

Rivulet crossing my ground,
And bringing me down from the Hall
This garden-rose that I found,
Forgetful of Maud and me,   840
And lost in trouble and moving round
Here at the head of a tinkling fall,
And trying to pass to the sea;
O rivulet, born at the Hall,
My Maud has sent it by thee—
If I read her sweet will right—
On a blushing mission to me,

Saying in odor and color, "Ah, be
Among the roses to-night."

XXII

I

Come into the garden, Maud,   850
  For the black bat, night, has flown,
Come into the garden, Maud,
  I am here at the gate alone;
And the woodbine spices are wafted abroad,
  And the musk of the rose is blown.

II

For a breeze of morning moves,
  And the planet of Love is on high,
Beginning to faint in the light that she loves
  On a bed of daffodil sky,
To faint in the light of the sun she loves,   860
  To faint in his light, and to die.

III

All night have the roses heard
  The flute, violin, bassoon;
All night has the casement jessamine stirr'd
  To the dancers dancing in tune;
Till a silence fell with the waking bird,
  And a hush with the setting moon.

IV

I said to the lily, "There is but one,
  With whom she has heart to be gay.
When will the dancers leave her alone?   870
  She is weary of dance and play."

Now half to the setting moon are gone,
    And half to the rising day;
Low on the sand and loud on the stone
    The last wheel echoes away.

V

I said to the rose, "The brief night goes
    In babble and revel and wine.
O young lord-lover, what sighs are those,
    For one that will never be thine?
But mine, but mine," so I sware to the rose,   880
    "For ever and ever, mine."

VI

And the soul of the rose went into my blood,
    As the music clash'd in the hall;
And long by the garden lake I stood,
    For I heard your rivulet fall
From the lake to the meadow and on to the wood,
    Our wood, that is dearer than all;

VII

From the meadow your walks have left so sweet
    That whenever a March-wind sighs
He sets the jewel-print of your feet   890
    In violets blue as your eyes,
To the woody hollows in which we meet
    And the valleys of Paradise.

VIII

The slender acacia would not shake
    One long milk-bloom on the tree;
The white lake-blossom fell into the lake
    As the pimpernel dozed on the lea;
But the rose was awake all night for your sake,
    Knowing your promise to me;
The lilies and roses were all awake,   900
    They sigh'd for the dawn and thee.

IX

Queen rose of the rosebud garden of girls,
    Come hither, the dances are done,
In gloss of satin and glimmer of pearls,
    Queen lily and rose in one;
Shine out, little head, sunning over with curls,
    To the flowers, and be their sun.

X

There has fallen a splendid tear
    From the passion-flower at the gate.
She is coming, my dove, my dear;   910
    She is coming, my life, my fate.
The red rose cries, "She is near, she is near;"
    And the white rose weeps, "She is late;"
The larkspur listens, "I hear, I hear;"
    And the lily whispers, "I wait."

XI

She is coming, my own, my sweet;
    Were it ever so airy a tread,
My heart would hear her and beat,
    Were it earth in an earthy bed;
My dust would hear her and beat,   920
    Had I lain for a century dead,
Would start and tremble under her feet,
    And blossom in purple and red.

PART II

I

"The fault was mine, the fault was mine"—
Why am I sitting here so stunn'd and still,

Plucking the harmless wild-flower on the hill?—
It is this guilty hand!—
And there rises ever a passionate cry
From underneath in the darkening land—
What is it, that has been done?
O dawn of Eden bright over earth and sky,
The fires of hell brake out of thy rising sun,
The fires of hell and of hate;   10
For she, sweet soul, had hardly spoken a word,
When her brother ran in his rage to the gate,
He came with the babe-faced lord,
Heap'd on her terms of disgrace;
And while she wept, and I strove to be cool,
He fiercely gave me the lie,
Till I with as fierce an anger spoke,
And he struck me, madman, over the face,
Struck me before the languid fool,
Who was gaping and grinning by;   20
Struck for himself an evil stroke,
Wrought for his house an irredeemable woe.
For front to front in an hour we stood,
And a million horrible bellowing echoes broke
From the red-ribb'd hollow behind the wood,
And thunder'd up into heaven the Christless code
That must have life for a blow.
Ever and ever afresh they seem'd to grow.
Was it he lay there with a fading eye?
"The fault was mine," he whisper'd, "fly!"   30
Then glided out of the joyous wood
The ghastly Wraith of one that I know,
And there rang on a sudden a passionate cry,
A cry for a brother's blood;
It will ring in my heart and my ears, till I die, till I die.

II

Is it gone? my pulses beat—
What was it? a lying trick of the brain?
Yet I thought I saw her stand,
A shadow there at my feet,
High over the shadowy land.   40

It is gone; and the heavens fall in a gentle rain,
When they should burst and drown with deluging storms
The feeble vassals of wine and anger and lust,
The little hearts that know not how to forgive.
Arise, my God, and strike, for we hold Thee just,
Strike dead the whole weak race of venomous worms,
That sting each other here in the dust;
We are not worthy to live.

II

I

See what a lovely shell,
Small and pure as a pearl,   50
Lying close to my foot,
Frail, but a work divine,
Made so fairily well
With delicate spire and whorl,
How exquisitely minute,
A miracle of design!

II

What is it? a learned man
Could give it a clumsy name.
Let him name it who can,
The beauty would be the same.   60

III

The tiny cell is forlorn,
Void of the little living will
That made it stir on the shore.
Did he stand at the diamond door
Of his house in a rainbow frill?
Did he push, when he was uncurl'd,
A golden foot or a fairy horn
Thro' his dim water-world?

IV

Slight, to be crush'd with a tap
Of my finger-nail on the sand,   **70**
Small, but a work divine,
Frail, but of force to withstand,
Year upon year, the shock
Of cataract seas that snap
The three-decker's oaken spine
Athwart the ledges of rock,
Here on the Breton strand!

V

Breton, not Briton; here
Like a shipwreck'd man on a coast
Of ancient fable and fear—   **80**
Plagued with a flitting to and fro,
A disease, a hard mechanic ghost
That never came from on high
Nor ever arose from below,
But only moves with the moving eye,
Flying along the land and the main—
Why should it look like Maud?
Am I to be overawed
By what I cannot but know
Is a juggle born of the brain?   **90**

VI

Back from the Breton coast,
Sick of a nameless fear,
Back to the dark sea-line
Looking, thinking of all I have lost;
An old song vexes my ear,
But that of Lamech is mine.

VII

For years, a measureless ill,
For years, for ever, to part—

But she, she would love me still;
And as long, O God, as she   **100**
Have a grain of love for me,
So long, no doubt, no doubt,
Shall I nurse in my dark heart,
However weary, a spark of will
Not to be trampled out.

VIII

Strange, that the mind, when fraught
With a passion so intense
One would think that it well
Might drown all life in the eye,—
That it should, by being so overwrought,   **110**
Suddenly strike on a sharper sense
For a shell, or a flower, little things
Which else would have been past by!
And now I remember, I,
When he lay dying there,
I noticed one of his many rings—
For he had many, poor worm—and thought,
It is his mother's hair.

IX

Who knows if he be dead?
Whether I need have fled?   **120**
Am I guilty of blood?
However this may be,
Comfort her, comfort her, all things good,
While I am over the sea!
Let me and my passionate love go by,
But speak to her all things holy and high,
Whatever happen to me!
'Me and my harmful love go by;
But come to her waking, find her asleep,
Powers of the height, Powers of the deep,   **130**
And comfort her tho' I die!

III

Courage, poor heart of stone!
I will not ask thee why
Thou canst not understand
That thou art left for ever alone;
Courage, poor stupid heart of stone!—
Or if I ask thee why,
Care not thou to reply:
She is but dead, and the time is at hand
When thou shalt more than die.   140

IV [1]

I

O that 'twere possible
After long grief and pain
To find the arms of my true love
Round me once again!

II

When I was wont to meet her
In the silent woody places
By the home that gave me birth,
We stood tranced in long embraces
Mixt with kisses sweeter, sweeter
Than anything on earth.   150

III

A shadow flits before me,
Not thou, but like to thee.
Ah, Christ, that it were possible
For one short hour to see
The souls we loved, that they might tell us
What and where they be!

[1] This lyric in its original form, printed in 1837, was the germ out of which *Maud* grew.

IV

It leads me forth at evening,
It lightly winds and steals
In a cold white robe before me,
When all my spirit reels   160
At the shouts, the leagues of lights,
And the roaring of the wheels.

V

Half the night I waste in sighs,
Half in dreams I sorrow after
The delight of early skies;
In a wakeful doze I sorrow
For the hand, the lips, the eyes,
For the meeting of the morrow,
The delight of happy laughter,
The delight of low replies.   170

VI

'T is a morning pure and sweet,
And a dewy splendor falls
On the little flower that clings
To the turrets and the walls;
'T is a morning pure and sweet,
And the light and shadow fleet.
She is walking in the meadow,
And the woodland echo rings;
In a moment we shall meet.
She is singing in the meadow,   180
And the rivulet at her feet
Ripples on in light and shadow
To the ballad that she sings.

VII

Do I hear her sing as of old,
My bird with the shining head,
My own dove with the tender eye?

But there rings on a sudden a passionate cry,
There is some one dying or dead,
And a sullen thunder is roll'd;
For a tumult shakes the city,   **190**
And I wake, my dream is fled.
In the shuddering dawn, behold,
Without knowledge, without pity,
By the curtains of my bed
That abiding phantom cold!

VIII

Get thee hence, nor come again,
Mix not memory with doubt,
Pass, thou deathlike type of pain,
Pass and cease to move about!
'T is the blot upon the brain   **200**
That *will* show itself without.

IX

Then I rise, the eave-drops fall,
And the yellow vapors choke
The great city sounding wide;
The day comes, a dull red ball
Wrapt in drifts of lurid smoke
On the misty river-tide.

X

Thro' the hubbub of the market
I steal, a wasted frame;
It crosses here, it crosses there,   **210**
Thro' all that crowd confused and loud,
The shadow still the same;
And on my heavy eyelids
My anguish hangs like shame.

XI

Alas for her that met me,
That heard me softly call,

Came glimmering thro' the laurels
At the quiet evenfall,
In the garden by the turrets
Of the old manorial hall!   220

XII

Would the happy spirit descend
From the realms of light and song,
In the chamber or the street,
As she looks among the blest,
Should I fear to greet my friend
Or to say "Forgive the wrong,"
Or to ask her, "Take me, sweet,
To the regions of thy rest"?

XIII

But the broad light glares and beats,
And the shadow flits and fleets   230
And will not let me be;
And I loathe the squares and streets,
And the faces that one meets,
Hearts with no love for me.
Always I long to creep
Into some still cavern deep,
There to weep, and weep, and weep
My whole soul out to thee.

V

I

Dead, long dead,
Long dead!   240
And my heart is a handful of dust,
And the wheels go over my head,
And my bones are shaken with pain,
For into a shallow grave they are thrust,
Only a yard beneath the street,
And the hoofs of the horses beat, beat,

The hoofs of the horses beat,
Beat into my scalp and my brain,
With never an end to the stream of passing feet,
Driving, hurrying, marrying, burying,   250
Clamor and rumble, and ringing and clatter;
And here beneath it is all as bad,
For I thought the dead had peace, but it is not so.
To have no peace in the grave, is that not sad?
But up and down and to and fro,
Ever about me the dead men go;
And then to hear a dead man chatter
Is enough to drive one mad.

II

Wretchedest age, since Time began,
They cannot even bury a man;   260
And tho' we paid our tithes in the days that are gone,
Not a bell was rung, not a prayer was read.
It is that which makes us loud in the world of the dead;
There is none that does his work, not one.
A touch of their office might have sufficed,
But the churchmen fain would kill their church,
As the churches have kill'd their Christ.

III

See, there is one of us sobbing,
No limit to his distress;
And another, a lord of all things, praying   270
To his own great self, as I guess;
And another, a statesman there, betraying
His party-secret, fool, to the press;
And yonder a vile physician, blabbing
The case of his patient—all for what?
To tickle the maggot born in an empty head,
And wheedle a world that loves him not,
For it is but a world of the dead.

IV

Nothing but idiot gabble!
For the prophecy given of old   286

And then not understood,
Has come to pass as foretold;
Not let any man think for the public good,
But babble, merely for babble.
For I never whisper'd a private affair
Within the hearing of cat or mouse,
No, not to myself in the closet alone,
But I heard it shouted at once from the top of the house;
Everything came to be known.
Who told *him* we were there?   290

V

Not that gray old wolf, for he came not back
From the wilderness, full of wolves, where he used to lie;
He has gather'd the bones for his o'ergrown whelp to crack—
Crack them now for yourself, and howl, and die.

VI

Prophet, curse me the blabbing lip,
And curse me the British vermin, the rat;
I know not whether he came in the Hanover ship,
But I know that he lies and listens mute
In an ancient mansion's crannies and holes.
Arsenic, arsenic, sure, would do it,   300
Except that now we poison our babes, poor souls!
It is all used up for that.

VII

Tell him now: she is standing here at my head;
Not beautiful now, not even kind;
He may take her now; for she never speaks her mind.
But is ever the one thing silent here.
She is not *of* us, as I divine;
She comes from another stiller world of the dead,
Stiller, not fairer than mine.

VIII

But I know where a garden grows,   310
Fairer than aught in the world beside,

All made up of the lily and rose
That blow by night, when the season is good,
To the sound of dancing music and flutes:
It is only flowers, they had no fruits,
And I almost fear they are not roses, but blood;
For the keeper was one, so full of pride,
He linkt a dead man there to a spectral bride;
For he, if he had not been a Sultan of brutes,
Would he have that hole in his side?   320

IX

But what will the old man say?
He laid a cruel snare in a pit
To catch a friend of mine one stormy day;
Yet now I could even weep to think of it;
For what will the old man say
When he comes to the second corpse in the pit?

X

Friend, to be struck by the public foe,
Then to strike him and lay him low,
That were a public merit, far,
Whatever the Quaker holds, from sin;   330
But the red life spilt for a private blow—
I swear to you, lawful and lawless war
Are scarcely even akin.

XI

O me, why have they not buried me deep enough?
Is it kind to have made me a grave so rough,
Me, that was never a quiet sleeper?
Maybe still I am but half-dead;
Then I cannot be wholly dumb.
I will cry to the steps above my head
And somebody, surely, some kind heart will come   340
To bury me, bury me
Deeper, ever so little deeper.

PART III

I

My life has crept so long on a broken wing
Thro' cells of madness, haunts of horror and fear,
That I come to be grateful at last for a little thing.
My mood is changed, for it fell at a time of year
When the face of night is fair on the dewy downs,
And the shining daffodil dies, and the Charioteer
And starry Gemini hang like glorious crowns
Over Orion's grave low down in the west,
That like a silent lightning under the stars
She seem'd to divide in a dream from a band of the blest,   **10**
And spoke of a hope for the world in the coming wars—
"And in that hope, dear soul, let trouble have rest,
Knowing I tarry for thee," and pointed to Mars
As he glow'd like a ruddy shield on the Lion's breast.

II

And it was but a dream, yet it yielded a dear delight
To have look'd, tho' but in a dream, upon eyes so fair,
That had been in a weary world my one thing bright;
And it was but a dream, yet it lighten'd my despair
When I thought that a war would arise in defence of **the right,**
That an iron tyranny now should bend or cease,   **20**
The glory of manhood stand on his ancient height,
Nor Britain's one sole God be the millionaire.
No more shall commerce be all in all, and Peace
Pipe on her pastoral hillock a languid note,
And watch her harvest ripen, her herd increase,
Nor the cannon-bullet rust on a slothful shore,
And the cobweb woven across the cannon's throat
Shall shake its threaded tears in the wind no more.

III

And as months ran on and rumor of battle grew,
"It is time, it is time, O passionate heart," said I,—   **30**

For I cleaved to a cause that I felt to be pure and true,—
"It is time, O passionate heart and morbid eye,
That old hysterical mock-disease should die."
And I stood on a giant deck and mixt my breath
With a loyal people shouting a battle-cry,
Till I saw the dreary phantom arise and fly
Far into the North, and battle, and seas of death.

IV

Let it go or stay, so I wake to the higher aims
Of a land that has lost for a little her lust of gold,
And love of a peace that was full of wrongs and shames,   40
Horrible, hateful, monstrous, not to be told;
And hail once more to the banner of battle unroll'd!
Tho' many a light shall darken, and many shall weep
For those that are crush'd in the clash of jarring claims,
Yet God's just wrath shall be wreak'd on a giant liar,
And many a darkness into the light shall leap,
And shine in the sudden making of splendid names,
And noble thought be freer under the sun,
And the heart of a people beat with one desire;
For the peace, that I deem'd no peace, is over and done,   50
And now by the side of the Black and the Baltic deep,
And deathful-grinning mouths of the fortress, flames
The blood-red blossom of war with a heart of fire.

V

Let it flame or fade, and the war roll down like a wind,
We have proved we have hearts in a cause, we are noble still,
And myself have awaked, as it seems, to the better mind.
It is better to fight for the good than to rail at the ill;
I have felt with my native land, I am one with my kind,
I embrace the purpose of God, and the doom assign'd.
                         [1854–55; publ. 1855, 1856]

EXPERIMENTS

IN QUANTITY

ON TRANSLATIONS OF HOMER

(Hexameters and Pentameters)

THESE lame hexameters the strong-wing'd music of Homer!
  No—but a most burlesque barbarous experiment.
When was a harsher sound ever heard, ye Muses, in England?
  When did a frog coarser croak upon our Helicon?
Hexameters no worse than daring Germany gave us,
  Barbarous experiment, barbarous hexameters.

MILTON

(Alcaics)

O MIGHTY-MOUTH'D inventor of harmonies,
O skill'd to sing of Time or Eternity,
    God-gifted organ-voice of England,
        Milton, a name to resound for ages;
Whose Titan angels, Gabriel, Abdiel,
Starr'd from Jehovah's gorgeous armories,
    Tower, as the deep-domed empyrean
        Rings to the roar of an angel onset!
Me rather all that bowery loneliness,
The brooks of Eden mazily murmuring,   10
    And bloom profuse and cedar arches
        Charm, as a wanderer out in ocean,
Where some refulgent sunset of India
Streams o'er a rich ambrosial ocean isle,
    And crimson-hued the stately palm-woods
        Whisper in odorous heights of even.

(Hendecasyllabics)

O you chorus of indolent reviewers,
Irresponsible, indolent reviewers,
Look, I come to the test, a tiny poem
All composed in a metre of Catullus,
All in quantity, careful of my motion,
Like the skater on ice that hardly bears him,
Lest I fall unawares before the people,
Waking laughter in indolent reviewers.
Should I flounder awhile without a tumble
Thro' this metrification of Catullus,   10
They should speak to me not without a welcome,
All that chorus of indolent reviewers.
Hard, hard, hard is it, only not to tumble,
So fantastical is the dainty metre.
Wherefore slight me not wholly, nor believe me
Too presumptuous, indolent reviewers.
O blatant Magazines, regard me rather—
Since I blush to belaud myself a moment—
As some rare little rose, a piece of inmost
Horticultural art, or half coquette-like   20
Maiden, not to be greeted unbenignly.

SPECIMEN OF A TRANSLATION OF THE ILIAD
IN BLANK VERSE

[ILIAD, VIII. 542–561]

So HECTOR spake; the Trojans roar'd applause;
Then loosed their sweating horses from the yoke,
And each beside his chariot bound his own;
And oxen from the city, and goodly sheep
In haste they drove, and honey-hearted wine
And bread from out the houses brought, and heap'd
Their firewood, and the winds from off the plain
Roll'd the rich vapor far into the heaven.
And these all night upon the bridge[1] of war

[1] Or, ridge. [Tennyson's note]

Sat glorying; many a fire before them blazed.   10
As when in heaven the stars about the moon
Look beautiful, when all the winds are laid,
And every height comes out, and jutting peak
And valley, and the immeasurable heavens
Break open to their highest, and all the stars
Shine, and the shepherd gladdens in his heart;
So many a fire between the ships and stream
Of Xanthus blazed before the towers of Troy,
A thousand on the plain; and close by each
Sat fifty in the blaze of burning fire;   20
And eating hoary grain and pulse the steeds,
Fixt by their cars, waited the golden dawn.

[publ. 1863]

IN THE VALLEY OF CAUTERETZ

ALL along the valley, stream that flashest white,
Deepening thy voice with the deepening of the night,
All along the valley, where thy waters flow,
I walk'd with one I loved two and thirty years ago.
All along the valley, while I walk'd to-day,
The two and thirty years were a mist that rolls away;
For all along the valley, down thy rocky bed,
Thy living voice to me was as the voice of the dead,
And all along the valley, by rock and cave and tree,
The voice of the dead was a living voice to me.   10

[1861; publ. 1864]

NORTHERN FARMER

OLD STYLE

I

WHEER 'asta beän saw long and meä liggin' 'ere aloän?
Noorse? thourt nowt o' a noorse; whoy, Doctor's abeän an' agoän;

1 *'asta beän,* hast thou been; *saw,* so; *liggin',* lying   2 *noorse,* nurse;
nowt, nought

Says that I moänt 'a naw moor aäle, but I beänt a fool;
Git ma my aäle, fur I beänt a-gawin' to breäk my rule.

II

Doctors, they knaws nowt, fur a says what 's nawways true,
Naw soort o' koind o' use to saäy the things that a do.
I've 'ed my point o' aäle ivry noight sin' I beän 'ere.
An' I've 'ed my quart ivry market-noight for foorty year.

III

Parson's a beän loikewoise, an' a sittin' ere o' my bed.
"The Amoighty's a taäkin o' you to 'issén, my friend," a
    said,   10
An' a towd ma my sins, an's toithe were due, an' I gied it in hond;
I done moy duty boy 'um, as I 'a done boy the lond.

IV

Larn'd a ma' beä. I reckons I 'annot sa mooch to iarn.
But a cast oop, thot a did, 'bout Bessy Marris's barne.
Thaw a knaws I hallus voäted wi' Squoire an' choorch an' staäte,
An' i' the woost o' toimes I wur niver agin the raäte.

V

An' I hallus coom'd to 's choorch afoor moy Sally wur deäd,
An' 'eärd 'um a bummin' awaäy loike a buzzard-clock ower my
    'eäd,
An' I niver knaw'd whot a meän'd but I thowt a 'ad summut to
    saäy,
An' I thowt a said whot a owt to 'a said, an' I coom'd awaäy.   20

3 *moänt 'a*, must not have   4 *ma*, me   5 *a*, he   7 *point*, pint   10
you, ou as in *hour; 'issen*, himself   11 *towd*, told; *toithe*, tithe   12
boy, by   13 *Larn'd a ma' beä*, learned he may be   14 *a cast oop*, he
cast up; *barne*, bairn   15 *Thaw*, though; *hallus*, always   16 *raäte*,
poor-tax   18 *buzzard-clock*. cockchafer   19 *summut*, somewhat   24
owt, ought.

VI

Bessy Marris's barne! tha knaws she laäid it to meä.
Mowt a beän, mayhap, for she wur a bad un, sheä.
'Siver, I kep 'um, I kep 'um, my lass, tha mun understond;
I done moy duty boy 'um, as I 'a done boy the lond.

VII

But Parson a cooms an' a goäs, an' a says it eäsy an' freeä:
"The Amoighty 's a taäkin o' you to 'issén, my friend," says 'eä
I weänt saäy men be loiars, thaw summun said it in 'aäste;
But 'e reäds wonn sarmin a weeäk, an' I 'a stubb'd Thurnaby
    waäste.

VIII

D' ya moind the waäste, my lass? naw, naw, tha was not borr
    then;
Theer wur a boggle in it, I often 'eärd 'um mysen;   30
Moäst loike a butter-bump, fur I 'eärd 'um about an' about,
But I stubb'd 'um oop wi' the lot, an' raäved an' rembled 'um out.

IX

Keäper's it wur; fo' they fun 'um theer a-laäid of 'is faäce
Down i' the woild 'enemies afoor I coom'd to the plaäce.
Noäks or Thimbleby—toäner 'ed shot 'um as deäd as a naäil.
Noäks wur 'ang'd for it oop at 'soize—but git ma my aäle.

X

Dubbut looök at the waäste; theer warn't not feeäd for a cow;
Nowt at all but bracken an' fuzz, an' looök at it now—

22 *Mowt a beän*, might have been   23 *'Siver*, howsoever; *mun*, must
27 *summun*, someone (David, Psalm cxvi)   28 *wonn sarmin*, one
sermon; *stubb'd*, cleared   30 *boggle*, bogy, ghost   31 *butter-bump*,
bittern   32 *raäved an' rembled*, tore up and threw away   33 *Keäper's*,
the gamekeeper's; *fun*, found   34 *'enemies*, anemones   35 *toäner*, one
or other   36 *'soize*, assizes   37 *Dobbut*, do but; *feeäd*, feed   38 *fuzz*,
furze

Warn't worth nowt a haäcre, an' now theer 's lots o' feeäd,
Fourscoor yows upon it, an' some on it down i' seeäd.   40

XI

Nobbut a bit on it 's left, an' I meän'd to 'a stubb'd it at fall,
Done it ta-year I meän'd, an' runn'd plow thruff it an' all,
If Godamoighty an' Parson 'ud nobbut let ma aloän,—
Meä, wi' haäte hoonderd haäcre o' Squoire's, an' lond o' my oän.

XII

Do Godamoighty knaw what a's doing a-taäkin' o' meä?
I beänt wonn as saws 'ere a beän an' yonder a peä;
An' Squoire 'ull be sa mad an' all—a' dear, a' dear!
And I 'a managed for Squoire coom Michaelmas thutty year.

XIII

A mowt 'a taäen owd Joänes, as 'ant not a 'aäpoth o' sense,
Or a mowt 'a taäen young Robins—a niver mended a fence;   50
But Godamoighty a moost taäke meä an' taäke ma now,
Wi' aäf the cows to cauve an' Thurnaby hoälms to plow!

XIV

Looök 'ow quoloty smoiles when they seeäs ma a passin' boy,
Says to thessén, naw doubt, "What a man a beä sewer-loy!"
Fur they knaws what I beän to Squoire sin' fust a coom'd to the
        'All;
I done moy duty by Squoire an' I done moy duty boy hall.

XV

Squoire 's i' Lunnon, an' summun I reckons 'ull 'a to wroite,
For whoä 's to howd the lond ater meä thot muddles ma quoit;
40 *fourscoor, ou* as in *hour; yows,* ewes; *seeäd,* clover   41 *Nobbut,*
nought but   42 *ta-year,* this year; *thruff,* through   43 *'ud nobbut,*
would only   46 *wonn as saws,* one that sows   49 *owd,* old; *'ant,* has
not; *'aäpoth,* halfpenny-worth   52 *aäf,* half; *cauve,* calve; *hoälms,*
low lands by a stream   53 *quoloty,* quality, the gentry   54 *thessen,*
themselves; *sewer-loy,* surely   55 *sin fust,* since first   58 *howd,* hold;
ater, after; *thot,* that; *quoit,* quite

Sartin-sewer I beä thot a weänt niver give it to Joänes,
Naw, nor a moänt to Robins—a niver rembles the stoäns.   60

XVI

But summun 'ull come ater meä mayhap wi' 'is kittle o' steäm
Huzzin' an' maäzin' the blessed feälds wi' the divil's oän teäm.
Sin' I mun doy I mun doy, thaw loife they says is sweet,
But sin' I mun doy I mun doy, for I couldn abeär to see it.

XVII

What atta stannin' theer fur, an' doesn bring ma the aäle?
Doctor 's a 'toättler, lass, an a 's hallus i' the owd taäle;
I weänt breäk rules fur Doctor, a knaws naw moor nor a floy;
Git ma my aäle, I tell tha, an' if I mun doy I mun doy.

[publ. 1864]

59 *Sartin-sewer*, certain sure; *a weänt niver*, he won't ever   60 *moänt*,
must not   61 *kittle o' steam*, steam thresher   62 *Huzzin' an' maäzin'*,
worrying and confusing   63 *doy*, die   66 *'toättler*, teetotaler; *taäle*,
tale   67 *floy*, fly

NORTHERN FARMER

NEW STYLE

I

Dosn't thou 'ear my 'erse's legs, as they canters awaäy?
Proputty, proputty, proputty—that's what I 'ears 'em saäy.
Proputty, proputty, proputty—Sam, thou 's an ass for thy paäins;
Theer's moor sense i' one o' 'is legs, nor in all thy braäins.

II

Woä—theer 's a craw to pluck wi' tha, Sam: yon 's Parson's
    'ouse—
Dosn't thou knaw that a man mun be eäther a man or a mouse?
Time to think on it then; for thou 'll be twenty to weeäk.
Proputty, proputty—woä then, woä—let ma 'ear mysén speäk.

1 *erse's*, horse's   2 *Proputty*, property   5 *craw*, crow   7 *to weeäk*,
this week   8 *mysén*, myself

III

Me an' thy muther, Sammy, 'as beän a-talkin' o' thee;
Thou 's beän talkin' to muther, an' she beän a-tellin' it me.   10
Thou 'll not marry for munny—thou 's sweet upo' Parson's lass—
Noä—thou 'll marry for luvv—an' we boäth on us thinks tha
     an ass.

IV

Seeä'd her to-daäy goä by—Saäint's-daäy—they was ringing the
     bells.
She 's a beauty, thou thinks—an' soä is scoors o' gells,
Them as 'as munny an' all—wot 's a beauty?—the flower as
     blaws.
But proputty, proputty sticks, an' proputty, proputty graws.

V

Do'ant be stunt; taäke time. I knaws what maäkes tha sa mad.
Warn't I craäzed fur the lasses mysén when I wur a lad?
But I knaw'd a Quaäker feller as often 'as towd ma this:
"Doänt thou marry for munny, but goä wheer munny is!"   20

VI

An' I went wheer munny war; an' thy muther coom to 'and,
Wi' lots o' munny laaïd by, an' a nicetish bit o' land.
Maäybe she warn't a beauty—I niver giv it a thowt—
But warn't she as good to cuddle an' kiss as a lass as 'ant nowt?

VII

Parson's lass 'ant nowt, an' she weänt 'a nowt when 'e 's deäd,
Mun be a guvness, lad, or summut, and addle her breäd.
Why? fur 'e 's nobbut a curate, an' weänt niver get hissén clear,
An' 'e maäde the bed as 'e ligs on afoor 'e coom'd to the shere.

14 *scoors o' gells*, scores of girls   17 *stunt*, stubborn   19 *towd*, told
24 *'ant nowt*, has nothing   25 *weänt 'a*, will not have   26 *addle*, earn
27 *nobbut*, nothing but   28 *ligs*, lies; *shere*, shire

VIII

An' thin 'e coom'd to the parish wi' lots o' Varsity debt,
Stook to his taaïl they did, an' 'e 'ant got shut on 'em yet.   30
An' 'e ligs on 'is back i' the grip, wi' noän to lend 'im a shuvv,
Woorse nor a far-welter'd yowe; fur, Sammy, 'e married fur luvv.

IX

Luvv? what's luvv? thou can luvv thy lass an' 'er munny too,
Maäkin' 'em goä togither, as they've good right to do.
Couldn I luvv thy muther by cause o' 'er munny laaïd by?
Naäy—fur I luvv'd 'er a vast sight moor fur it; reäson why.

X

Ay, an' thy muther says thou wants to marry the lass,
Cooms of a gentleman burn; an' we boäth on us thinks tha an ass.
Woä then, proputty, wiltha?—an ass as near as mays nowt—
Woä then, wiltha? dangtha!—the bees is as fell as owt.   40

XI

Breäk me a bit o' the esh for his 'eäd, lad, out o' the fence!
Gentleman burn! what 's gentleman burn? is it shillins an' pence?
Proputty, proputty's ivrything 'ere, an', Sammy, I'm blest
If it is n't the saäme oop yonder, fur them as 'as it 's the best.

XII

Tis 'n them as 'as munny as breäks into 'ouses an' steäls,
Them as 'as coäts to their backs an' taäkes their regular meäls.
Noä, but it 's them as niver knaws wheer a meäl 's to be 'ad.
Taäke my word for it, Sammy, the poor in a loomp is bad.

30 *shut on,* clear of   31 *grip,* ditch; *shuvv,* shove   32 *far-welter'd
yowe,* ewe lying on her back   38 *burn,* born   39 *u iltha,* wilt thou;
mays nowt, makes no difference   40 *bees is as fell as owt,* flies are as
fierce as anything   41 *esh,* ash

XIII

Them or thir feythers, tha sees, mun 'a beän a laäzy lot,
Fur work mun 'a gone to the gittin' whiniver munny was got. 50
Feyther 'ad ammost nowt; leästways 'is munny was 'id.
But 'e tued an' moil'd issén deäd, an' 'e died a good un, 'e did.

XIV

Looök thou theer wheer Wrigglesby beck cooms out by the 'ill!
Feyther run oop to the farm, an' I runs oop to the mill;
An' I 'll run oop to the brig, an' that thou 'll live to see;
And if thou marries a good un I 'll leäve the land to thee.

XV

Thim 's my noätions, Sammy, wheerby I meäns to stick;
But if thou marries a bad un, I 'll leäve the land to Dick.—
Coom oop, proputty, proputty—that 's what I 'ears 'im saäy—
Proputty, proputty, proputty—canter an' canter awaäy. 60
[publ. 1869]

52 *tued an' moil'd,* toiled and drudged 53 *beck,* brook 55 *brig,* bridge

LUCRETIUS

Lucilia, wedded to Lucretius, found
Her master cold; for when the morning flush
Of passion and the first embrace had died
Between them, tho' he loved her none the less,
Yet often when the woman heard his foot
Return from pacings in the field, and ran
To greet him with a kiss, the master took
Small notice, or austerely, for—his mind
Half buried in some weightier argument,
Or fancy-borne perhaps upon the rise 10
And long roll of the hexameter—he past
To turn and ponder those three hundred scrolls
Left by the Teacher, whom he held divine.

She brook'd it not, but wrathful, petulant,
Dreaming some rival, sought and found a witch
Who brew'd the philtre which had power, they said,
To lead an errant passion home again.
And this, at times, she mingled with his drink,
And this destroy'd him; for the wicked broth
Confused the chemic labor of the blood,   20
And tickling the brute brain within the man's
Made havoc among those tender cells, and check'd
His power to shape. He loathed himself, and once
After a tempest woke upon a morn
That mock'd him with returning calm, and cried:

    "Storm in the night! for thrice I heard the rain
Rushing; and once the flash of a thunderbolt—
Methought I never saw so fierce a fork—
Struck out the streaming mountain-side, and show'd
A riotous confluence of watercourses   30
Blanching and billowing in a hollow of it,
Where all but yester-eve was dusty-dry.

    "Storm, and what dreams, ye holy Gods, what dreams!
For thrice I waken'd after dreams. Perchance
We do but recollect the dreams that come
Just ere the waking. Terrible: for it seem'd
A void was made in Nature; all her bonds
Crack'd; and I saw the flaring atom-streams
And torrents of her myriad universe,
Ruining along the illimitable inane,   40
Fly on to clash together again, and make
Another and another frame of things
For ever. That was mine, my dream, I knew it—
Of and belonging to me, as the dog
With inward yelp and restless forefoot plies
His function of the woodland; but the next!
I thought that all the blood by Sylla shed
Came driving rainlike down again on earth,
And where it dash'd the reddening meadow, sprang
No dragon warriors from Cadmean teeth,   50
For these I thought my dream would show to me,
But girls, Hetairai, curious in their art,
Hired animalisms, vile as those that made

The mulberry-faced Dictator's orgies worse
Than aught they fable of the quiet Gods.
And hands they mixt, and yell'd and round me drove
In narrowing circles till I yell'd again
Half-suffocated, and sprang up, and saw—
Was it the first beam of my latest day?

"Then, then, from utter gloom stood out the breasts,   60
The breasts of Helen, and hoveringly a sword
Now over and now under, now direct,
Pointed itself to pierce, but sank down shamed
At all that beauty; and as I stared, a fire,
The fire that left a roofless Ilion,
Shot out of them, and scorch'd me that I woke.

"Is this thy vengeance, holy Venus, thine,
Because I would not one of thine own doves,
Not even a rose, were offer'd to thee? thine,
Forgetful how my rich proœmion makes   70
Thy glory fly along the Italian field,
In lays that will outlast thy deity?

"Deity? nay, thy worshippers. My tongue
Trips, or I speak profanely. Which of these
Angers thee most, or angers thee at all?
Not if thou be'st of those who, far aloof
From envy, hate and pity, and spite and scorn,
Live the great life which all our greatest fain
Would follow, centred in eternal calm.

"Nay, if thou canst, O Goddess, like ourselves   80
Touch, and be touch'd, then would I cry to thee
To kiss thy Mavors, roll thy tender arms
Round him, and keep him from the lust of blood
That makes a steaming slaughter-house of Rome.

"Ay, but I meant not thee; I meant not her
Whom all the pines of Ida shook to see
Slide from that quiet heaven of hers, and tempt
The Trojan, while his neatherds were abroad;
Nor her that o'er her wounded hunter wept
Her deity false in human-amorous tears;   90

Nor whom her beardless apple-arbiter
Decided fairest. Rather, O ye Gods,
Poet-like, as the great Sicilian called
Calliope to grace his golden verse—
Ay, and this Kypris also—did I take
That popular name of thine to shadow forth
The all-generating powers and genial heat
Of Nature, when she strikes thro' the thick blood
Of cattle, and light is large, and lambs are glad
Nosing the mother's udder, and the bird   100
Makes his heart voice amid the blaze of flowers;
Which things appear the work of mighty Gods.

   "The Gods! and if I go *my* work is left
Unfinish'd—*if* I go. The Gods, who haunt
The lucid interspace of world and world,
Where never creeps a cloud, or moves a wind,
Nor ever falls the least white star of snow,
Nor ever lowest roll of thunder moans,
Nor sound of human sorrow mounts to mar
Their sacred everlasting calm! and such,   110
Not all so fine, nor so divine a calm,
Not such, nor all unlike it, man may gain
Letting his own life go. The Gods, the Gods!
If all be atoms, how then should the Gods
Being atomic not be dissoluble,
Not follow the great law? My master held
That Gods there are, for all men so believe.
I prest my footsteps into his, and meant
Surely to lead my Memmius in a train
Of flowery clauses onward to the proof   120
That Gods there are, and deathless. Meant? I meant?
I have forgotten what I meant; my mind
Stumbles, and all my faculties are lamed.

   "Look where another of our Gods, the Sun,
Apollo, Delius, or of older use
All-seeing Hyperion—what you will—
Has mounted yonder; since he never sware,
Except his wrath were wreak'd on wretched man,
That he would only shine among the dead
Hereafter—tales! for never yet on earth   130

Could dead flesh creep, or bits of roasting ox
Moan round the spit—nor knows he what he sees;
King of the East altho' he seem, and girt
With song and flame and fragrance, slowly lifts
His golden feet on those empurpled stairs
That climb into the windy halls of heaven.
And here he glances on an eye new-born,
And gets for greeting but a wail of pain;
And here he stays upon a freezing orb
That fain would gaze upon him to the last;   140
And here upon a yellow eyelid fallen
And closed by those who mourn a friend in vain,
Not thankful that his troubles are no more.
And me, altho' his fire is on my face
Blinding, he sees not, nor at all can tell
Whether I mean this day to end myself,
Or lend an ear to Plato where he says,
That men like soldiers may not quit the post
Allotted by the Gods. But he that holds
The Gods are careless, wherefore need he care   150
Greatly for them, nor rather plunge at once,
Being troubled, wholly out of sight, and sink
Past earthquake—ay, and gout and stone, that break
Body toward death, and palsy, death-in-life,
And wretched age—and worst disease of all,
These prodigies of myriad nakednesses,
And twisted shapes of lust, unspeakable,
Abominable, strangers at my hearth
Not welcome, harpies miring every dish,
The phantom husks of something foully done,   160
And fleeting thro' the boundless universe,
And blasting the long quiet of my breast
With animal heat and dire insanity?

    "How should the mind, except it loved them, clasp
These idols to herself? or do they fly
Now thinner, and now thicker, like the flakes
In a fall of snow, and so press in, perforce
Of multitude, as crowds that in an hour
Of civic tumult jam the doors, and bear
The keepers down, and throng, their rags and they   170
The basest, far into that council-hall
Where sit the best and stateliest of the land?

"Can I not fling this horror off me again,
Seeing with how great ease Nature can smile,
Balmier and nobler from her bath of storm,
At random ravage? and how easily
The mountain there has cast his cloudy slough,
Now towering o'er him in serenest air,
A mountain o'er a mountain,—ay, and within
All hollow as the hopes and fears of men?   180

"But who was he that in the garden snared
Picus and Faunus, rustic Gods? a tale
To laugh at—more to laugh at in myself—
For look! what is it? there? yon arbutus
Totters; a noiseless riot underneath
Strikes through the wood, sets all the tops quivering—
The mountain quickens into Nymph and Faun;
And here an Oread—how the sun delights
To glance and shift about her slippery sides,
And rosy knees and supple roundedness,   190
And budded bosom-peaks—who this way runs
Before the rest!—A satyr, a satyr, see,
Follows; but him I proved impossible;
Twy-natured is no nature. Yet he draws
Nearer and nearer, and I scan him now
Beastlier than any phantom of his kind
That ever butted his rough brother-brute
For lust or lusty blood or provender.
I hate, abhor, spit, sicken at him; and she
Loathes him as well; such a precipitate heel,   200
Fledged as it were with Mercury's ankle-wing,
Whirls her to me—but will she fling herself
Shameless upon me? Catch her, goat-foot! nay,
Hide, hide them, million-myrtled wilderness,
And cavern-shadowing laurels, hide! do I wish—
What?—that the bush were leafless? or to whelm
All of them in one massacre? O ye Gods,
I know you careless, yet, behold, to you
From childly wont and ancient use I call—
I thought I lived securely as yourselves—   210
No lewdness, narrowing envy, monkey-spite,
No madness of ambition, avarice, none;
No larger feast than under plane or pine

With neighbors laid along the grass, to take
Only such cups as left us friendly-warm,
Affirming each his own philosophy—
Nothing to mar the sober majesties
Of settled, sweet, Epicurean life.
But now it seems some unseen monster lays
His vast and filthy hands upon my will,   224
Wrenching it backward into his, and spoils
My bliss in being; and it was not great,
For save when shutting reasons up in rhythm,
Or Heliconian honey in living words,
To make a truth less harsh, I often grew
Tired of so much within our little life,
Or of so little in our little life—
Poor little life that toddles half an hour
Crown'd with a flower or two, and there an end—
And since the nobler pleasure seems to fade,   230
Why should I, beastlike as I find myself,
Not manlike end myself?—our privilege—
What beast has heart to do it? And what man,
What Roman would be dragg'd in triumph thus?
Not I; not he, who bears one name with her
Whose death-blow struck the dateless doom of kings,
When, brooking not the Tarquin in her veins,
She made her blood in sight of Collatine
And all his peers, flushing the guiltless air,
Spout from the maiden fountain in her heart.   240
And from it sprang the Commonwealth, which breaks
As I am breaking now!

                "And therefore now
Let her, that is the womb and tomb of all,
Great Nature, take, and forcing far apart
Those blind beginnings that have made me man,
Dash them anew together at her will
Thro' all her cycles—into man once more,
Or beast or bird or fish, or opulent flower.
But till this cosmic order everywhere
Shatter'd into one earthquake in one day   250
Cracks all to pieces,—and that hour perhaps
Is not so far when momentary man
Shall seem no more a something to himself,

But he, his hopes and hates, his homes and fanes,
And even his bones long laid within the grave,
The very sides of the grave itself shall pass,
Vanishing, atom and void, atom and void,
Into the unseen for ever,—till that hour,
My golden work in which I told a truth
That stays the rolling Ixionian wheel,   260
And numbs the Fury's ringlet-snake, and plucks
The mortal soul from out immortal hell,
Shall stand. Ay, surely; then it fails at last
And perishes as I must; for O Thou,
Passionless bride, divine Tranquillity,
Yearn'd after by the wisest of the wise,
Who fail to find thee, being as thou art
Without one pleasure and without one pain,
Howbeit I know thou surely must be mine
Or soon or late, yet out of season, thus   270
I woo thee roughly, for thou carest not
How roughly men may woo thee so they win—
Thus—thus—the soul flies out and dies in the air."

   With that he drove the knife into his side.
She heard him raging, heard him fall, ran in,
Beat breast, tore hair, cried out upon herself
As having fail'd in duty to him, shriek'd
That she but meant to win him back, fell on him,
Clasp'd, kiss'd him, wail'd. He answer'd, "Care not thou!
Thy duty? What is duty? Fare thee well!"   280
                               [publ. 1868]

THE HIGHER PANTHEISM

THE sun, the moon, the stars, the seas, the hills and the plains,—
Are not these, O Soul, the Vision of Him who reigns?

Is not the Vision He, tho' He be not that which He seems?
Dreams are true while they last, and do we not live in dreams?

Earth, these solid stars, this weight of body and limb,
Are they not sign and symbol of thy division from Him?

Dark is the world to thee; thyself art the reason why,
For is He not all but thou, that hast power to feel "I am I"?

Glory about thee, without thee; and thou fulfillest thy doom,
Making Him broken gleams and a stifled splendor and gloom. 10

Speak to Him, thou, for He hears, and Spirit with Spirit can
         meet—
Closer is He than breathing, and nearer than hands and feet.

God is law, say the wise; O Soul, and let us rejoice,
For if He thunder by law the thunder is yet His voice.

Law is God, say some; no God at all, says the fool,
For all we have power to see is a straight staff bent in a pool;

And the ear of man cannot hear, and the eye of man cannot see;
But if we could see and hear, this Vision—were it not He?
                                        [publ. 1869]

FLOWER IN THE CRANNIED WALL

FLOWER in the crannied wall,
I pluck you out of the crannies,
I hold you here, root and all, in my hand,
Little flower—but *if* I could understand
What you are, root and all, and all in all,
I should know what God and man is.
                                        [publ. 1869]

IN THE GARDEN AT SWAINSTON [1]

NIGHTINGALES warbled without,
    Within was weeping for thee;
Shadows of three dead men

---

[1] The home of Sir John Simeon (d. 1870). The other two of the
"three dead men" were Arthur Hallam and Henry Lushington.

Walk'd in the walks with me,
Shadows of three dead men, and thou wast one of the three,

Nightingales sang in his woods,
  The Master was far away;
Nightingales warbled and sang
  Of a passion that lasts but a day;
  Still in the house in his coffin the Prince of courtesy lay.   **10**

Two dead men have I known
  In courtesy like to thee;
Two dead men have I loved
  With a love that ever will be;
  Three dead men have I loved. and thou art last of the three

[1870; publ. 1874]

IDYLLS OF THE KING

IN TWELVE BOOKS

"Flos Regum Arthurus."—Joseph of Exeter.

DEDICATION

THESE to His Memory—since he held them dear,
Perchance as finding there unconsciously
Some image of himself—I dedicate,
I dedicate, I consecrate with tears—
These Idylls.

       And indeed he seems to me
Scarce other than my king's ideal knight,
"Who reverenced his conscience as his king;
Whose glory was, redressing human wrong;
Who spake no slander, no, nor listen'd to it;
Who loved one only and who clave to her—"   10
Her—over all whose realms to their last isle,
Commingled with the gloom of imminent war,
The shadow of his loss drew like eclipse,
Darkening the world. We have lost him; he is gone.
We know him now; all narrow jealousies
Are silent, and we see him as he moved,
How modest, kindly, all-accomplish'd, wise,
With what sublime repression of himself,
And in what limits, and how tenderly;
Not swaying to this faction or to that;   20
Not making his high place the lawless perch
Of wing'd ambitions, nor a vantage-ground
For pleasure; but thro' all this tract of years
Wearing the white flower of a blameless life,
Before a thousand peering littlenesses,
In that fierce light which beats upon a throne
And blackens every blot; for where is he
Who dares foreshadow for an only son
A lovelier life, a more unstain'd, than his?
Or how should England dreaming of *his* sons   30
Hope more for these than some inheritance

320

Of such a life, a heart, a mind as thine,
Thou noble Father of her Kings to be,
Laborious for her people and her poor—
Voice in the rich dawn of an ampler day—
Far-sighted summoner of War and Waste
To fruitful strifes and rivalries of peace——
Sweet nature gilded by the gracious gleam
Of letters, dear to Science, dear to Art,
Dear to thy land and ours, a Prince indeed,   **40**
Beyond all titles, and a household name,
Hereafter, thro' all times, Albert the Good.

Break not, O woman's-heart, but still endure;
Break not, for thou art royal, but endure,
Remembering all the beauty of that star
Which shone so close beside thee that ye made
One light together, but has past and leaves
The Crown a lonely splendor.

                              May all love,
His love, unseen but felt, o'ershadow thee,
The love of all thy sons encompass thee,   **50**
The love of all thy daughters cherish thee,
The love of all thy people comfort thee,
Till God's love set thee at his side again!
                              [publ. 1862]

THE COMING OF ARTHUR

LEODOGRAN, the king of Cameliard,
Had one fair daughter, and none other child;
And she was fairest of all flesh on earth,
Guinevere, and in her his one delight.

For many a petty king ere Arthur came
Ruled in this isle and, ever waging war
Each upon other, wasted all the land;
And still from time to time the heathen host
Swarm'd over-seas, and harried what was left.
And so there grew great tracts of wilderness,   **10**

Wherein the beast was ever more and more,
But man was less and less, till Arthur came.
For first Aurelius lived and fought and died,
And after him King Uther fought and died,
But either fail'd to make the kingdom one.
And after these King Arthur for a space,
And thro' the puissance of his Table Round,
Drew all their petty princedoms under him,
Their king and head, and made a realm and reign'd.

   And thus the land of Cameliard was waste,   20
Thick with wet woods, and many a beast therein,
And none or few to scare or chase the beast;
So that wild dog and wolf and boar and bear
Came night and day, and rooted in the fields,
And wallow'd in the gardens of the King.
And ever and anon the wolf would steal
The children and devour, but now and then,
Her own brood lost or dead, lent her fierce teat
To human sucklings; and the children, housed
In her foul den, there at their meat would growl,   30
And mock their foster-mother on four feet,
Till, straighten'd, they grew up to wolf-like men,
Worse than the wolves. And King Leodogran
Groan'd for the Roman legions here again
And Cæsar's eagle. Then his brother king,
Urien, assail'd him; last a heathen horde,
Reddening the sun with smoke and earth with blood,
And on the spike that split the mother's heart
Spitting the child, brake on him, till, amazed,
He knew not whither he should turn for aid.   40

   But—for he heard of Arthur newly crown'd,
Tho' not without an uproar made by those
Who cried, "He is not Uther's son"—the King
Sent to him, saying, "Arise, and help us thou!
For here between the man and beast we die."

   And Arthur yet had done no deed of arms,
But heard the call and came; and Guinevere
Stood by the castle walls to watch him pass;
But since he neither wore on helm or shield

The golden symbol of his kinglihood,   50
But rode a simple knight among his knights,
And many of these in richer arms than he,
She saw him not, or mark'd not, if she saw,
One among many, tho' his face was bare.
But Arthur, looking downward as he past,
Felt the light of her eyes into his life
Smite on the sudden, yet rode on, and pitch'd
His tents beside the forest. Then he drave
The heathen; after, slew the beast, and fell'd
The forest, letting in the sun, and made   60
Broad pathways for the hunter and the knight,
And so return'd.

              For while he linger'd there,
A doubt that ever smoulder'd in the hearts
Of those great lords and barons of his realm
Flash'd forth and into war; for most of these,
Colleaguing with a score of petty kings,
Made head against him, crying: "Who is he
That he should rule us? who hath proven him
King Uther's son? for lo! we look at him,
And find nor face nor bearing, limbs nor voice,   70
Are like to those of Uther whom we knew.
This is the son of Gorloïs, not the King;
This is the son of Anton, not the King."

   And Arthur, passing thence to battle, felt
Travail, and throes and agonies of the life,
Desiring to be join'd with Guinevere,
And thinking as he rode: "Her father said
That there between the man and beast they die.
Shall I not lift her from this land of beasts
Up to my throne and side by side with me?   80
What happiness to reign a lonely king,
Vext—O ye stars that shudder over me,
O earth that soundest hollow under me,
Vext with waste dreams? for saving I be join'd
To her that is the fairest under heaven,
I seem as nothing in the mighty world,
And cannot will my will nor work my work
Wholly, nor make myself in mine own realm

Victor and lord. But were I join'd with her,
Then might we live together as one life,   **90**
And reigning with one will in everything
Have power on this dark land to lighten it,
And power on this dead world to make it live."

    Thereafter—as he speaks who tells the tale—
When Arthur reach'd a field of battle bright
With pitch'd pavilions of his foe, the world
Was all so clear about him that he saw
The smallest rock far on the faintest hill,
And even in high day the morning star.
So when the King had set his banner broad,   **100**
At once from either side, with trumpet-blast,
And shouts, and clarions shrilling unto blood,
The long-lanced battle let their horses run.
And now the barons and the kings prevail'd,
And now the King, as here and there that war
Went swaying; but the Powers who walk the world
Made lightnings and great thunders over him,
And dazed all eyes, till Arthur by main might,
And mightier of his hands with every blow,
And leading all his knighthood threw the kings,   **110**
Carádos, Urien, Cradlemont of Wales,
Claudius, and Clariance of Northumberland,
The King Brandagoras of Latangor,
With Anguisant of Erin, Morganore,
And Lot of Orkney. Then, before a voice
As dreadful as the shout of one who sees
To one who sins, and deems himself alone
And all the world asleep, they swerved and brake
Flying, and Arthur call'd to stay the brands
That hack'd among the flyers, "Ho! they yield!"   **120**
So like a painted battle the war stood
Silenced, the living quiet as the dead,
And in the heart of Arthur joy was lord.
He laugh'd upon his warrior whom he loved
And honor'd most. "Thou dost not doubt me King,
So well thine arm hath wrought for me to-day."
"Sir and my liege," he cried, "the fire of God
Descends upon thee in the battle-field.
I know thee for my King!" Whereat the two,

For each had warded either in the fight,   130
Sware on the field of death a deathless love.
And Arthur said, "Man's word is God in man;
Let chance what will, I trust thee to the death."

Then quickly from the foughten field he sent
Ulfius, and Brastias, and Bedivere,
His new-made knights, to King Leodogran,
Saying, "If I in aught have served thee well,
Give me thy daughter Guinevere to wife."

Whom when he heard, Leodogran in heart
Debating—"How should I that am a king,   140
However much he holp me at my need,
Give my one daughter saving to a king,
And a king's son?"—lifted his voice, and call'd
A hoary man, his chamberlain, to whom
He trusted all things, and of him required
His counsel: "Knowest thou aught of Arthur's birth?"

Then spake the hoary chamberlain and said:
"Sir King, there be but two old men that know;
And each is twice as old as I; and one
Is Merlin, the wise man that ever served   150
King Uther thro' his magic art, and one
Is Merlin's master—so they call him—Bleys,
Who taught him magic; but the scholar ran
Before the master, and so far that Bleys
Laid magic by, and sat him down, and wrote
All things and whatsoever Merlin did
In one great annal-book, where after-years
Will learn the secret of our Arthur's birth."

To whom the King Leodogran replied:
"O friend, had I been holpen half as well   160
By this King Arthur as by thee to-day,
Then beast and man had had their share of me;
But summon here before us yet once more
Ulfius, and Brastias, and Bedivere."

Then, when they came before him, the king said:
"I have seen the cuckoo chased by lesser fowl,

And reason in the chase; but wherefore now
Do these your lords stir up the heat of war,
Some calling Arthur born of Gorloïs,
Others of Anton? Tell me, ye yourselves,   **170**
Hold ye this Arthur for King Uther's son?"

And Ulfius and Brastias answer'd, "Ay."
Then Bedivere, the first of all his knights
Knighted by Arthur at his crowning, spake—
For bold in heart and act and word was he,
Whenever slander breathed against the King—

"Sir, there be many rumors on this head;
For there be those who hate him in their hearts,
Call him baseborn, and since his ways are sweet,
And theirs are bestial, hold him less than man;   **180**
And there be those who deem him more than man,
And dream he dropt from heaven. But my belief
In all this matter—so ye care to learn—
Sir, for ye know that in King Uther's time
The prince and warrior Gorloïs, he that held
Tintagil castle by the Cornish sea,
Was wedded with a winsome wife, Ygerne;
And daughters had she borne him,—one whereof,
Lot's wife, the Queen of Orkney, Bellicent,
Hath ever like a loyal sister cleaved   **190**
To Arthur,—but a son she had not borne.
And Uther cast upon her eyes of love;
But she, a stainless wife to Gorloïs,
So loathed the bright dishonor of his love
That Gorloïs and King Uther went to war,
And overthrown was Gorloïs and slain.
Then Uther in his wrath and heat besieged
Ygerne within Tintagil, where her men,
Seeing the mighty swarm about their walls,
Left her and fled, and Uther enter'd in,   **200**
And there was none to call to but himself.
So, compass'd by the power of the king,
Enforced she was to wed him in her tears,
And with a shameful swiftness; afterward,
Not many moons, King Uther died himself,
Moaning and wailing for an heir to rule

After him, lest the realm should go to wrack.
And that same night, the night of the new year,
By reason of the bitterness and grief
That vext his mother, all before his time   **210**
Was Arthur born, and all as soon as born
Deliver'd at a secret postern-gate
To Merlin, to be holden far apart
Until his hour should come, because the lords
Of that fierce day were as the lords of this,
Wild beasts, and surely would have torn the child
Piecemeal among them, had they known; for each
But sought to rule for his own self and hand,
And many hated Uther for the sake
Of Gorloïs. Wherefore Merlin took the child,   **220**
And gave him to Sir Anton, an old knight
And ancient friend of Uther; and his wife
Nursed the young prince, and rear'd him with her own;
And no man knew. And ever since the lords
Have foughten like wild beasts among themselves,
So that the realm has gone to wrack; but now,
This year, when Merlin—for his hour had come—
Brought Arthur forth, and set him in the hall,
Proclaiming, 'Here is Uther's heir, your king,'
A hundred voices cried: 'Away with him!   **230**
No king of ours! a son of Gorloïs he,
Or else the child of Anton, and no king,
Or else baseborn.' Yet Merlin thro' his craft,
And while the people clamor'd for a king,
Had Arthur crown'd; but after, the great lords
Banded, and so brake out in open war."

Then while the king debated with himself
If Arthur were the child of shamefulness,
Or born the son of Gorloïs after death,
Or Uther's son and born before his time,   **240**
Or whether there were truth in anything
Said by these three, there came to Cameliard,
With Gawain and young Modred, her two sons,
Lot's wife, the Queen of Orkney, Bellicent;
Whom as he could, not as he would, the king
Made feast for, saying, as they sat at meat:
"A doubtful throne is ice on summer seas.

Ye come from Arthur's court. Victor his men
Report him! Yea, but ye—think ye this king—
So many those that hate him, and so strong,   250
So few his knights, however brave they be—
Hath body enow to hold his foemen down?"

    "O King," she cried, "and I will tell thee: few,
Few, but all brave, all of one mind with him;
For I was near him when the savage yells
Of Uther's peerage died, and Arthur sat
Crowned on the daïs, and his warriors cried,
'Be thou the king, and we will work thy will
Who love thee.' Then the King in low deep tones,
And simple words of great authority,   260
Bound them by so strait vows to his own self
That when they rose, knighted from kneeling, some
Were pale as at the passing of a ghost,
Some flush'd, and others dazed, as one who wakes
Half-blinded at the coming of a light.

    "But when he spake, and cheer'd his Table Round
With large, divine, and comfortable words,
Beyond my tongue to tell thee—I beheld
From eye to eye thro' all their Order flash
A momentary likeness of the King;   270
And ere it left their faces, thro' the cross
And those around it and the Crucified,
Down from the casement over Arthur, smote
Flame-color, vert, and azure, in three rays,
One falling upon each of three fair queens
Who stood in silence near his throne, the friends
Of Arthur, gazing on him, tall, with bright
Sweet faces, who will help him at his need.

    "And there I saw mage Merlin, whose vast wit
And hundred winters are but as the hands   280
Of loyal vassals toiling for their liege.

    "And near him stood the Lady of the Lake,
Who knows a subtler magic than his own—
Clothed in white samite, mystic, wonderful.
She gave the King his huge cross-hilted sword,

Whereby to drive the heathen out. A mist
Of incense curl'd about her, and her face
Wellnigh was hidden in the minster gloom;
But there was heard among the holy hymns
A voice as of the waters, for she dwells   290
Down in a deep—calm, whatsoever storms
May shake the world—and when the surface rolls,
Hath power to walk the waters like our Lord.

"There likewise I beheld Excalibur
Before him at his crowning borne, the sword
That rose from out the bosom of the lake,
And Arthur row'd across and took it—rich
With jewels, elfin Urim, on the hilt,
Bewildering heart and eye—the blade so bright
That men are blinded by it—on one side,   300
Graven in the oldest tongue of all this world,
'Take me,' but turn the blade and ye shall see,
And written in the speech ye speak yourself,
'Cast me away!' And sad was Arthur's face
Taking it, but old Merlin counsell'd him,
'Take thou and strike! the time to cast away
Is yet far-off.' So this great brand the king
Took, and by this will beat his foemen down."

Thereat Leodogran rejoiced, but thought
To sift his doubtings to the last, and ask'd,   310
Fixing full eyes of question on her face,
"The swallow and the swift are near akin,
But thou art closer to this noble prince,
Being his own dear sister;" and she said,
"Daughter of Gorloïs and Ygerne am I;"
"And therefore Arthur's sister?" ask'd the king.
She answer'd, "These be secret things," and sign'd
To those two sons to pass, and let them be.
And Gawain went, and breaking into song
Sprang out, and follow'd by his flying hair   320
Ran like a colt, and leapt at all he saw;
But Modred laid his ear beside the doors,
And there half-heard—the same that afterward
Struck for the throne, and striking found his doom.

And then the Queen made answer: "What know I?
For dark my mother was in eyes and hair,
And dark in hair and eyes am I; and dark
Was Gorloïs; yea, and dark was Uther too,
Wellnigh to blackness; but this king is fair
Beyond the race of Britons and of men.   330
Moreover, always in my mind I hear
A cry from out the dawning of my life,
A mother weeping, and I hear her say,
'O that ye had some brother, pretty one,
To guard thee on the rough ways of the world.'"

"Ay," said the king, "and hear ye such a cry?
But when did Arthur chance upon thee first?"

"O King!" she cried, "and I will tell thee true.
He found me first when yet a little maid.
Beaten I had been for a little fault   340
Whereof I was not guilty; and out I ran
And flung myself down on a bank of heath,
And hated this fair world and all therein,
And wept, and wish'd that I were dead; and he—
I know not whether of himself he came,
Or brought by Merlin, who, they say, can walk
Unseen at pleasure—he was at my side,
And spake sweet words, and comforted my heart,
And dried my tears, being a child with me.
And many a time he came, and evermore   350
As I grew greater grew with me; and sad
At times he seem'd, and sad with him was I,
Stern too at times, and then I loved him not,
But sweet again, and then I loved him well.
And now of late I see him less and less,
But those first days had golden hours for me,
For then I surely thought he would be king.

"But let me tell thee now another tale:
For Bleys, our Merlin's master, as they say,
Died but of late, and sent his cry to me,   360
To hear him speak before he left his life.
Shrunk like a fairy changeling lay the mage;
And when I enter'd told me that himself

And Merlin ever served about the king,
Uther, before he died; and on the night
When Uther in Tintagil past away
Moaning and wailing for an heir, the two
Left the still king, and passing forth to breathe,
Then from the castle gateway by the chasm
Descending thro' the dismal night—a night   370
In which the bounds of heaven and earth were lost—
Beheld, so high upon the dreary deeps
It seem'd in heaven, a ship, the shape thereof
A dragon wing'd, and all from-stem to stern
Bright with a shining people on the decks,
And gone as soon as seen. And then the two
Dropt to the cove, and watch'd the great sea fall.
Wave after wave, each mightier than the last.
Till last, a ninth one, gathering half the deep
And full of voices, slowly rose and plunged   380
Roaring, and all the wave was in a flame;
And down the wave and in the flame was borne
A naked babe, and rode to Merlin's feet,
Who stoopt and caught the babe, and cried, 'The King!
Here is an heir for Uther!' And the fringe
Of that great breaker, sweeping up the strand,
Lash'd at the wizard as he spake the word,
And all at once all round him rose in fire,
So that the child and he were clothed in fire.
And presently thereafter follow'd calm,   390
Free sky and stars. 'And this same child,' he said,
'Is he who reigns; nor could I part in peace
Till this were told.' And saying this the seer
Went thro' the strait and dreadful pass of death,
Not ever to be question'd any more
Save on the further side; but when I met
Merlin, and ask'd him if these things were truth—
The shining dragon and the naked child
Descending in the glory of the seas—
He laugh'd as is his wont, and answer'd me   400
In riddling triplets of old time, and said:—

    " 'Rain, rain, and sun! a rainbow in the sky!
A young man will be wiser by and by;
An old man's wit may wander ere he die.

" 'Rain, rain, and sun! a rainbow on the lea!
And truth is this to me, and that to thee;
And truth or clothed or naked let it be.

" 'Rain, sun, and rain! and the free blossom blows;
Sun, rain, and sun! and where is he who knows?
From the great deep to the great deep he goes.'   **410**

"So Merlin riddling anger'd me; but thou
Fear not to give this King thine only child,
Guinevere; so great bards of him will sing
Hereafter, and dark sayings from of old
Ranging and ringing thro' the minds of men,
And echo'd by old folk beside their fires
For comfort after their wage-work is done,
Speak of the King; and Merlin in our time
Hath spoken also, not in jest, and sworn
Tho' men may wound him that he will not die,   **420**
But pass, again to come, and then or now
Utterly smite the heathen underfoot,
Till these and all men hail him for their king."

She spake and King Leodogran rejoiced,
But musing "Shall I answer yea or nay?"
Doubted, and drowsed, nodded and slept, and saw,
Dreaming, a slope of land that ever grew,
Field after field, up to a height, the peak
Haze-hidden, and thereon a phantom king,
Now looming, and now lost; and on the slope   **430**
The sword rose, the hind fell, the herd was driven,
Fire glimpsed; and all the land from roof and rick,
In drifts of smoke before a rolling wind,
Stream'd to the peak, and mingled with the haze
And made it thicker; while the phantom king
Sent out at times a voice; and here or there
Stood one who pointed toward the voice, the rest
Slew on and burnt, crying, 'No king of ours,
No son of Uther, and no king of ours;'
Till with a wink his dream was changed, the haze   **440**
Descended, and the solid earth became
As nothing, but the King stood out in heaven,
Crown'd. And Leodogran awoke, and sent

Ulfius, and Brastias, and Bedivere,
Back to the court of Arthur answering yea.

Then Arthur charged his warrior whom he loved
And honor'd most, Sir Lancelot, to ride forth
And bring the Queen, and watch'd him from the gates;
And Lancelot past away among the flowers—
For then was latter April—and return'd   450
Among the flowers, in May, with Guinevere.
To whom arrived, by Dubric the high saint,
Chief of the church in Britain, and before
The stateliest of her altar-shrines, the King
That morn was married, while in stainless white,
The fair beginners of a nobler time,
And glorying in their vows and him, his knights
Stood round him, and rejoicing in his joy.
Far shone the fields of May thro' open door,
The sacred altar blossom'd white with May,   460
The sun of May descended on their King,
They gazed on all earth's beauty in their Queen,
Roll'd incense, and there past along the hymns
A voice as of the waters, while the two
Sware at the shrine of Christ a deathless love.
And Arthur said, "Behold, thy doom is mine.
Let chance what will, I love thee to the death!"
To whom the Queen replied with drooping eyes,
"King and my lord, I love thee to the death!"
And holy Dubric spread his hands and spake: 470
"Reign ye, and live and love, and make the world
Other, and may thy Queen be one with thee,
And all this Order of thy Table Round
Fulfil the boundless purpose of their King!"

So Dubric said; but when they left the shrine
Great lords from Rome before the portal stood,
In scornful stillness gazing as they past;
Then while they paced a city all on fire
With sun and cloth of gold, the trumpets blew,
And Arthur's knighthood sang before the King:—   480

"Blow trumpet, for the world is white with May!
Blow trumpet, the long night hath roll'd away!
Blow thro' the living world—'Let the King reign!'

"Shall Rome or Heathen rule in Arthur's realm?
Flash brand and lance, fall battle-axe upon helm,
Fall battle-axe, and flash brand! Let the King reign!

"Strike for the King and live! his knights have heard
That God hath told the King a secret word.
Fall battle-axe, and flash brand! Let the King reign!

"Blow trumpet! he will lift us from the dust.   490
Blow trumpet! live the strength, and die the lust!
Clang battle-axe, and clash brand! Let the King reign!

"Strike for the King and die! and if thou diest,
The King is king, and ever wills the highest.
Clang battle-axe, and clash brand! Let the King reign!

"Blow, for our Sun is mighty in his May!
Blow, for our Sun is mightier day by day!
Clang battle-axe, and clash brand! Let the King reign! ·

"The King will follow Christ, and we the King,
In whom high God hath breathed a secret thing.   500
Fall battle-axe, and clash brand! Let the King reign!"

So sang the knighthood, moving to their hall.
There at the banquet those great lords from Rome,
The slowly-fading mistress of the world,
Strode in and claim'd their tribute as of yore.
But Arthur spake: "Behold, for these have sworn
To wage my wars, and worship me their King;
The old order changeth, yielding place to new,
And we that fight for our fair father Christ,
Seeing that ye be grown too weak and old   510
To drive the heathen from your Roman wall,
No tribute will we pay." So those great lords
Drew back in wrath, and Arthur strove with Rome.

And Arthur and his knighthood for a space
Were all one will, and thro' that strength the King
Drew in the petty princedoms under him,
Fought, and in twelve great battles overcame
The heathen hordes, and made a realm and reign'd.
                                        [publ. 1869]

THE HOLY GRAIL

FROM noiseful arms, and acts of prowess done
In tournament or tilt, Sir Percivale,
Whom Arthur and his knighthood call'd the Pure,
Had past into the silent life of prayer,
Praise, fast, and alms; and leaving for the cowl
The helmet in an abbey far away
From Camelot, there, and not long after, died.

And one, a fellow-monk among the rest,
Ambrosius, loved him much beyond the rest,
And honor'd him, and wrought into his heart   10
A way by love that waken'd love within,
To answer that which came; and as they sat
Beneath a world-old yew-tree, darkening half
The cloisters, on a gustful April morn
That puff'd the swaying branches into smoke
Above them, ere the summer when he died,
The monk Ambrosius question'd Percivale:

"O brother, I have seen this yew-tree smoke,
Spring after spring, for half a hundred years;
For never have I known the world without,   20
Nor ever stray'd beyond the pale. But thee,
When first thou camest—such a courtesy
Spake thro' the limbs and in the voice—I knew
For one of those who eat in Arthur's hall;
For good ye are and bad, and like to coins,
Some true, some light, but every one of you
Stamp'd with the image of the King; and now
Tell me, what drove thee from the Table Round,
My brother? was it earthly passion crost?"

"Nay," said the knight; "for no such passion mine,   30
But the sweet vision of the Holy Grail
Drove me from all vainglories, rivalries,
And earthly heats that spring and sparkle out
Among us in the jousts, while women watch

Who wins, who falls, and waste the spiritual strength
Within us, better offer'd up to heaven."

To whom the monk: "The Holy Grail!—I trust
We are green in Heaven's eyes; but here too much
We moulder—as to things without I mean—
Yet one of your own knights, a guest of ours,   40
Told us of this in our refectory,
But spake with such a sadness and so low
We heard not half of what he said. What is it?
The phantom of a cup that comes and goes?"

"Nay, monk! what phantom?" answer'd Percivale.
"The cup, the cup itself, from which our Lord
Drank at the last sad supper with his own.
This, from the blessed land of Aromat—
After the day of darkness, when the dead
Went wandering o'er Moriah—the good saint   50
Arimathæan Joseph, journeying brought
To Glastonbury, where the winter thorn
Blossoms at Christmas, mindful of our Lord.
And there awhile it bode; and if a man
Could touch or see it, he was heal'd at once,
By faith, of all his ills. But then the times
Grew to such evil that the holy cup
Was caught away to heaven, and disappear'd."

To whom the monk: "From our old books I know
That Joseph came of old to Glastonbury,   60
And there the heathen Prince, Arviragus,
Gave him an isle of marsh whereon to build;
And there he built with wattles from the marsh
A little lonely church in days of yore,
For so they say, these books of ours, but seem
Mute of this miracle, far as I have read.
But who first saw the holy thing to-day?"

"A woman," answer'd Percivale, "a nun,
And one no further off in blood from me
Than sister; and if ever holy maid   70
With knees of adoration wore the stone,
A holy maid; tho' never maiden glow'd,

But that was in her earlier maidenhood,
With such a fervent flame of human love,
Which, being rudely blunted, glanced and shot
Only to holy things; to prayer and praise
She gave herself, to fast and alms. And yet,
Nun as she was, the scandal of the Court,
Sin against Arthur and the Table Round,
And the strange sound of an adulterous race,   80
Across the iron grating of her cell
Beat, and she pray'd and fasted all the more.

"And he to whom she told her sins, or what
Her all but utter whiteness held for sin,
A man wellnigh a hundred winters old,
Spake often with her of the Holy Grail,
A legend handed down thro' five or six,
And each of these a hundred winters old,
From our Lord's time. And when King Arthur made
His Table Round, and all men's hearts became   90
Clean for a season, surely he had thought
That now the Holy Grail would come again;
But sin broke out. Ah, Christ, that it would come,
And heal the world of all their wickedness!
'O Father!' ask'd the maiden, 'might it come
To me by prayer and fasting?' 'Nay,' said he,
'I know not, for thy heart is pure as snow.'
And so she pray'd and fasted, till the sun
Shone, and the wind blew, thro' her, and I thought
She might have risen and floated when I saw her.   100

"For on a day she sent to speak with me.
And when she came to speak, behold her eyes
Beyond my knowing of them, beautiful,
Beyond all knowing of them, wonderful,
Beautiful in the light of holiness!
And 'O my brother Percivale,' she said,
'Sweet brother, I have seen the Holy Grail;
For, waked at dead of night, I heard a sound
As of a silver horn from o'er the hills
Blown, and I thought, "It is not Arthur's use   110
To hunt by moonlight." And the slender sound
As from a distance beyond distance grew

Coming upon me—O never harp nor horn,
Nor aught we blow with breath, or touch with hand,
Was like that music as it came; and then
Stream'd thro' my cell a cold and silver beam,
And down the long beam stole the Holy Grail,
Rose-red with beatings in it, as if alive,
Till all the white walls of my cell were dyed
With rosy colors leaping on the wall;   120
And then the music faded, and the Grail
Past, and the beam decay'd, and from the walls
The rosy quiverings died into the night.
So now the Holy Thing is here again
Among us, brother, fast thou too and pray,
And tell thy brother knights to fast and pray,
That so perchance the vision may be seen
By thee and those, and all the world be heal'd.'

"Then leaving the pale nun, I spake of this
To all men; and myself fasted and pray'd   130
Always, and many among us many a week
Fasted and pray'd even to the uttermost,
Expectant of the wonder that would be.

"And one there was among us, ever moved
Among us in white armor, Galahad.
'God make thee good as thou art beautiful!'
Said Arthur, when he dubb'd him knight, and none
In so young youth was ever made a knight
Till Galahad; and this Galahad, when he heard
My sister's vision, fill'd me with amaze;   140
His eyes became so like her own, they seem'd
Hers, and himself her brother more than I.

"Sister or brother none had he; but some
Call'd him a son of Lancelot, and some said
Begotten by enchantment—chatterers they,
Like birds of passage piping up and down,
That gape for flies—we know not whence they come;
For when was Lancelot wanderingly lewd?

"But she, the wan sweet maiden, shore away
Clean from her forehead all that wealth of hair   150

Which made a silken mat-work for her feet;
And out of this she plaited broad and long
A strong sword-belt, and wove with silver thread
And crimson in the belt a strange device,
A crimson grail within a silver beam;
And saw the bright boy-knight, and bound it on him,
Saying: 'My knight, my love, my knight of heaven,
O thou, my love, whose love is one with mine,
I, maiden, round thee, maiden, bind my belt.
Go forth, for thou shalt see what I have seen,   **160**
And break thro' all, till one will crown thee king
Far in the spiritual city;' and as she spake
She sent the deathless passion in her eyes
Thro' him, and made him hers, and laid her mind
On him, and he believed in her belief.

"Then came a year of miracle. O brother,
In our great hall there stood a vacant chair,
Fashion'd by Merlin ere he past away,
And carven with strange figures; and in and out
The figures, like a serpent, ran a scroll   **170**
Of letters in a tongue no man could read.
And Merlin call'd it 'the Siege Perilous,'
Perilous for good and ill; 'for there,' he said,
'No man could sit but he should lose himself.'
And once by misadvertence Merlin sat
In his own chair, and so was lost; but he,
Galahad, when he heard of Merlin's doom,
Cried, 'If I lose myself, I save myself!'

"Then on a summer night it came to pass,
While the great banquet lay along the hall,   **180**
That Galahad would sit down in Merlin's chair.

"And all at once, as there we sat, we heard
A cracking and a riving of the roofs,
And rending, and a blast, and overhead
Thunder, and in the thunder was a cry.
And in the blast there smote along the hall
A beam of light seven times more clear than day;
And down the long beam stole the Holy Grail
All over cover'd with a luminous cloud,

And none might see who bare it, and it past.   190
But every knight beheld his fellow's face
As in a glory, and all the knights arose,
And staring each at other like dumb men
Stood, till I found a voice and sware a vow.

"I sware a vow before them all, that I,
Because I had not seen the Grail, would ride
A twelvemonth and a day in quest of it,
Until I found and saw it, as the nun
My sister saw it; and Galahad sware the vow,
And good Sir Bors, our Lancelot's cousin, sware,   200
And Lancelot sware, and many among the knights,
And Gawain sware, and louder than the rest."

Then spake the monk Ambrosius, asking him,
"What said the King? Did Arthur take the vow?"

"Nay, for my lord," said Percivale, "the King,
Was not in hall; for early that same day,
Scaped thro' a cavern from a bandit hold,
An outraged maiden sprang into the hall
Crying on help; for all her shining hair
Was smear'd with earth, and either milky arm   210
Red-rent with hooks of bramble, and all she wore
Torn as a sail that leaves the rope is torn
In tempest. So the King arose and went
To smoke the scandalous hive of those wild bees
That made such honey in his realm. Howbeit
Some little of this marvel he too saw,
Returning o'er the plain that then began
To darken under Camelot; whence the King
Look'd up, calling aloud, 'Lo, there! the roofs
Of our great hall are roll'd in thunder-smoke!   220
Pray heaven, they be not smitten by the bolt!'
For dear to Arthur was that hall of ours,
As having there so oft with all his knights
Feasted, and as the stateliest under heaven.

"O brother, had you known our mighty hall,
Which Merlin built for Arthur long ago!
For all the sacred mount of Camelot,

And all the dim rich city, roof by roof,
Tower after tower, spire beyond spire,
By grove, and garden-lawn, and rushing brook, 230
Climbs to the mighty hall that Merlin built.
And four great zones of sculpture, set betwixt
With many a mystic symbol, gird the hall:
And in the lowest beasts are slaying men,
And in the second men are slaying beasts,
And on the third are warriors, perfect men,
And on the fourth are men with growing wings,
And over all one statue in the mould
Of Arthur, made by Merlin, with a crown,
And peak'd wings pointed to the Northern Star. 240
And eastward fronts the statue, and the crown
And both the wings are made of gold, and flame
At sunrise till the people in far fields,
Wasted so often by the heathen hordes,
Behold it, crying, 'We have still a king.'

"And, brother, had you known our hall within,
Broader and higher than any in all the lands!
Where twelve great windows blazon Arthur's wars,
And all the light that falls upon the board
Streams thro' the twelve great battles of our King. 250
Nay, one there is, and at the eastern end,
Wealthy with wandering lines of mount and mere,
Where Arthur finds the brand Excalibur.
And also one to the west, and counter to it,
And blank; and who shall blazon it? when and how?—
O, there, perchance, when all our wars are done,
The brand Excalibur will be cast away!

"So to this hall full quickly rode the King,
In horror lest the work by Merlin wrought,
Dreamlike, should on the sudden vanish, wrapt 260
In unremorseful folds of rolling fire.
And in he rode, and up I glanced, and saw
The golden dragon sparkling over all;
And many of those who burnt the hold, their arms
Hack'd, and their foreheads grimed with smoke and sear'd,
Follow'd, and in among bright faces, ours,
Full of the vision, prest; and then the King

Spake to me, being nearest, 'Percivale,'—
Because the hall was all in tumult—some
Vowing, and some protesting,—'what is this?'   270

"O brother, when I told him what had chanced,
My sister's vision and the rest, his face
Darken'd, as I have seen it more than once,
When some brave deed seem'd to be done in vain,
Darken; and 'Woe is me, my knights,' he cried,
'Had I been here, ye had not sworn the vow.'
Bold was mine answer, 'Had thyself been here
My King, thou wouldst have sworn.' 'Yea, yea,' said he,
'Art thou so bold and hast not seen the Grail?'

"'Nay, lord, I heard the sound, I saw the light,   280
But since I did not see the holy thing,
I sware a vow to follow it till I saw.'

"Then when he ask'd us, knight by knight, if any
Had seen it, all their answers were as one:
'Nay, lord, and therefore have we sworn our vows.'

"'Lo, now,' said Arthur, 'have ye seen a cloud?
What go ye into the wilderness to see?'

"Then Galahad on the sudden, and in a voice
Shrilling along the hall to Arthur, call'd,
'But I, Sir Arthur, saw the Holy Grail,   290
I saw the Holy Grail and heard a cry—
"O Galahad, and O Galahad, follow me!"'

"'Ah, Galahad, Galahad,' said the King, 'for such
As thou art is the vision, not for these.
Thy holy nun and thou have seen a sign—
Holier is none, my Percivale, than she—
A sign to maim this Order which I made.
But ye that follow but the leader's bell,'—
Brother, the King was hard upon his knights,—
'Taliessin is our fullest throat of song,   300
And one hath sung and all the dumb will sing.
Lancelot is Lancelot, and hath overborne
Five knights at once, and every younger knight,

Unproven, holds himself as Lancelot,
Till overborne by one, he learns—and ye,
What are ye? Galahads?—no, nor Percivales'—
For thus it pleased the King to range me close
After Sir Galahad;—'nay,' said he, 'but men
With strength and will to right the wrong'd, of power
To lay the sudden heads of violence flat,   316
Knights that in twelve great battles splash'd and dyed
The strong White Horse in his own heathen blood—
But one hath seen, and all the blind will see.
Go, since your vows are sacred, being made.
Yet—for ye know the cries of all my realm
Pass thro' this hall—how often, O my knights,
Your places being vacant at my side,
This chance of noble deeds will come and go
Unchallenged, while ye follow wandering fires
Lost in the quagmire! Many of you, yea most,   320
Return no more. Ye think I show myself
Too dark a prophet. Come now, let us meet
The morrow morn once more in one full field
Of gracious pastime, that once more the King,
Before ye leave him for this quest, may count
The yet-unbroken strength of all his knights,
Rejoicing in that Order which he made.'

"So when the sun broke next from underground,
All the great Table of our Arthur closed
And clash'd in such a tourney and so full,   330
So many lances broken—never yet
Had Camelot seen the like since Arthur came;
And I myself and Galahad, for a strength
Was in us from the vision, overthrew
So many knights that all the people cried,
And almost burst the barriers in their heat,
Shouting, 'Sir Galahad and Sir Percivale!'

"But when the next day brake from underground—
O brother, had you known our Camelot,
Built by old kings, age after age, so old   340
The King himself had fears that it would fall,
So strange, and rich, and dim; for where the roofs
Totter'd toward each other in the sky,

Met foreheads all along the street of those
Who watch'd us pass; and lower, and where the long
Rich galleries, lady-laden, weigh'd the necks
Of dragons clinging to the crazy walls,
Thicker than drops from thunder, showers of flowers
Fell as we past; and men and boys astride
On wyvern, lion, dragon, griffin, swan,   350
At all the corners, named us each by name,
Calling 'God speed!' but in the ways below
The knights and ladies wept, and rich and poor
Wept, and the King himself could hardly speak
For grief, and all in middle street the Queen,
Who rode by Lancelot, wail'd and shriek'd aloud,
'This madness has come on us for our sins.'
So to the Gate of the Three Queens we came,
Where Arthur's wars are render'd mystically,   360
And thence departed every one his way.

"And I was lifted up in heart, and thought
Of all my late-shown prowess in the lists,
How my strong lance had beaten down the knights,
So many and famous names; and never yet
Had heaven appear'd so blue, nor earth so green,
For all my blood danced in me, and I knew
That I should light upon the Holy Grail.

"Thereafter, the dark warning of our King,
That most of us would follow wandering fires,   370
Came like a driving gloom across my mind.
Then every evil word I had spoken once,
And every evil thought I had thought of old,
And every evil deed I ever did,
Awoke and cried, 'This quest is not for thee.'
And lifting up mine eyes, I found myself
Alone, and in a land of sand and thorns,
And I was thirsty even unto death;
And I, too, cried, 'This quest is not for thee.'

"And on I rode, and when I thought my thirst
Would slay me, saw deep lawns, and then a brook,   380
With one sharp rapid, where the crisping white
Play'd ever back upon the sloping wave
And took both ear and eye; and o'er the brook

Were apple-trees, and apples by the brook
Fallen, and on the lawns. 'I will rest here,'
I said, 'I am not worthy of the quest;'
But even while I drank the brook, and ate
The goodly apples, all these things at once
Fell into dust, and I was left alone
And thirsting in a land of sand and thorns.   390

   "And then behold a woman at a door
Spinning; and fair the house whereby she sat,
And kind the woman's eyes and innocent,
And all her bearing gracious; and she rose
Opening her arms to meet me, as who should say,
'Rest here;' but when I touch'd her, lo! she, too,
Fell into dust and nothing, and the house
Became no better than a broken shed,
And in it a dead babe; and also this
Fell into dust, and I was left alone.   400

   "And on I rode, and greater was my thirst.
Then flash'd a yellow gleam across the world,
And where it smote the plowshare in the field
The plowman left his plowing and fell down
Before it; where it glitter'd on her pail
The milkmaid left her milking and fell down
Before it, and I knew not why, but thought
'The sun is rising,' tho' the sun had risen.
Then was I ware of one that on me moved
In golden armor with a crown of gold   410
About a casque all jewels, and his horse
In golden armor jewelled everywhere;
And on the splendor came, flashing me blind,
And seem'd to me the lord of all the world,
Being so huge. But when I thought he meant
To crush me, moving on me, lo! he, too,
Open'd his arms to embrace me as he came,
And up I went and touch'd him, and he, too,
Fell into dust, and I was left alone
And wearying in a land of sand and thorns.   420

   "And I rode on and found a mighty hill,
And on the top a city wall'd; the spires
Prick'd with incredible pinnacles into heaven.

And by the gateway stirr'd a crowd; and these
Cried to me climbing, 'Welcome, Percivale!
Thou mightiest and thou purest among men!'
And glad was I and clomb, but found at top
No man, nor any voice. And thence I past
Far thro' a ruinous city, and I saw
That man had once dwelt there; but there I found   430
Only one man of an exceeding age.
'Where is that goodly company,' said I,
'That so cried out upon me?' and he had
Scarce any voice to answer, and yet gasp'd,
'Whence and what art thou?' and even as he spoke
Fell into dust and disappear'd, and I
Was left alone once more and cried in grief,
'Lo, if I find the Holy Grail itself
And touch it, it will crumble into dust!'

  "And thence I dropt into a lowly vale,   440
Low as the hill was high, and where the vale
Was lowest found a chapel, and thereby
A holy hermit in a hermitage,
To whom I told my phantoms, and he said:

  " 'O son, thou hast not true humility,
The highest virtue, mother of them all;
For when the Lord of all things made Himself
Naked of glory for His mortal change,
"Take thou my robe," she said, "for all is thine,"
And all her form shone forth with sudden light   450
So that the angels were amazed, and she
Follow'd Him down, and like a flying star
Led on the gray-hair'd wisdom of the east.
But her thou hast not known; for what is this
Thou thoughtest of thy prowess and thy sins?
Thou hast not lost thyself to save thyself
As Galahad.' When the hermit made an end,
In silver armor suddenly Galahad shone
Before us, and against the chapel door
Laid lance and enter'd, and we knelt in prayer.   460
And there the hermit slaked my burning thirst,
And at the sacring of the mass I saw
The holy elements alone; but he,

'Saw ye no more? I, Galahad, saw the **Grail,**
The Holy Grail, descend upon the shrine.
I saw the fiery face as of a child
That smote itself into the bread and went;
And hither am I come; and never yet
Hath what thy sister taught me first to see,
This holy thing, fail'd from my side, nor come   470
Cover'd, but moving with me night and day,
Fainter by day, but always in the night
Blood-red, and sliding down the blacken'd marsh
Blood-red, and on the naked mountain top
Blood-red, and in the sleeping mere below
Blood-red. And in the strength of this I rode,
Shattering all evil customs everywhere,
And past thro' Pagan realms, and made them **mine,**
And clash'd with Pagan hordes, and bore them **down,**
And broke thro' all, and in the strength of this   480
Come victor. But my time is hard at hand,
And hence I go, and one will crown me **king**
Far in the spiritual city; and come thou, too,
For thou shalt see the vision when I go.'

    "While thus he spake, his eye, dwelling on **mine,**
Drew me, with power upon me, till I grew
One with him, to believe as he believed.
Then, when the day began to wane, we went.

    "There rose a hill that none but man could climb,
Scarr'd with a hundred wintry watercourses—   490
Storm at the top, and when we gain'd it, storm
Round us and death; for every moment glanced
His silver arms and gloom'd, so quick and thick
The lightnings here and there to left and right
Struck, till the dry old trunks about us, dead,
Yea, rotten with a hundred years of death,
Sprang into fire. And at the base we found
On either hand, as far as eye could see,
A great black swamp and of an evil smell,
Part black, part whiten'd with the bones of men,   500
Not to be crost, save that some ancient king
Had built a way, where, link'd with many a bridge.
A thousand piers ran into the great Sea.

And Galahad fled along them bridge by bridge,
And every bridge as quickly as he crost
Sprang into fire and vanish'd, tho' I yearn'd
To follow; and thrice above him all the heavens
Open'd and blazed with thunder such as seem'd
Shoutings of all the sons of God. And first
At once I saw him far on the great Sea,   510
In silver-shining armor starry-clear;
And o'er his head the Holy Vessel hung
Clothed in white samite or a luminous cloud.
And with exceeding swiftness ran the boat,
If boat it were—I saw not whence it came.
And when the heavens open'd and blazed again
Roaring, I saw him like a silver star—
And had he set the sail, or had the boat
Become a living creature clad with wings?
And o'er his head the Holy Vessel hung   520
Redder than any rose, a joy to me,
For now I knew the veil had been withdrawn.
Then in a moment when they blazed again
Opening, I saw the least of little stars
Down on the waste, and straight beyond the star
I saw the spiritual city and all her spires
And gateways in a glory like one pearl—
No larger, tho' the goal of all the saints—
Strike from the sea; and from the star there shot
A rose-red sparkle to the city, and there   530
Dwelt, and I knew it was the Holy Grail,
Which never eyes on earth again shall see.
Then fell the floods of heaven drowning the deep.
And how my feet recrost the deathful ridge
No memory in me lives; but that I touch'd
The chapel-doors at dawn I know, and thence
Taking my war-horse from the holy man,
Glad that no phantom vext me more, return'd
To whence I came, the gate of Arthur's wars."

"O brother," ask'd Ambrosius,—"for in sooth   540
These ancient books—and they would win thee—teem,
Only I find not there this Holy Grail,
With miracles and marvels like to these,
Not all unlike: which oftentime I read,

Who read but on my breviary with ease,
Till my head swims, and then go forth and pass
Down to the little thorpe that lies so close,
And almost plaster'd like a martin's nest
To these old walls—and mingle with our folk;
And knowing every honest face of theirs 550
As well as ever shepherd knew his sheep,
And every homely secret in their hearts,
Delight myself with gossip and old wives,
And ills and aches, and teethings, lyings-in,
And mirthful sayings, children of the place,
That have no meaning half a league away;
Or lulling random squabbles when they rise,
Chafferings and chatterings at the market-cross,
Rejoice, small man, in this small world of mine,
Yea, even in their hens and in their eggs— 560
O brother, saving this Sir Galahad,
Came ye on none but phantoms in your quest,
No man, no woman?"

            Then Sir Percivale:
"All men, to one so bound by such a vow,
And women were as phantoms. O, my brother,
Why wilt thou shame me to confess to thee
How far I falter'd from my quest and vow?
For after I had lain so many nights,
A bed-mate of the snail and eft and snake,
In grass and burdock, I was changed to wan 570
And meagre, and the vision had not come;
And then I chanced upon a goodly town
With one great dwelling in the middle of it.
Thither I made, and there was I disarm'd
By maidens each as fair as any flower;
But when they led me into hall, behold,
The princess of that castle was the one,
Brother, and that one only, who had ever
Made my heart leap; for when I moved of old
A slender page about her father's hall, 580
And she a slender maiden, all my heart
Went after her with longing, yet we twain
Had never kiss'd a kiss or vow'd a vow.
And now I came upon her once again,

And one had wedded her, and he was dead,
And all his land and wealth and state were hers,
And while I tarried, every day she set
A banquet richer than the day before
By me, for all her longing and her will
Was toward me as of old; till one fair morn,   590
I walking to and fro beside a stream
That flash'd across her orchard underneath
Her castle-walls, she stole upon my walk,
And calling me the greatest of all knights,
Embraced me, and so kiss'd me the first time,
And gave herself and all her wealth to me.
Then I remember'd Arthur's warning word,
That most of us would follow wandering fires,
And the quest faded in my heart. Anon,
The heads of all her people drew to me,   600
With supplication both of knees and tongue:
'We have heard of thee; thou art our greatest knight,
Our Lady says it, and we well believe.
Wed thou our Lady, and rule over us,
And thou shalt be as Arthur in our land.'
O me, my brother! but one night my vow
Burnt me within, so that I rose and fled,
But wail'd and wept, and hated mine own self,
And even the holy quest, and all but her;
Then after I was join'd with Galahad   610
Cared not for her nor anything upon earth."

Then said the monk: "Poor men, when yule is cold,
Must be content to sit by little fires.
And this am I, so that ye care for me
Ever so little; yea, and blest be heaven
That brought thee here to this poor house of ours
Where all the brethren are so hard, to warm
My cold heart with a friend; but O the pity
To find thine own first love once more—to hold,
Hold her a wealthy bride within thine arms,   620
Or all but hold, and then—cast her aside,
Foregoing all her sweetness, like a weed!
For we that want the warmth of double life,
We that are plagued with dreams of something sweet
Beyond all sweetness in a life so rich,—

Ah, blessed Lord, I speak too earthly-wise,
Seeing I never stray'd beyond the cell,
But live like an old badger in his earth,
With earth about him everywhere, despite
All fast and penance. Saw ye none beside,   630
None of your knights?"

                   "Yea, so," said Percivale:
"One night my pathway swerving east, I saw
The pelican on the casque of our Sir Bors
All in the middle of the rising moon,
And toward him spurr'd, and hail'd him, and he me,
And each made joy of either. Then he ask'd:
'Where is he? hast thou seen him—Lancelot?—Once,'
Said good Sir Bors, 'he dash'd across me—mad,
And maddening what he rode; and when I cried,
"Ridest thou then so hotly on a quest   640
So holy?" Lancelot shouted, "Stay me not!
I have been the sluggard, and I ride apace,
For now there is a lion in the way!"
So vanish'd.'

            "Then Sir Bors had ridden on
Softly, and sorrowing for our Lancelot,
Because his former madness, once the talk
And scandal of our table, had return'd;
For Lancelot's kith and kin so worship him
That ill to him is ill to them, to Bors
Beyond the rest. He well had been content   650
Not to have seen, so Lancelot might have seen,
The Holy Cup of healing; and, indeed,
Being so clouded with his grief and love,
Small heart was his after the holy quest.
If God would send the vision, well; if not,
The quest and he were in the hands of Heaven.

  "And then, with small adventure met, Sir Bors
Rode to the lonest tract of all the realm,
And found a people there among their crags,
Our race and blood, a remnant that were left   660
Paynim amid their circles, and the stones
They pitch up straight to heaven; and their wise men

Were strong in that old magic which can trace
The wandering of the stars, and scoff'd at him
And this high quest as at a simple thing,
Told him he follow'd—almost Arthur's words—
A mocking fire: 'what other fire than he
Whereby the blood beats, and the blossom blows,
And the sea rolls, and all the world is warm'd?'
And when his answer chafed them, the rough crowd,   670
Hearing he had a difference with their priests,
Seized him, and bound and plunged him into a cell
Of great piled stones; and lying bounden there
In darkness thro' innumerable hours
He heard the hollow-ringing heavens sweep
Over him till by miracle—what else?—
Heavy as it was, a great stone slipt and fell,
Such as no wind could move; and thro' the gap
Glimmer'd the streaming scud. Then came a night
Still as the day was loud, and thro' the gap   680
The seven clear stars of Arthur's Table Round—
For, brother, so one night, because they roll
Thro' such a round in heaven, we named the stars,
Rejoicing in ourselves and in our King—
And these, like bright eyes of familiar friends,
In on him shone: 'And then to me, to me,'
Said good Sir Bors, 'beyond all hopes of mine,
Who scarce had pray'd or ask'd it for myself—
Across the seven clear stars—O grace to me!—
In color like the fingers of a hand   690
Before a burning taper, the sweet Grail
Glided and past, and close upon it peal'd
A sharp quick thunder.' Afterwards, a maid,
Who kept our holy faith among her kin
In secret, entering, loosed and let him go."

To whom the monk: "And I remember now
That pelican on the casque. Sir Bors it was
Who spake so low and sadly at our board,
And mighty reverent at our grace was he;
A square-set man and honest, and his eyes,   700
An outdoor sign of all the warmth within,
Smiled with his lips—a smile beneath a cloud,
But heaven had meant it for a sunny one.

Ay, ay, Sir Bors, who else? But when ye reach'd
The city, found ye all your knights return'd,
Or was there sooth in Arthur's prophecy,
Tell me, and what said each, and what the King?"

Then answer'd Percivale: "And that can I,
Brother, and truly; since the living words
Of so great men as Lancelot and our King   710
Pass not from door to door and out again,
But sit within the house. O, when we reach'd
The city, our horses stumbling as they trode
On heaps of ruin, hornless unicorns,
Crack'd basilisks, and splinter'd cockatrices,
And shatter'd talbots, which had left the stones
Raw that they fell from, brought us to the hall.

"And there sat Arthur on the dais-throne,
And those that had gone out upon the quest,
Wasted and worn, and but a tithe of them,   720
And those that had not, stood before the King,
Who, when he saw me, rose and bade me hail,
Saying: 'A welfare in thine eyes reproves
Our fear of some disastrous chance for thee
On hill or plain, at sea or flooding ford.
So fierce a gale made havoc here of late
Among the strange devices of our kings,
Yea, shook this newer, stronger hall of ours,
And from the statue Merlin moulded for us
Half-wrench'd a golden wing; but now—the quest,   730
This vision—hast thou seen the Holy Cup
That Joseph brought of old to Glastonbury?'

"So when I told him all thyself hast heard,
Ambrosius, and my fresh but fixt resolve
To pass away into the quiet life,
He answer'd not, but, sharply turning, ask'd
Of Gawain, 'Gawain, was this quest for thee?'

" 'Nay, lord,' said Gawain, 'not for such as I.
Therefore I communed with a saintly man,
Who made me sure the quest was not for me;   740
For I was much a-wearied of the quest,

But found a silk pavilion in a field,
And merry maidens in it; and then this gale
Tore my pavilion from the tenting-pin,
And blew my merry maidens all about
With all discomfort; yea, and but for this,
My twelvemonth and a day were pleasant to me.'

"He ceased; and Arthur turn'd to whom at first
He saw not, for Sir Bors, on entering, push'd
Athwart the throng to Lancelot, caught his hand,   750
Held it, and there, half-hidden by him, stood,
Until the King espied him, saying to him,
'Hail, Bors! if ever loyal man and true
Could see it, thou hast seen the Grail;' and Bors,
'Ask me not, for I may not speak of it;
I saw it;' and the tears were in his eyes.

"Then there remain'd but Lancelot, for the rest
Spake but of sundry perils in the storm.
Perhaps, like him of Cana in Holy Writ,
Our Arthur kept his best until the last;   760
'Thou, too, my Lancelot,' ask'd the King, 'my friend,
Our mightiest, hath this quest avail'd for thee?'

" 'Our mightiest!' answer'd Lancelot, with a groan;
'O King!'—and when he paused methought I spied
A dying fire of madness in his eyes—
'O King, my friend, if friend of thine I be,
Happier are those that welter in their sin,
Swine in the mud, that cannot see for slime,
Slime of the ditch; but in me lived a sin
So strange, of such a kind, that all of pure,   770
Noble, and knightly in me twined and clung
Round that one sin, until the wholesome flower
And poisonous grew together, each as each,
Not to be pluck'd asunder; and when thy knights
Sware, I sware with them only in the hope
That could I touch or see the Holy Grail
They might be pluck'd asunder. Then I spake
To one most holy saint, who wept and said
That, save they could be pluck'd asunder, all
My quest were but in vain; to whom I vow'd   780

That I would work according as he will'd.
And forth I went, and while I yearn'd and strove
To tear the twain asunder in my heart,
My madness came upon me as of old,
And whipt me into waste fields far away.
There was I beaten down by little men,
Mean knights, to whom the moving of my sword
And shadow of my spear had been enow
To scare them from me once; and then I came
All in my folly to the naked shore, 790
Wide flats, where nothing but coarse grasses grew;
But such a blast, my King, began to blow,
So loud a blast along the shore and sea,
Ye could not hear the waters for the blast,
Tho' heapt in mounds and ridges all the sea
Drove like a cataract, and all the sand
Swept like a river, and the clouded heavens
Were shaken with the motion and the sound.
And blackening in the sea-foam sway'd a boat,
Half-swallow'd in it, anchor'd with a chain; 800
And in my madness to myself I said,
"I will embark and I will lose myself,
And in the great sea wash away my sin."
I burst the chain, I sprang into the boat.
Seven days I drove along the dreary deep,
And with me drove the moon and all the stars;
And the wind fell, and on the seventh night
I heard the shingle grinding in the surge,
And felt the boat shock earth, and looking up,
Behold, the enchanted towers of Carbonek, 810
A castle like a rock upon a rock,
With chasm-like portals open to the sea,
And steps that met the breaker! There was none
Stood near it but a lion on each side
That kept the entry, and the moon was full.
Then from the boat I leapt, and up the stairs,
There drew my sword. With sudden-flaring manes
Those two great beasts rose upright like a man,
Each gript a shoulder, and I stood between,
And, when I would have smitten them, heard a voice, 820
"Doubt not, go forward; if thou doubt, the beasts
Will tear thee piecemeal." Then with violence

The sword was dash'd from out my hand, and fell.
And up into the sounding hall I past;
But nothing in the sounding hall I saw,
No bench nor table, painting on the wall
Or shield of knight, only the rounded moon
Thro' the tall oriel on the rolling sea.
But always in the quiet house I heard,
Clear as a lark, high o'er me as a lark,   830
A sweet voice singing in the topmost tower
To the eastward. Up I climb'd a thousand steps
With pain; as in a dream I seem'd to climb
For ever; at the last I reach'd a door,
A light was in the crannies, and I heard,
"Glory and joy and honor to our Lord
And to the Holy Vessel of the Grail!"
Then in my madness I essay'd the door;
It gave, and thro' a stormy glare, a heat
As from a seven-times-heated furnace, I,   840
Blasted and burnt, and blinded as I was,
With such a fierceness that I swoon'd away—
O, yet methought I saw the Holy Grail,
All pall'd in crimson samite, and around
Great angels, awful shapes, and wings and eyes!
And but for all my madness and my sin,
And then my swooning, I had sworn I saw
That which I saw; but what I saw was veil'd
And cover'd, and this quest was not for me.'

   "So speaking, and here ceasing, Lancelot left   850
The hall long silent, till Sir Gawain—nay,
Brother, I need not tell thee foolish words,—
A reckless and irreverent knight was he,
Now bolden'd by the silence of his King,—
Well, I will tell thee: 'O King, my liege,' he said,
'Hath Gawain fail'd in any quest of thine?
When have I stinted stroke in foughten field?
But as for thine, my good friend Percivale,
Thy holy nun and thou have driven men mad,
Yea, made our mightiest madder than our least.   860
But by mine eyes and by mine ears I swear,
I will be deafer than the blue-eyed cat,
And thrice as blind as any noonday owl,

To holy virgins in their ecstasies,
Henceforward.'

        " 'Deafer,' said the blameless King,
'Gawain, and blinder unto holy things,
Hope not to make thyself by idle vows,
Being too blind to have desire to see.
But if indeed there came a sign from heaven,
Blessed are Bors, Lancelot, and Percivale,   870
For these have seen according to their sight.
For every fiery prophet in old times,
And all the sacred madness of the bard,
When God made music thro' them, could but speak
His music by the framework and the chord;
And as ye saw it ye have spoken truth.

      " 'Nay—but thou errest, Lancelot; never yet
Could all of true and noble in knight and man
Twine round one sin, whatever it might be,
With such a closeness but apart there grew,   880
Save that he were the swine thou spakest of,
Some root of knighthood and pure nobleness;
Whereto see thou, that it may bear its flower.

      " 'And spake I not too truly, O my knights?
Was I too dark a prophet when I said
To those who went upon the Holy Quest,
That most of them would follow wandering fires,
Lost in the quagmire?—lost to me and gone,
And left me gazing at a barren board,
And a lean Order—scarce return'd a tithe—   890
And out of those to whom the vision came
My greatest hardly will believe he saw.
Another hath beheld it afar off,
And, leaving human wrongs to right themselves,
Cares but to pass into the silent life.
And one hath had the vision face to face,
And now his chair desires him here in vain,
However they may crown him otherwhere.

      " 'And some among you held that if the King
Had seen the sight he would have sworn the vow.   900

Not easily, seeing that the King must guard
That which he rules, and is but as the hind
To whom a space of land is given to plow,
Who may not wander from the allotted field
Before his work be done, but, being done,
Let visions of the night or of the day
Come as they will; and many a time they come,
Until this earth he walks on seems not earth,
This light that strikes his eyeball is not light,
This air that smites his forehead is not air   910
But vision—yea, his very hand and foot—
In moments when he feels he cannot die,
And knows himself no vision to himself,
Nor the high God a vision, nor that One
Who rose again. Ye have seen what ye have seen.'

    "So spake the King; I knew not all he meant."
                                    [publ. 1869]

            THE LAST TOURNAMENT

DAGONET, the fool, whom Gawain in his mood
Had made mock-knight of Arthur's Table Round,
At Camelot, high above the yellowing woods,
Danced like a wither'd leaf before the hall.
And toward him from the hall, with harp in hand,
And from the crown thereof a carcanet
Of ruby swaying to and fro, the prize
Of Tristram in the jousts of yesterday,
Came Tristram, saying, "Why skip ye so, Sir Fool?"

    For Arthur and Sir Lancelot riding once   10
Far down beneath a winding wall of rock
Heard a child wail. A stump of oak half-dead,
From roots like some black coil of carven snakes,
Clutch'd at the crag, and started thro' mid air
Bearing an eagle's nest; and thro' the tree
Rush'd ever a rainy wind, and thro' the wind
Pierced ever a child's cry; and crag and tree
Scaling, Sir Lancelot from the perilous nest,
This ruby necklace thrice around her neck,

And all unscarr'd from beak or talon, brought   20
A maiden babe, which Arthur pitying took,
Then gave it to his Queen to rear. The Queen,
But coldly acquiescing, in her white arms
Received, and after loved it tenderly,
And named it Nestling; so forgot herself
A moment, and her cares; till that young life
Being smitten in mid heaven with mortal cold
Past from her, and in time the carcanet
Vext her with plaintive memories of the child.
So she, delivering it to Arthur, said,   30
"Take thou the jewels of this dead innocence,
And make them, an thou wilt, a tourney-prize."

To whom the King: "Peace to thine eagle-borne
Dead nestling, and this honor after death,
Following thy will! but, O my Queen, I muse
Why ye not wear on arm, or neck, or zone
Those diamonds that I rescued from the tarn,
And Lancelot won, methought, for thee to wear."

"Would rather you had let them fall," she cried,
"Plunge and be lost—ill-fated as they were,   40
A bitterness to me!—ye look amazed,
Not knowing they were lost as soon as given—
Slid from my hands when I was leaning out
Above the river—that unhappy child
Past in her barge; but rosier luck will go
With these rich jewels, seeing that they came
Not from the skeleton of a brother-slayer,
But the sweet body of a maiden babe.
Perchance—who knows?—the purest of thy knights
May win them for the purest of my maids."   50

She ended, and the cry of a great jousts
With trumpet-blowings ran on all the ways
From Camelot in among the faded fields
To furthest towers; and everywhere the knights
Arm'd for a day of glory before the King.

But on the hither side of that loud morn
Into the hall stagger'd, his visage ribb'd
From ear to ear with dogwhip-weals, his nose

Bridge-broken, one eye out, and one hand off,
And one with shatter'd fingers dangling lame,   60
A churl, to whom indignantly the King:

"My churl, for whom Christ died, what evil beast
Hath drawn his claws athwart thy face? or fiend?
Man was it who marr'd heaven's image in thee thus?"

Then, sputtering thro' the hedge of splinter'd teeth,
Yet strangers to the tongue, and with blunt stump
Pitch-blacken'd sawing the air, said the maim'd churl:

"He took them and he drave them to his tower—
Some hold he was a table-knight of thine—
A hundred goodly ones—the Red Knight, he—   70
Lord, I was tending swine, and the Red Knight
Brake in upon me and drave them to his tower;
And when I call'd upon thy name as one
That doest right by gentle and by churl,
Maim'd me and maul'd, and would outright have slain,
Save that he sware me to a message, saying:
'Tell thou the King and all his liars that I
Have founded my Round Table in the North,
And whatsoever his own knights have sworn
My knights have sworn the counter to it—and say   80
My tower is full of harlots, like his court,
But mine are worthier, seeing they profess
To be none other than themselves—and say
My knights are all adulterers like his own,
But mine are truer, seeing they profess
To be none other; and say his hour is come,
The heathen are upon him, his long lance
Broken, and his Excalibur a straw.'"

Then Arthur turn'd to Kay the seneschal:
"Take thou my churl, and tend him curiously   90
Like a king's heir, till all his hurts be whole.
The heathen—but that ever-climbing wave,
Hurl'd back again so often in empty foam,
Hath lain for years at rest—and renegades,
Thieves, bandits, leavings of confusion, whom
The wholesome realm is purged of otherwhere,
Friends, thro' your manhood and your fealty,—now

Make their last head like Satan in the North.
My younger knights, new-made, in whom your flower
Waits to be solid fruit of golden deeds,   100
Move with me toward their quelling, which achieved,
The loneliest ways are safe from shore to shore.
But thou, Sir Lancelot, sitting in my place
Enchair'd to-morrow, arbitrate the field;
For wherefore shouldst thou care to mingle with it,
Only to yield my Queen her own again?
Speak, Lancelot, thou art silent; is it well?"

Thereto Sir Lancelot answer'd: "It is well;
Yet better if the King abide, and leave
The leading of his younger knights to me.   110
Else, for the King has will'd it, it is well."

Then Arthur rose and Lancelot follow'd him,
And while they stood without the doors, the King
Turn'd to him saying: "Is it then so well?
Or mine the blame that oft I seem as he
Of whom was written, 'A sound is in his ears'?
The foot that loiters, bidden go,—the glance
That only seems half-loyal to command,—
A manner somewhat fallen from reverence—
Or have I dream'd the bearing of our knights   120
Tells of a manhood ever less and lower?
Or whence the fear lest this my realm, uprear'd,
By noble deeds at one with noble vows,
From flat confusion and brute violences,
Reel back into the beast, and be no more?"

He spoke, and taking all his younger knights,
Down the slope city rode, and sharply turn'd
North by the gate. In her high bower the Queen,
Working a tapestry, lifted up her head,
Watch'd her lord pass, and knew not that she sigh'd.   130
Then ran across her memory the strange rhyme
Of bygone Merlin, "Where is he who knows?
From the great deep to the great deep he goes."

But when the morning of a tournament,
By these in earnest those in mockery call'd
The Tournament of the Dead Innocence,

Brake with a wet wind blowing, Lancelot,
Round whose sick head all night, like birds of prey,
The words of Arthur flying shriek'd, arose,
And down a streetway hung with folds of pure   **140**
White samite, and by fountains running wine,
Where children sat in white with cups of gold,
Moved to the lists, and there, with slow sad steps
Ascending, fill'd his double-dragon'd chair.

He glanced and saw the stately galleries,
Dame, damsel, each thro' worship of their Queen
White-robed in honor of the stainless child,
And some with scatter'd jewels, like a bank
Of maiden snow mingled with sparks of fire.
He look'd but once, and vail'd his eyes again.   **150**

The sudden trumpet sounded as in a dream
To ears but half-awaked, then one low roll
Of autumn thunder, and the jousts began;
And ever the wind blew, and yellowing leaf,
And gloom and gleam, and shower and shorn plume
Went down it. Sighing weariedly, as one
Who sits and gazes on a faded fire,
When all the goodlier guests are past away,
Sat their great umpire looking o'er the lists.
He saw the laws that ruled the tournament   **160**
Broken, but spake not; once, a knight cast down
Before his throne of arbitration cursed
The dead babe and the follies of the King;
And once the laces of a helmet crack'd,
And show'd him, like a vermin in its hole,
Modred, a narrow face. Anon he heard
The voice that billow'd round the barriers roar
An ocean-sounding welcome to one knight,
But newly-enter'd, taller than the rest,
And armor'd all in forest green, whereon   **170**
There tript a hundred tiny silver deer,
And wearing but a holly-spray for crest,
With ever-scattering berries, and on shield
A spear, a harp, a bugle—Tristram—late
From over-seas in Brittany return'd,
And marriage with a princess of that realm,

Isolt the White—Sir Tristram of the Woods—
Whom Lancelot knew, had held sometime with pain
His own against him, and now yearn'd to shake
The burthen off his heart in one full shock   180
With Tristram even to death. His strong hands gript
And dinted the gilt dragons right and left,
Until he groan'd for wrath—so many of those
That ware their ladies' colors on the casque
Drew from before Sir Tristram to the bounds,
And there with gibes and flickering mockeries
Stood, while he mutter'd, "Craven crests! O shame!
What faith have these in whom they sware to love?
The glory of our Round Table is no more."

    So Tristram won, and Lancelot gave, the gems,   190
Not speaking other word than, "Hast thou won?
Art thou the purest, brother? See, the hand
Wherewith thou takest this is red!" to whom
Tristram, half plagued by Lancelot's languorous mood,
Made answer: "Ay, but wherefore toss me this
Like a dry bone cast to some hungry hound?
Let be thy fair Queen's fantasy. Strength of heart
And might of limb, but mainly use and skill,
Are winners in this pastime of our King.
My hand—belike the lance hath dript upon it—   200
No blood of mine, I trow; but O chief knight,
Right arm of Arthur in the battle-field,
Great brother, thou nor I have made the world;
Be happy in thy fair Queen as I in mine."

    And Tristram round the gallery made his horse
Caracole; then bow'd his homage, bluntly saying,
"Fair damsels, each to him who worships each
Sole Queen of Beauty and of love, behold
This day my Queen of Beauty is not here."
And most of these were mute, some anger'd, one   210
Murmuring, "All courtesy is dead," and one,
"The glory of our Round Table is no more."

    Then fell thick rain, plume droopt and mantle clung,
And pettish cries awoke, and the wan day
Went glooming down in wet and weariness;

But under her black brows a swarthy one
Laugh'd shrilly, crying: "Praise the patient saints,
Our one white day of Innocence hath past,
Tho' somewhat draggled at the skirt. So be it.
The snowdrop only, flowering thro' the year,　　　　220
Would make the world as blank as wintertide.
Come—let us gladden their sad eyes, our Queen's
And Lancelot's, at this night's solemnity
With all the kindlier colors of the field."

So dame and damsel glitter'd at the feast
Variously gay; for he that tells the tale
Liken'd them, saying, as when an hour of cold
Falls on the mountain in midsummer snows,
And all the purple slopes of mountain flowers
Pass under white, till the warm hour returns　　　　230
With veer of wind and all are flowers again,
So dame and damsel cast the simple white,
And glowing in all colors, the live grass,
Rose-campion, bluebell, kingcup, poppy, glanced
About the revels, and with mirth so loud
Beyond all use, that, half-amazed, the Queen,
And wroth at Tristram and the lawless jousts,
Brake up their sports, then slowly to her bower
Parted, and in her bosom pain was lord.

And little Dagonet on the morrow morn,　　　　240
High over all the yellowing autumn-tide,
Danced like a wither'd leaf before the hall.
Then Tristram saying, "Why skip ye so, Sir Fool?"
Wheel'd round on either heel, Dagonet replied,
"Belike for lack of wiser company;
Or being fool, and seeing too much wit
Makes the world rotten, why, belike I skip
To know myself the wisest knight of all."
"Ay, fool," said Tristram, "but 'tis eating dry
To dance without a catch, a roundelay　　　　250
To dance to." Then he twangled on his harp,
And while he twangled little Dagonet stood
Quiet as any water-sodden log
Stay'd in the wandering warble of a brook,
But when the twangling ended, skipt again;

And being ask'd, "Why skipt ye not, Sir Fool?"
Made answer, "I had liefer twenty years
Skip to the broken music of my brains
Than any broken music thou canst make."
Then Tristram, waiting for the quip to come, 265
"Good now, what music have I broken, fool?"
And little Dagonet, skipping, "Arthur, the King's;
For when thou playest that air with Queen Isolt,
Thou makest broken music with thy bride,
Her daintier namesake down in Brittany—
And so thou breakest Arthur's music too."
"Save for that broken music in thy brains,
Sir Fool," said Tristram, "I would break thy head.
Fool, I came late, the heathen wars were o'er,
The life had flown, we sware but by the shell— 270
I am but a fool to reason with a fool—
Come, thou art crabb'd and sour; but lean me down,
Sir Dagonet, one of thy long asses' ears,
And harken if my music be not true.

" 'Free love—free field—we love but while we may.
The woods are hush'd, their music is no more;
The leaf is dead, the yearning past away.
New leaf, new life—the days of frost are o'er;
New life, new love, to suit the newer day;
New loves are sweet as those that went before. 280
Free love—free field—we love but while we may.'

"Ye might have moved slow-measure to my tune,
Not stood stock-still. I made it in the woods,
And heard it ring as true as tested gold."

But Dagonet with one foot poised in his hand:
"Friend, did ye mark that fountain yesterday,
Made to run wine?—but this had run itself
All out like a long life to a sour end—
And them that round it sat with golden cups
To hand the wine to whosoever came— 290
The twelve small damosels white as Innocence,
In honor of poor Innocence the babe,
Who left the gems which Innocence the Queen
Lent to the King, and Innocence the King

Gave for a prize—and one of those white slips
Handed her cup and piped, the pretty one,
'Drink, drink, Sir Fool,' and thereupon I drank,
Spat—pish—the cup was gold, the draught was mud."

And Tristram: "Was it muddier than thy gibes?
Is all the laughter gone dead out of thee?—   300
Not marking how the knighthood mock thee, fool—
'Fear God: honor the King—his one true knight—
Sole follower of the vows'—for here be they
Who knew thee swine enow before I came,
Smuttier than blasted grain. But when the King
Had made thee fool, thy vanity so shot up
It frighted all free fool from out thy heart;
Which left thee less than fool, and less than swine,
A naked aught—yet swine I hold thee still,
For I have flung thee pearls and find thee swine."   310

And little Dagonet mincing with his feet:
"Knight, an ye fling those rubies round my neck
In lieu of hers, I'll hold thou hast some touch
Of music, since I care not for thy pearls.
Swine? I have wallow'd, I have wash'd—the world
Is flesh and shadow—I have had my day.
The dirty nurse, Experience, in her kind
Hath foul'd me—an I wallow'd, then I wash'd—
I have had my day and my philosophies—
And thank the Lord I am King Arthur's fool.   320
Swine, say ye? swine, goats, asses, rams, and geese
Troop'd round a Paynim harper once, who thrumm'd
On such a wire as musically as thou
Some such fine song—but never a king's fool."

And Tristram, "Then were swine, goats, asses, geese
The wiser fools, seeing thy Paynim bard
Had such a mastery of his mystery
That he could harp his wife up out of hell."

Then Dagonet, turning on the ball of his foot,
"And whither harp'st thou thine? down! and thyself   330
Down! and two more; a helpful harper thou,
That harpest downward! Dost thou know the star
We call the Harp of Arthur up in heaven?"

And Tristram, "Ay, Sir Fool, for when our King
Was victor wellnigh day by day, the knights,
Glorying in each new glory, set his name
High on all hills and in the signs of heaven."

And Dagonet answer'd: "Ay, and when the land
Was freed, and the Queen false, ye set yourself
To babble about him, all to show your wit—   340
And whether he were king by courtesy,
Or king by right—and so went harping down
The black king's highway, got so far and grew
So witty that ye play'd at ducks and drakes
With Arthur's vows on the great lake of fire.
Tuwhoo! do ye see it? do ye see the star?"

"Nay, fool," said Tristram, "not in open day."
And Dagonet: "Nay, nor will; I see it and hear.
It makes a silent music up in heaven,
And I and Arthur and the angels hear,   350
And then we skip." "Lo, fool," he said, "ye talk
Fool's treason; is the King thy brother fool?"
Then little Dagonet clapt his hands and shrill'd:
"Ay, ay, my brother fool, the king of fools!
Conceits himself as God that he can make
Figs out of thistles, silk from bristles, milk
From burning spurge, honey from hornet-combs,
And men from beasts—Long live the king of fools!"

And down the city Dagonet danced away;
But thro' the slowly-mellowing avenues   360
And solitary passes of the wood
Rode Tristram toward Lyonnesse and the west.
Before him fled the face of Queen Isolt
With ruby-circled neck, but evermore
Past, as a rustle or twitter in the wood
Made dull his inner, keen his outer eye
For all that walk'd, or crept, or perch'd, or flew.
Anon the face, as, when a gust hath blown,
Unruffling waters re-collect the shape
Of one that in them sees himself, return'd;   370
But at the slot or fewmets of a deer,
Or even a fallen feather, vanish'd again.

So on for all that day from lawn to lawn
Thro' many a league-long bower he rode. At length
A lodge of intertwisted beechen-boughs,
Furze-cramm'd and bracken-rooft, the which himself
Built for a summer day with Queen Isolt
Against a shower, dark in the golden grove
Appearing, sent his fancy back to where
She lived a moon in that low lodge with him;   386
Till Mark her lord had past, the Cornish King,
With six or seven, when Tristram was away,
And snatch'd her thence, yet, dreading worse than shame
Her warrior Tristram, spake not any word,
But bode his hour, devising wretchedness.

And now that desert lodge to Tristram lookt
So sweet that, halting, in he past and sank
Down on a drift of foliage random-blown;
But could not rest for musing how to smooth
And sleek his marriage over to the queen.   390
Perchance in lone Tintagil far from all
The tonguesters of the court she had not heard.
But then what folly had sent him over-seas
After she left him lonely here? a name?
Was it the name of one in Brittany,
Isolt, the daughter of the king? "Isolt
Of the White Hands" they call'd her: the sweet name
Allured him first, and then the maid herself,
Who served him well with those white hands of hers,
And loved him well, until himself had thought   400
He loved her also, wedded easily,
But left her all as easily, and return'd.
The black-blue Irish hair and Irish eyes
Had drawn him home—what marvel? then he laid
His brows upon the drifted leaf and dream'd.

He seem'd to pace the strand of Brittany
Between Isolt of Britain and his bride,
And show'd them both the ruby-chain, and both
Began to struggle for it, till his queen
Graspt it so hard that all her hand was red.   410
Then cried the Breton, "Look, her hand is red!
These be no rubies, this is frozen blood,

And melts within her hand—her hand is hot
With ill desires, but this I gave thee, look,
Is all as cool and white as any flower."
Follow'd a rush of eagle's wings, and then
A whimpering of the spirit of the child,
Because the twain had spoil'd her carcanet.

He dream'd; but Arthur with a hundred spears
Rode far, till o'er the illimitable reed,   420
And many a glancing plash and sallowy isle,
The wide-wing'd sunset of the misty marsh
Glared on a huge machicolated tower
That stood with open doors, whereout was roll'd
A roar of riot, as from men secure
Amid their marshes, ruffians at their ease
Among their harlot-brides, an evil song.
"Lo there," said one of Arthur's youth, for there,
High on a grim dead tree before the tower,
A goodly brother of the Table Round   430
Swung by the neck; and on the boughs a shield
Showing a shower of blood in a field noir,
And therebeside a horn, inflamed the knights
At that dishonor done the gilded spur,
Till each would clash the shield and blow the horn.
But Arthur waved them back. Alone he rode.
Then at the dry harsh roar of the great horn,
That sent the face of all the marsh aloft
An ever upward-rushing storm and cloud
Of shriek and plume, the Red Knight heard, and all,   440
Even to tipmost lance and topmost helm,
In blood-red armor sallying, howl'd to the King:

"The teeth of Hell flay bare and gnash thee flat!—
Lo! art thou not that eunuch-hearted king
Who fain had clipt free manhood from the world—
The woman-worshipper? Yea, God's curse, and I!
Slain was the brother of my paramour
By a knight of thine, and I that heard her whine
And snivel, being eunuch-hearted too,
Sware by the scorpion-worm that twists in hell   450
And stings itself to everlasting death,
To hang whatever knight of thine I fought
And tumbled. Art thou king?—Look to thy life!"

He ended. Arthur knew the voice; the face
Wellnigh was helmet-hidden, and the name
Went wandering somewhere darkling in his mind.
And Arthur deign'd not use of word or sword,
But let the drunkard, as he stretch'd from horse
To strike him, overbalancing his bulk,
Down from the causeway heavily to the swamp   460
Fall, as the crest of some slow-arching wave,
Heard in dead night along that table-shore,
Drops flat, and after the great waters break
Whitening for half a league, and thin themselves,
Far over sands marbled with moon and cloud,
From less and less to nothing; thus he fell
Head-heavy. Then the knights, who watch'd him, roar'd
And shouted and leapt down upon the fallen,
There trampled out his face from being known,
And sank his head in mire, and slimed themselves;   470
Nor heard the King for their own cries, but sprang
Thro' open doors, and swording right and left
Men, women, on their sodden faces, hurl'd
The tables over and the wines, and slew
Till all the rafters rang with woman-yells,
And all the pavement stream'd with massacre.
Then, echoing yell with yell, they fired the tower,
Which half that autumn night, like the live North,
Red-pulsing up thro' Alioth and Alcor,
Made all above it, and a hundred meres   480
About it, as the water Moab saw
Come round by the east, and out beyond them flush'd
The long low dune and lazy-plunging sea.

So all the ways were safe from shore to shore,
But in the heart of Arthur pain was lord.

Then, out of Tristram waking, the red dream
Fled with a shout, and that low lodge return'd,
Mid-forest, and the wind among the boughs.
He whistled his good war-horse left to graze
Among the forest greens, vaulted upon him,   490
And rode beneath an ever-showering leaf,
Till one lone woman, weeping near a cross,
Stay'd him. "Why weep ye?" "Lord," she said, "my man

Hath left me or is dead;" whereon he thought—
"What, if she hate me now? I would not this.
What, if she love me still? I would not that.
I know not what I would"—but said to her,
"Yet weep not thou, lest, if thy mate return,
He find thy favor changed and love thee not"—
Then pressing day by day thro' Lyonnesse   500
Last in a roky hollow, belling, heard
The hounds of Mark, and felt the goodly hounds
Yelp at his heart, but, turning, past and gain'd
Tintagil, half in sea and high on land,
A crown of towers.

           Down in a casement sat,
A low sea-sunset glorying round her hair
And glossy-throated grace, Isolt the queen.
And when she heard the feet of Tristram grind
The spiring stone that scaled about her tower,
Flush'd, started, met him at the doors, and there   510
Belted his body with her white embrace,
Crying aloud: "Not Mark—not Mark, my soul!
The footstep flutter'd me at first—not he!
Catlike thro' his own castle steals my Mark,
But warrior-wise thou stridest thro' his halls
Who hates thee, as I him—even to the death.
My soul, I felt my hatred for my Mark
Quicken within me, and knew that thou wert nigh."
To whom Sir Tristram smiling, "I am here;
Let be thy Mark, seeing he is not thine."   520

    And drawing somewhat backward she replied:
"Can he be wrong'd who is not even his own,
But save for dread of thee had beaten me,
Scratch'd, bitten, blinded, marr'd me somehow—Mark?
What rights are his that dare not strike for them?
Not lift a hand—not, tho' he found me thus!
But harken! have ye met him? hence he went
To-day for three days' hunting—as he said—
And so returns belike within an hour.
Mark's way, my soul!—but eat not thou with Mark,   530
Because he hates thee even more than fears,
Nor drink; and when thou passest any wood

Close vizor, lest an arrow from the bush
Should leave me all alone with Mark and hell.
My God, the measure of my hate for Mark
Is as the measure of my love for thee!"

So, pluck'd one way by hate and one by love,
Drain'd of her force, again she sat, and spake
To Tristram, as he knelt before her, saying:
"O hunter, and O blower of the horn,   540
Harper, and thou hast been a rover too,
For, ere I mated with my shambling king,
Ye twain had fallen out about the bride
Of one—his name is out of me—the prize,
If prize she were—what marvel?—she could see—
Thine, friend; and ever since my craven seeks
To wreck thee villainously—but, O Sir Knight,
What dame or damsel have ye kneel'd to last?"

And Tristram, "Last to my Queen Paramount,
Here now to my queen paramount of love   550
And loveliness—ay, lovelier than when first
Her light feet fell on our rough Lyonnesse,
Sailing from Ireland."

                    Softly laugh'd Isolt:
"Flatter me not, for hath not our great Queen
My dole of beauty trebled?" and he said:
"Her beauty is her beauty, and thine thine,
And thine is more to me—soft, gracious, kind—
Save when thy Mark is kindled on thy lips
Most gracious; but she, haughty, even to him,
Lancelot; for I have seen him wan enow   560
To make one doubt if ever the great Queen
Have yielded him her love."

                    To whom Isolt:
"Ah, then, false hunter and false harper, thou
Who brakest thro' the scruple of my bond,
Calling me thy white hind, and saying to me
That Guinevere had sinn'd against the highest,
And I—misyoked with such a want of man—
That I could hardly sin against the lowest."

He answer'd: "O my soul, be comforted!
If this be sweet, to sin in leading-strings,   570
If here be comfort, and if ours be sin,
Crown'd warrant had we for the crowning sin
That made us happy; but how ye greet me—fear
And fault and doubt—no word of that fond tale—
Thy deep heart-yearnings, thy sweet memories
Of Tristram in that year he was away."

And, saddening on the sudden, spake Isolt:
"I had forgotten all in my strong joy
To see thee—yearnings?—ay! for, hour by hour,
Here in the never-ended afternoon,   580
O, sweeter than all memories of thee,
Deeper than any yearnings after thee
Seem'd those far-rolling, westward-smiling seas,
Watch'd from this tower. Isolt of Britain dash'd
Before Isolt of Brittany on the strand,
Would that have chill'd her bride-kiss? Wedded her?
Fought in her father's battles? wounded there?
The King was all fulfill'd with gratefulness,
And she, my namesake of the hands, that heal'd
Thy hurt and heart with unguent and caress—   590
Well—can I wish her any huger wrong
Than having known thee? her too hast thou left
To pine and waste in those sweet memories.
O, were I not my Mark's, by whom all men
Are noble, I should hate thee more than love."

And Tristram, fondling her light hands, replied:
"Grace, queen, for being loved; she loved me well.
Did I love her? the name at least I loved.
Isolt?—I fought his battles, for Isolt!
The night was dark; the true star set. Isolt!   600
The name was ruler of the dark—Isolt?
Care not for her! patient, and prayerful, meek,
Pale-blooded, she will yield herself to God."

And Isolt answer'd: "Yea, and why not I?
Mine is the larger need, who am not meek,
Pale-blooded, prayerful. Let me tell thee now.
Here one black, mute midsummer night I sat,

Lonely, but musing on thee, wondering where,
Murmuring a light song I had heard thee sing,
And once or twice I spake thy name aloud.   610
Then flash'd a levin-brand; and near me stood,
In fuming sulphur blue and green, a fiend—
Mark's way to steal behind one in the dark—
For there was Mark: 'He has wedded her,' he said.
Not said, but hiss'd it; then this crown of towers
So shook to such a roar of all the sky,
That here in utter dark I swoon'd away,
And woke again in utter dark, and cried,
'I will flee hence and give myself to God'—
And thou wert lying in thy new leman's arms."   620

    Then Tristram, ever dallying with her hand,
"May God be with thee, sweet, when old and gray,
And past desire!" a saying that anger'd her.
" 'May God be with thee, sweet, when thou art old,
And sweet no more to me!' I need Him now.
For when had Lancelot utter'd aught so gross
Even to the swineherd's malkin in the mast?
The greater man the greater courtesy.
Far other was the Tristram, Arthur's knight!
But thou, thro' ever harrying thy wild beasts—   630
Save that to touch a harp, tilt with a lance
Becomes thee well—art grown wild beast thyself.
How darest thou, if lover, push me even
In fancy from thy side, and set me far
In the gray distance, half a life away,
Her to be loved no more? Unsay it, unswear!
Flatter me rather, seeing me so weak,
Broken with Mark and hate and solitude,
Thy marriage and mine own, that I should suck
Lies like sweet wines. Lie to me; I believe.   640
Will ye not lie? not swear, as there ye kneel,
And solemnly as when ye sware to him,
The man of men, our King—My God, the power
Was once in vows when men believed the King!
They lied not then who sware, and thro' their vows
The King prevailing made his realm—I say,
Swear to me thou wilt love me even when old,
Gray-hair'd, and past desire, and in despair."

Then Tristram, pacing moodily up and down:
"Vows! did you keep the vow you made to Mark   650
More than I mine? Lied, say ye? Nay, but learnt,
The vow that binds too strictly snaps itself—
My knighthood taught me this—ay, being snapt—
We run more counter to the soul thereof
Than had we never sworn. I swear no more.
I swore to the great King, and am forsworn.
For once—even to the height—I honor'd him.
'Man, is he man at all?' methought, when first
I rode from our rough Lyonnesse, and beheld
That victor of the Pagan throned in hall—   660
His hair, a sun that ray'd from off a brow
Like hill-snow high in heaven, the steel-blue eyes,
The golden beard that clothed his lips with light—
Moreover, that weird legend of his birth,
With Merlin's mystic babble about his end
Amazed me; then, his foot was on a stool
Shaped as a dragon; he seem'd to me no man,
But Michael trampling Satan; so I sware,
Being amazed. But this went by—The vows!
O, ay—the wholesome madness of an hour—   670
They served their use, their time; for every knight
Believed himself a greater than himself,
And every follower eyed him as a God;
Till he, being lifted up beyond himself,
Did mightier deeds than elsewise he had done,
And so the realm was made. But then their vows—
First mainly thro' that sullying of our Queen—
Began to gall the knighthood, asking whence
Had Arthur right to bind them to himself?
Dropt down from heaven? wash'd up from out the deep? 680
They fail'd to trace him thro' the flesh and blood
Of our old kings. Whence then? a doubtful lord
To bind them by inviolable vows,
Which flesh and blood perforce would violate;
For feel this arm of mine—the tide within
Red with free chase and heather-scented air,
Pulsing full man. Can Arthur make me pure
As any maiden child? lock up my tongue
From uttering freely what I freely hear?
Bind me to one? The wide world laughs at it.   690

And worldling of the world am I, and know
The ptarmigan that whitens ere his hour
Woos his own end; we are not angels here
Nor shall be. Vows—I am woodman of the woods.
And hear the garnet-headed yaffingale
Mock them—my soul, we love but while we may;
And therefore is my love so large for thee,
Seeing it is not bounded save by love."

Here ending, he moved toward her, and she said:
"Good; an I turn'd away my love for thee   700
To some one thrice as courteous as thyself—
For courtesy wins woman all as well
As valor may, but he that closes both
Is perfect, he is Lancelot—taller indeed,
Rosier and comelier, thou—but say I loved
This knightliest of all knights, and cast thee back
Thine own small saw, 'We love but while we may,'
Well then, what answer?"

                              He that while she spake,
Mindful of what he brought to adorn her with,
The jewels, had let one finger lightly touch   710
The warm white apple of her throat, replied,
"Press this a little closer, sweet, until—
Come, I am hunger'd and half-anger'd—meat,
Wine, wine—and I will love thee to the death,
And out beyond into the dream to come."

So then, when both were brought to full accord,
She rose, and set before him all he will'd;
And after these had comforted the blood
With meats and wines, and satiated their hearts—
Now talking of their woodland paradise,   720
The deer, the dews, the fern, the founts, the lawns;
Now mocking at the much ungainliness,
And craven shifts, and long crane legs of Mark—
Then Tristram laughing caught the harp and sang:

"Ay, ay, O, ay—the winds that bend the brier!
A star in heaven, a star within the mere!
Ay, ay, O, ay—a star was my desire,
And one was far apart and one was near.

Ay, ay, O, ay—the winds that bow the grass!
And one was water and one star was fire,   730
And one will ever shine and one will pass.
Ay, ay, O, ay—the winds that move the mere!"

Then in the light's last glimmer Tristram show'd
And swung the ruby carcanet. She cried,
"The collar of some Order, which our King
Hath newly founded, all for thee, my soul,
For thee, to yield thee grace beyond thy peers."

"Not so, my queen," he said, "but the red fruit
Grown on a magic oak-tree in mid-heaven,
And won by Tristram as a tourney-prize,   740
And hither brought by Tristram for his last
Love-offering and peace-offering unto thee."

He spoke, he turn'd, then, flinging round her neck,
Claspt it, and cried, "Thine Order, O my queen!"
But, while he bow'd to kiss the jewell'd throat,
Out of the dark, just as the lips had touch'd,
Behind him rose a shadow and a shriek—
"Mark's way," said Mark, and clove him thro' the brain.

That night came Arthur home, and while he climb'd,
All in a death-dumb autumn-dripping gloom,   750
The stairway to the hall, and look'd and saw
The great Queen's bower was dark,—about his feet
A voice clung sobbing till he question'd it,
"What art thou?" and the voice about his feet
Sent up an answer, sobbing, "I am thy fool,
And I shall never make thee smile again."

                                        [publ. 1871]

THE REVENGE

A BALLAD OF THE FLEET

I

At Flores in the Azores Sir Richard Grenville lay,
And a pinnace, like a flutter'd bird, came flying from far away:

"Spanish ships of war at sea! we have sighted fifty-three!"
Then sware Lord Thomas Howard: " 'Fore God I am no coward;
But I cannot meet them here, for my ships are out of gear,
And the half my men are sick. I must fly, but follow quick.
We are six ships of the line; can we fight with fifty-three?"

II

Then spake Sir Richard Grenville: "I know you are no coward;
You fly them for a moment to fight with them again.
But I've ninety men and more that are lying sick ashore.   10
I should count myself the coward if I left them, my Lord Howard,
To these Inquisition dogs and the devildoms of Spain."

III

So Lord Howard past away with five ships of war that day,
Till he melted like a cloud in the silent summer heaven;
But Sir Richard bore in hand all his sick men from the land
Very carefully and slow,
Men of Bideford in Devon,
And we laid them on the ballast down below;
For we brought them all aboard,
And they blest him in their pain, that they were not left to
        Spain,   20
To the thumb-screw and the stake, for the glory of the Lord.

IV

He had only a hundred seamen to work the ship and to fight,
And he sailed away from Flores till the Spaniard came in sight,
With his huge sea-castles heaving upon the weather bow
"Shall we fight or shall we fly?
Good Sir Richard, tell us now,
For to fight is but to die!
There'll be little of us left by the time this sun be set."
And Sir Richard said again: "We be all good English men.
Let us bang these dogs of Seville, the children of the devil,   30
For I never turn'd my back upon Don or devil yet."

V

Sir Richard spoke and he laugh'd, and we roar'd a hurrah, and so
The little Revenge ran on sheer into the heart of the foe,
With her hundred fighters on deck, and her ninety sick below;
For half of their fleet to the right and half to the left were seen,
And the little Revenge ran on thro' the long sea-lane between.

VI

Thousands of their soldiers look'd down from their decks and
    laugh'd,
Thousands of their seamen made mock at the mad little craft
Running on and on, till delay'd
By their mountain-like San Philip that, of fifteen hundred
    tons,   40
And up-shadowing high above us with her yawning tiers of guns,
Took the breath from our sails, and we stay'd.

VII

And while now the great San Philip hung above us like a cloud
Whence the thunderbolt will fall
Long and loud,
Four galleons drew away
From the Spanish fleet that day,
And two upon the larboard and two upon the starboard lay,
And the battle-thunder broke from them all.

VIII

But anon the great San Philip, she bethought herself and
    went,   50
Having that within her womb that had left her ill content;
And the rest they came aboard us, and they fought us hand to
    hand,
For a dozen times they came with their pikes and musqueteers,
And a dozen times we shook 'em off as a dog that shakes his ears
When he leaps from the water to the land.

IX

And the sun went down, and the stars came out far over the
    summer sea,
But never a moment ceased the fight of the one and the fifty-
    three.
Ship after ship, the whole night long, their high-built galleons
    came,
Ship after ship, the whole night long, with her battle-thunder
    and flame;
Ship after ship, the whole night long, drew back with her dead
    and her shame.   60
For some were sunk and many were shatter'd, and so could fight
    us no more—
God of battles, was ever a battle like this in the world before?

X

For he said, "Fight on! fight on!"
Tho' his vessel was all but a wreck;
And it chanced that, when half of the short summer night was
    gone,
With a grisly wound to be drest he had left the deck,
But a bullet struck him that was dressing it suddenly dead,
And himself he was wounded again in the side and the head,
And he said, "Fight on! fight on!"

XI

And the night went down, and the sun smiled out far over the
    summer sea,   70
And the Spánish fleet with broken sides lay round us all in a ring;
But they dared not touch us again, for they fear'd that we still
    could sting,
So they watch'd what the end would be.
And we had not fought them in vain,
But in perilous plight were we,
Seeing forty of our poor hundred were slain,
And half of the rest of us maim'd for life
In the crash of the cannonades and the desperate strife;

And the sick men down in the hold were most of them stark and
    cold,
And the pikes were all broken or bent, and the powder was all
    of it spent;   80
And the masts and the rigging were lying over the side;
But Sir Richard cried in his English pride:
"We have fought such a fight for a day and a night
As may never be fought again!
We have won great glory, my men!
And a day less or more
At sea or ashore,
We die—does it matter when?
Sink me the ship, Master Gunner—sink her, split her in twain!
Fall into the hands of God, not into the hands of Spain!"   90

XII

And the gunner said, "Ay, ay," but the seamen made reply:
"We have children, we have wives,
And the Lord hath spared our lives.
We will make the Spaniard promise, if we yield, to let us go;
We shall live to fight again and to strike another blow."
And the lion there lay dying, and they yielded to the foe.

XIII

And the stately Spanish men to their flagship bore him then,
Where they laid him by the mast, old Sir Richard caught at last,
And they praised him to his face with their courtly foreign grace;
But he rose upon their decks, and he cried: 100
"I have fought for Queen and Faith like a valiant man and true;
I have only done my duty as a man is bound to do.
With a joyful spirit I Sir Richard Grenville die!"
And he fell upon their decks, and he died.

XIV

And they stared at the dead that had been so valiant and true,
And had holden the power and glory of Spain so cheap
That he dared her with one little ship and his English few;
Was he devil or man? He was devil for aught they knew,
But they sank his body with honor down into the deep,

And they mann'd the Revenge with a swarthier alien crew, 110
And away she sail'd with her loss and long'd for her own;
When a wind from the lands they had ruin'd awoke from sleep,
And the water began to heave and the weather to moan,
And or ever that evening ended a great gale blew,
And a wave like the wave that is raised by an earthquake grew,
Till it smote on their hulls and their sails and their masts and
   their flags,
And the whole sea plunged and fell on the shot-shatter'd navy of
   Spain,
And the little Revenge herself went down by the island crags
To be lost evermore in the main.

                       [publ. 1878]

THE VOYAGE OF MAELDUNE

(FOUNDED ON AN IRISH LEGEND A.D. 700)

I

I was the chief of the race—he had stricken my father dead—
But I gather'd my fellows together, I swore I would strike off his
   head.
Each of them look'd like a king, and was noble in birth as in
   worth,
And each of them boasted he sprang from the oldest race upon
   earth.
Each was as brave in the fight as the bravest hero of song,
And each of them liefer had died than have done one another
   a wrong.
He lived on an isle in the ocean—we sail'd on a Friday morn—
He that had slain my father the day before I was born.

II

And we came to the isle in the ocean, and there on the shore was
   he.
But a sudden blast blew us out and away thro' a boundless
   sea.   10

III

And we came to the Silent Isle that we never had touch'd at
    before,
Where a silent ocean always broke on a silent shore,
And the brooks glitter'd on in the light without sound, and the
    long waterfalls
Pour'd in a thunderless plunge to the base of the mountain walls,
And the poplar and cypress unshaken by storm flourish'd up
    beyond sight,
And the pine shot aloft from the crag to an unbelievable height,
And high in the heaven above it there flicker'd a songless lark,
And the cock couldn't crow, and the bull couldn't low, and the
    dog couldn't bark.
And round it we went, and thro' it, but never a murmur, a
    breath—
It was all of it fair as life, it was all of it quiet as death,   20
And we hated the beautiful isle, for whenever we strove to speak
Our voices were thinner and fainter than any flittermouse-shriek;
And the men that were mighty of tongue and could raise such a
    battle-cry
That a hundred who heard it would rush on a thousand lances
    and die—
O, they to be dumb'd by the charm!—so fluster'd with anger
    were they
They almost fell on each other; but after we sail'd away.

IV

And we came to the Isle of Shouting; we landed, a score of wild
    birds
Cried from the topmost summit with human voices and words.
Once in an hour they cried, and whenever their voices peal'd
The steer fell down at the plow and the harvest died from the
    field,   30
And the men dropt dead in the valleys and half of the cattle went
    lame,
And the roof sank in on the hearth, and the dwelling broke into
    flame;
And the shouting of these wild birds ran into the hearts of my
    crew,

Till they shouted along with the shouting and seized one another
and slew.
But I drew them the one from the other; I saw that we could not
stay,
And we left the dead to the birds, and we sail'd with our
wounded away.

V

And we came to the Isle of Flowers; their breath met us out on
the seas,
For the Spring and the middle Summer sat each on the lap of the
breeze;
And the red passion-flower to the cliffs, and the dark-blue clema-
tis, clung,
And starr'd with a myriad blossom the long convolvulus
hung;   40
And the topmost spire of the mountain was lilies in lieu of snow,
And the lilies like glaciers winded down, running out below
Thro' the fire of the tulip and poppy, the blaze of gorse, and the
blush
Of millions of roses that sprang without leaf or a thorn from the
bush;
And the whole isle-side flashing down from the peak without
ever a tree
Swept like a torrent of gems from the sky to the blue of the sea.
And we roll'd upon capes of crocus and vaunted our kith and
our kin,
And we wallow'd in beds of lilies, and chanted the triumph of
Finn,
Till each like a golden image was pollen'd from head to feet
And each was as dry as a cricket, with thirst in the middle-day
heat.   50
Blossom and blossom, and promise of blossom, but never a fruit!
And we hated the Flowering Isle, as we hated the isle that was
mute,
And we tore up the flowers by the million and flung them in
bight and bay,
And we left but a naked rock, and in anger we sail'd away.

VI

And we came to the Isle of Fruits; all round from the cliffs and
the capes,

Purple or amber, dangled a hundred fathom of grapes,
And the warm melon lay like a little sun on the tawny sand,
And the fig ran up from the beach and rioted over the land,
And the mountain arose like a jewell'd throne thro' the fragrant air,
Glowing with all-color'd plums and with golden masses of pear, 60
And the crimson and scarlet of berries that flamed upon bine and vine,
But in every berry and fruit was the poisonous pleasure of wine;
And the peak of the mountain was apples, the hugest that ever were seen,
And they prest, as they grew, on each other, with hardly a leaflet between,
And all of them redder than rosiest health or than utterest shame,
And setting, when Even descended, the very sunset aflame.
And we stay'd three days, and we gorged and we madden'd, till every one drew
His sword on his fellow to slay him, and ever they struck and they slew;
And myself, I had eaten but sparely, and fought till I sunder'd the fray,
Then I bade them remember my father's death, and we sail'd away. 70

VII

And we came to the Isle of Fire; we were lured by the light from afar,
For the peak sent up one league of fire to the Northern Star;
Lured by the glare and the blare, but scarcely could stand upright,
For the whole isle shudder'd and shook like a man in a mortal affright.
We were giddy besides with the fruits we had gorged, and so crazed that at last
There were some leap'd into the fire; and away we sail'd, and we past
Over that undersea isle, where the water is clearer than air.
Down we look'd—what a garden! O bliss, what a Paradise there!
Towers of a happier time, low down in a rainbow deep
Silent palaces, quiet fields of eternal sleep! 80

And three of the gentlest and best of my people, whate'er I could
    say,
Plunged head-down in the sea, and the Paradise trembled away.

VIII

And we came to the Bounteous Isle, where the heavens lean low
    on the land,
And ever at dawn from the cloud glitter'd o'er us a sun-bright
    hand,
Then it open'd and dropt at the side of each man, as he rose
    from his rest,
Bread enough for his need till the laborless day dipt under the
    west;
And we wander'd about it and thro' it. O, never was time so
    good!
And we sang of the triumphs of Finn, and the boast of our an-
    cient blood,
And we gazed at the wandering wave as we sat by the gurgle
    of springs,
And we chanted the songs of the Bards and the glories of fairy
    kings.   90
But at length we began to be weary, to sigh, and to stretch and
    yawn,
Till we hated the Bounteous Isle and the sun-bright hand of the
    dawn,
For there was not an enemy near, but the whole green isle was
    our own,
And we took to playing at ball, and we took to throwing the
    stone,
And we took to playing at battle, but that was a perilous play,
For the passion of battle was in us, we slew and we sail'd away.

IX

And we came to the Isle of Witches and heard their musical
    cry—
"Come to us, O, come, come!" in the stormy red of a sky
Dashing the fires and the shadows of dawn on the beautiful
    shapes,
For a wild witch naked as heaven stood on each of the loftiest
    capes,   100

And a hundred ranged on the rock like white sea-birds in a row,
And a hundred gamboll'd and pranced on the wrecks in the sand
 below,
And a hundred splash'd from the ledges, and bosom'd the burst
 of the spray;
But I knew we should fall on each other, and hastily sail'd away.

X

And we came in an evil time to the Isle of the Double Towers,
One was of smooth-cut stone, one carved all over with flowers,
But an earthquake always moved in the hollows under the dells,
And they shock'd on each other and butted each other with
 clashing of bells,
And the daws flew out of the towers and jangled and wrangled
 in vain,
And the clash and boom of the bells rang into the heart and the
 brain,   110
Till the passion of battle was on us, and all took sides with the
 towers,
There were some for the clean-cut stone, there were more for the
 carven flowers,
And the wrathful thunder of God peal'd over us all the day,
For the one half slew the other, and after we sail'd away.

XI

And we came to the Isle of a Saint who had sail'd with Saint
 Brendan of yore,
He had lived ever since on the isle and his winters were fifteen
 score,
And his voice was low as from other worlds, and his eyes were
 sweet,
And his white hair sank to his heels, and his white beard fell to
 his feet,
And he spake to me: "O Maeldune, let be this purpose of thine!
Remember the words of the Lord when he told us, 'Vengeance
 is mine!'   120
His fathers have slain thy fathers in war or in single strife,
Thy fathers have slain his fathers, each taken a life for a life,
Thy father had slain his father, how long shall the murder last?
Go back to the Isle of Finn and suffer the Past to be Past."

And we kiss'd the fringe of his beard, and we pray'd as we heard
    him pray,
And the holy man he assoil'd us, and sadly we sail'd away.

XII

And we came to the isle we were blown from, and there on the
    shore was he,
The man that had slain my father. I saw him and let him be.
O, weary was I of the travel, the trouble, the strife, and the sin,
When I landed again with a tithe of my men, on the Isle of
    Finn!   130
                    [publ. 1880]

BATTLE OF BRUNANBURH [1]

[A translation, printed in *Ballads, and Other Poems* (1880),
with this note: "Constantinus, King of the Scots, after having
sworn allegiance to Athelstan, allied himself with the Danes of
Ireland under Anlaf, and invading England, was defeated by
Athelstan and his brother Edmund with great slaughter at
Brunanburh in the year 937."]

I

    ATHELSTAN King,
    Lord among Earls,
    Bracelet-bestower and
    Baron of Barons,
    He with his brother,
    Edmund Atheling,
    Gaining a lifelong
    Glory in battle,
    Slew with the sword-edge
    There by Brunanburh,   10
    Brake the shield-wall,
    Hew'd the linden-wood,[2]
    Hack'd the battle-shield,
Sons of Edward with hammer'd brands.

[1] I have more or less availed myself of my son's prose translation of
this poem in the "Contemporary Review" (November, 1876). [Tennyson's note]

[2] Shields of lindenwood. [Tennyson's note]

II

Theirs was a greatness
Got from their grandsires—
Theirs that so often in
Strife with their enemies
Struck for their hoards and their hearths and their homes.

III

Bow'd the spoiler,   **20**
Bent the Scotsman,
Fell the ship-crews
Doom'd to the death.
All the field with blood of the fighters
Flow'd, from when first the great
Sun-star of morning-tide,
Lamp of the Lord God
Lord everlasting,
Glode over earth till the glorious creature
Sank to his setting.   **30**

IV

There lay many a man
Marr'd by the javelin,
Men of the Northland
Shot over shield.
There was the Scotsman
Weary of war.

V

We the West-Saxons,
Long as the daylight
Lasted, in companies
Troubled the track of the host that we hated;   **40**
Grimly with swords that were sharp from the grindstone,
Fiercely we hack'd at the flyers before us.

VI

Mighty the Mercian,
Hard was his hand-play,
Sparing not any of
Those that with Anlaf,
Warriors over the
Weltering waters
Borne in the bark's-bosom,
Drew to this island—   50
Doom'd to the death.

VII

Five young kings put asleep by the sword-stroke,
Seven strong earls of the army of Anlaf
Fell on the war-field, numberless numbers,
Shipmen and Scotsmen.

VIII

Then the Norse leader—
Dire was his need of it,
Few were his following—
Fled to his war-ship;
Fleeted his vessel to sea with the king in it,   60
Saving his life on the fallow flood.

IX

Also the crafty one,
Constantinus,
Crept to his North again,
Hoar-headed hero!

X

Slender warrant had
He to be proud of
The welcome of war-knives—
He that was reft of his
Folk and his friends that had   70

Fallen in conflict,
Leaving his son too
Lost in the carnage,
Mangled to morsels,
A youngster in war!

XI

Slender reason had
He to be glad of
The clash of the war-glaive—
Traitor and trickster
And spurner of treaties—   **80**
He nor had Anlaf
With armies so broken
A reason for bragging
That they had the better
In perils of battle
On places of slaughter—
The struggle of standards,
The rush of the javelins,
The crash of the charges,[1]
The wielding of weapons—   **90**
The play that they play'd with
The children of Edward.

XII

Then with their nail'd prows
Parted the Norsemen, a
Blood-redden'd relic of
Javelins over
The jarring breaker, the deep-sea billow,
Shaping their way toward Dyflen[2] again,
Shamed in their souls.

XIII

Also the brethren,   **100**
King and Atheling,

[1] Lit. "the gathering of men." [Tennyson's note]
[2] Dublin. [Tennyson's note]

Each in his glory,
Went to his own in his own West-Saxon land,
Glad of the war.

XIV

Many a carcase they left to be carrion,
Many a livid one, many a sallow-skin—
Left for the white-tail'd eagle to tear it, and
Left for the horny-nibb'd raven to rend it, and
Gave to the garbaging war-hawk to gorge it, and
That gray beast, the wolf of the weald.   110

XV

Never had huger
Slaughter of heroes
Slain by the sword-edge—
Such as old writers
Have writ of in histories—
Hapt in this isle, since
Up from the East hither
Saxon and Angle from
Over the broad billow
Broke into Britain with   120
Haughty war-workers who
Harried the Welshman, when
Earls that were lured by the
Hunger of glory gat
Hold of the land.

RIZPAH

17—

I

WAILING, wailing, wailing, the wind over land and sea—
And Willy's voice in the wind, "O mother, come out to me!"
Why should he call me to-night, when he knows that I cannot go?
For the downs are as bright as day, and the full moon stares at
    the snow.

II

We should be seen, my dear; they would spy us out of the town.
The loud black nights for us, and the storm rushing over the
down,
When I cannot see my own hand, but am led by the creak of the
chain,
And grovel and grope for my son till I find myself drenched with
the rain.

III

Anything fallen again? nay—what was there left to fall?
I have taken them home, I have number'd the bones, I have
hidden them all.   10
What am I saying? and what are *you*? do you come as a spy?
Falls? what falls? who knows? As the tree falls so must it lie.

IV

Who let her in? how long has she been? you—what have you
heard?
Why did you sit so quiet? you never have spoken a word.
O—to pray with me—yes—a lady—none of their spies—
But the night has crept into my heart, and begun to darken my
eyes.

V

Ah—you, that have lived so soft, what should *you* know of the
night,
The blast and the burning shame and the bitter frost and the
fright?
I have done it, while you were asleep—you were only made for
the day.
I have gather'd my baby together—and now you may go your
way.   20

VI

Nay—for it's kind of you, madam, to sit by an old dying wife
But say nothing hard of my boy, I have only an hour of life.
I kiss'd my boy in the prison, before he went out to die.

"They dared me to do it," he said, and he never has told me a lie.
I whipt him for robbing an orchard once when he was but a
　　　child—
"The farmer dared me to do it," he said; he was always so wild—
And idle—and couldn't be idle—my Willy—he never could rest.
The King should have made him a soldier, he would have been
　　　one of his best.

VII

But he lived with a lot of wild mates, and they never would let
　　　him be good;
They swore that he dare not rob the mail, and he swore that he
　　　would;　　　　　　　　　　　　　　　　　　　　　　　30
And he took no life, but he took one purse, and when all was
　　　done
He flung it among his fellows—"I'll none of it," said my son.

VIII

I came into court to the judge and the lawyers. I told them my
　　　tale,
God's own truth—but they kill'd him, they kill'd him for robbing
　　　the mail.
They hang'd him in chains for a show—we had always borne a
　　　good name—
To be hang'd for a thief—and then put away—isn't that enough
　　　shame?
Dust to dust—low down—let us hide! but they set him so high
That all the ships of the world could stare at him, passing by.
God'ill pardon the hell-black raven and horrible fowls of the air,
But not the black heart of the lawyer who kill'd him and hang'd
　　　him there.　　　　　　　　　　　　　　　　　　　　40

IX

And the jailer forced me away. I had bid him my last good-bye;
They had fasten'd the door of his cell. "O mother!" I heard him
　　　cry.
I couldn't get back tho' I tried, he had something further to say,
And now I never shall know it. The jailer forced me away.

X

Then since I couldn't but hear that cry of my boy that was dead,
They seized me and shut me up: they fasten'd me down on my
bed.
"Mother, O mother!"—he call'd in the dark to me year after
year—
They beat me for that, they beat me—you know that I couldn't
but hear;
And then at the last they found I had grown so stupid and still
They let me abroad again—but the creatures had worked their
will.   50

XI

Flesh of my flesh was gone, but bone of my bone was left—
I stole them all from the lawyers—and you, will you call it a
theft?—
My baby, the bones that had suck'd me, the bones that had
laughed and had cried—
Theirs? O, no! they are mine—not theirs—they had moved in
my side.

XII

Do you think I was scared by the bones? I kiss'd 'em, I buried
'em all—
I can't dig deep, I am old—in the night by the churchyard wall.
My Willy 'ill rise up whole when the trumpet of judgment 'ill
sound,
But I charge you never to say that I laid him in holy ground.

XIII

They would scratch him up—they would hang him again on the
cursed tree.
Sin? O, yes, we are sinners, I know—let all that be,   60
And read me a Bible verse of the Lord's goodwill toward men—
"Full of compassion and mercy, the Lord"—let me hear it again;
"Full of compassion and mercy—long-suffering." Yes, O, yes!
For the lawyer is born but to murder—the Saviour lives but to
bless.
He'll never put on the black cap except for the worst of the
worst,

And the first may be last—I have heard it in church—and the
    last may be first.
Suffering—O, long-suffering—yes, as *t*he Lord must know,
Year after year in the mist and the wind and the shower and
    the snow.

XIV

Heard, have you? what? they have told you he never repented
    his sin.
How do they know it? are *they* his mother? are *you* of his
    kin?   70
Heard! have you ever heard, when the storm on the downs began,
The wind that 'ill wail like a child and the sea that 'ill moan like
    a man?

XV

Election, Election, and Reprobation—it's all very well.
But I go to-night to my boy, and I shall not find him in hell.
For I cared so much for my boy that the Lord has look'd into
    my care,
And He means me I'm sure to be happy with Willy, I know not
    where.

XVI

And if *he* be lost—but to save *my* soul, that is all your desire—
Do you think that I care for *my* soul if my boy be gone to the
    fire?
I have been with God in the dark—go, go, you may leave me
    alone—
You never have borne a child—you are just as hard as a
    stone.   80

XVII

Madam, I beg your pardon! I think that you mean to be kind,
But I cannot hear what you say for my Willy's voice in the
    wind—
The snow and the sky so bright—he used but to call in the dark,
And he calls to me now from the church and not from the gib-
    bet—for hark!
Nay—you can hear it yourself—it is coming—shaking the
    walls—
Willy—the moon's in a cloud——Good-night. I am going. He
    calls.

[publ. 1880]

"FRATER AVE ATQUE VALE"

Row us out from Desenzano, to your Sirmione row!
So they row'd, and there we landed—"O venusta Sirmio!"
There to me thro' all the groves of olive in the summer glow,
There beneath the Roman ruin where the purple flowers grow,
Came that "Ave atque Vale" of the Poet's hopeless woe,
Tenderest of Roman poets nineteen hundred years ago,
"Frater Ave atque Vale"—as we wander'd to and fro
Gazing at the Lydian laughter of the Garda Lake below
Sweet Catullus's all-but-island, olive-silvery Sirmio!

[1880; publ. 1883]

TO VIRGIL

WRITTEN AT THE REQUEST OF THE MANTUANS FOR THE NINETEENTH CENTENARY OF VIRGIL'S DEATH

I

ROMAN VIRGIL, thou that singest
  Ilion's lofty temples robed in fire,
Ilion falling, Rome arising,
  wars, and filial faith, and Dido's pyre;

II

Landscape-lover, lord of language
  more than he that sang the "Works and Days,"
All the chosen coin of fancy
  flashing out from many a golden phrase;

III

Thou that singest wheat and woodland,
  tilth and vineyard, hive and horse and herd;
All the charm of all the Muses
  often flowering in a lonely word;

IV

Poet of the happy Tityrus
      piping underneath his beechen bowers;
Poet of the poet-satyr
      whom the laughing shepherd bound with flowers;

V

Chanter of the Pollio, glorying
      in the blissful years again to be,
Summers of the snakeless meadow,
      unlaborious earth and oarless sea;   10

VI

Thou that seest Universal
      Nature moved by Universal Mind;
Thou majestic in thy sadness
      at the doubtful doom of human kind;

VII

Light among the vanish'd ages;
      star that gildest yet this phantom shore;
Golden branch amid the shadows,
      kings and realms that pass to rise no more;

VIII

Now thy Forum roars no longer,
      fallen every purple Cæsar's dome—
Tho' thine ocean-roll of rhythm
      sound for ever of Imperial Rome—

IX

Now the Rome of slaves hath perish'd,
      and the Rome of freemen holds her place,
I, from out the Northern Island
      sunder'd once from all the human race,

x

I salute thee, Mantovano,
  I that loved thee since my day began,
Wielder of the stateliest measure
   ever moulded by the lips of man.   20

        [publ. 1882]

VASTNESS

I

MANY a hearth upon our dark globe sighs after many a vanish'd
  face,
Many a planet by many a sun may roll with the dust of a vanish'd race.

II

Raving politics, never at rest—as this poor earth's pale history
  runs,—
What is it all but a trouble of ants in the gleam of a million million of suns?

III

Lies upon this side, lies upon that side, truthless violence mourn'd
  by the wise,
Thousands of voices drowning his own in a popular torrent of
  lies upon lies;

IV

Stately purposes, valor in battle, glorious annals of army and
  fleet,
Death for the right cause, death for the wrong cause, trumpets of
  victory, groans of defeat;

V

Innocence seethed in her mother's milk, and Charity setting the
  martyr aflame;

Thraldom who walks with the banner of Freedom, and recks not
    to ruin a realm in her name.   **10**

VI

Faith at her zenith, or all but lost in the gloom of doubts that
    darken the schools;
Craft with a bunch of all-heal in her hand, follow'd up by her
    vassal legion of fools;

VII

Trade flying over a thousand seas with her spice and her vintage,
    her silk and her corn;
Desolate offing, sailorless harbors, famishing populace, wharves
    forlorn;

VIII

Star of the morning, Hope in the sunrise; gloom of the evening,
    Life at a close;
Pleasure who flaunts on her wide downway with her flying robe
    and her poison'd rose;

IX

Pain, that has crawl'd from the corpse of Pleasure, a worm which
    writhes all day, and at night
Stirs up again in the heart of the sleeper, and stings him back to
    the curse of the light;

X

Wealth with his wines and his wedded harlots; honest Poverty,
    bare to the bone;
Opulent Avarice, lean as Poverty; Flattery gilding the rift in a
    throne;   **20**

XI

Fame blowing out from her golden trumpet a jubilant challenge
    to Time and to Fate;
Slander, her shadow, sowing the nettle on all the laurell'd graves
    of the great;

XII

Love for the maiden, crown'd with marriage, no regrets for aught
that has been,
Household happiness, gracious children, debtless competence,
golden mean;

XIII

National hatreds of whole generations, and pigmy spites of the
village spire;
Vows that will last to the last death-ruckle, and vows that are
snapt in a moment of fire;

XIV

He that has lived for the lust of the minute, and died in the doing
it, flesh without mind;
He that has nail'd all flesh to the Cross, till Self died out in the
love of his kind;

XV

Spring and Summer and Autumn and Winter, and all these old
revolutions of earth;
All new-old revolutions of Empire—change of the tide—what is
all of it worth?   30

XVI

What the philosophies, all the sciences, poesy, varying voices of
prayer,
All that is noblest, all that is basest, all that is filthy with all that
is fair?

XVII

What is it all, if we all of us end but in being our own corpse-
coffins at last?
Swallow'd in Vastness, lost in Silence, drown'd in the deeps of
a meaningless Past?

XVIII

What but a murmur of gnats in the gloom, or a moment's anger
    of bees in their hive?—

Peace, let it be! for I loved him, and love him for ever: the dead
    are not dead but alive.

                        [publ. 1885]

THE ANCIENT SAGE

A THOUSAND summers ere the time of Christ,
From out his ancient city came a Seer
Whom one that loved and honor'd him, and yet
Was no disciple, richly garb'd, but worn
From wasteful living, follow'd—in his hand
A scroll of verse—till that old man before
A cavern whence an affluent fountain pour'd
From darkness into daylight, turn'd and spoke:

"This wealth of waters might but seem to draw
From yon dark cave, but, son, the source is higher,   10
Yon summit half-a-league in air—and higher
The cloud that hides it—higher still the heavens
Whereby the cloud was moulded, and whereout
The cloud descended. Force is from the heights.
I am wearied of our city, son, and go
To spend my one last year among the hills.
What hast thou there? Some death-song for the Ghouls
To make their banquet relish? let me read.

   " 'How far thro' all the bloom and brake
      That nightingale is heard!   20
   What power but the bird's could make
      This music in the bird?
   How summer-bright are yonder skies,
      And earth as fair in hue!
   And yet what sign of aught that lies
      Behind the green and blue?
   But man to-day is fancy's fool
      As man hath ever been.

The nameless Power, or Powers, that rule
Were never heard or seen.'   **30**

If thou wouldst hear the Nameless, and wilt dive
Into the temple-cave of thine own self,
There, brooding by the central altar, thou
Mayst haply learn the Nameless hath a voice,
By which thou wilt abide, if thou be wise,
As if thou knewest, tho' thou canst not know;
For Knowledge is the swallow on the lake
That sees and stirs the surface-shadow there
But never yet hath dipt into the abysm,
The abysm of all abysms, beneath, within   **40**
The blue of sky and sea, the green of earth,
And in the million-millionth of a grain
Which cleft and cleft again for evermore,
And ever vanishing, never vanishes,
To me, my son, more mystic than myself,
Or even than the Nameless is to me.
  "And when thou sendest thy free soul thro' heaven,
Nor understandest bound nor boundlessness,
Thou seest the Nameless of the hundred names.
  "And if the Nameless should withdraw from all   **50**
Thy frailty counts most real, all thy world
Might vanish like thy shadow in the dark.

          "'And since—from when this earth began—
              The Nameless never came
            Among us, never spake with nan,
              And never named the Name—

Thou canst not prove the Nameless, O my son,
Nor canst thou prove the world thou movest in,
Thou canst not prove that thou art body alone,
Nor canst thou prove that thou art spirit alone,   **60**
Nor canst thou prove that thou art both in one.
Thou canst not prove thou art immortal, no,
Nor yet that thou art mortal—nay, my son,
Thou canst not prove that I, who speak with thee,
Am not thyself in converse with thyself,
For nothing worthy proving can be proven,
Nor yet disproven. Wherefore thou be wise,
Cleave ever to the sunnier side of doubt,
And cling to Faith beyond the forms of Faith!

She reels not in the storm of warring words,   **70**
She brightens at the clash of 'Yes' and 'No,'
She sees the best that glimmers thro' the worst,
She feels the sun is hid but for a night,
She spies the summer thro' the winter bud,
She tastes the fruit before the blossom falls,
She hears the lark within the songless egg,
She finds the fountain where they wail'd 'Mirage!'

> " 'What Power? aught akin to Mind,
>   The mind in me and you?
>   Or power as of the Gods gone blind   **80**
>   Who see not what they do?'

But some in yonder city hold, my son,
That none but gods could build this house of ours,
So beautiful, vast, various, so beyond
All work of man, yet, like all work of man,
A beauty with defect—till That which knows,
And is not known, but felt thro' what we feel
Within ourselves is highest, shall descend
On this half-deed, and shape it at the last
According to the Highest in the Highest.   **90**

> " 'What Power but the Years that make
>   And break the vase of clay,
>   And stir the sleeping earth, and wake
>   The bloom that fades away?
>   What rulers but the Days and Hours
>   That cancel weal with woe,
>   And wind the front of youth with flowers,
>   And cap our age with snow?'

The days and hours are ever glancing by,
And seem to flicker past thro' sun and shade,   **100**
Or short, or long, as Pleasure leads, or Pain,
But with the Nameless is nor day nor hour;
Tho' we, thin minds, who creep from thought to thought,
Break into 'Thens' and 'Whens' the Eternal Now—
This double seeming of the single world!—
My words are like the babblings in a dream
Of nightmare, when the babblings break the dream.
But thou be wise in this dream-world of ours,
Nor take thy dial for thy deity,
But make the passing shadow serve thy will.   **110**

" 'The years that made the stripling wise
    Undo their work again,
And leave him, blind of heart and eyes,
    The last and least of men;
Who clings to earth, and once would dare
    Hell-heat or Arctic cold,
And now one breath of cooler air
    Would loose him from his hold.
His winter chills him to the root,
    He withers marrow and mind;   **120**
The kernel of the shrivell'd fruit
    Is jutting thro' the rind;
The tiger spasms tear his chest,
    The palsy wags his head;
The wife, the sons, who love him best
    Would fain that he were dead;
The griefs by which he once was wrung
    Were never worth the while'—

Who knows? or whether this earth-narrow life
Be yet but yolk, and forming in the shell?   **130**

    " 'The shaft of scorn that once had stung
        But wakes a dotard smile.'

The placid gleam of sunset after storm!

    " 'The statesman's brain that sway'd the past
        Is feebler than his knees;
The passive sailor wrecks at last
    In ever-silent seas;
The warrior hath forgot his arms,
    The learned all his lore;
The changing market frets or charms   **140**
    The merchant's hope no more:
The prophet's beacon burn'd in vain,
    And now is lost in cloud;
The plowman passes, bent with pain,
    To mix with what he plow'd;
The poet whom his age would quote
    As heir of endless fame—
He knows not even the book he wrote,
    Not even his own name.
For man has overlived his day,   **150**
    And, darkening in the light,
Scarce feels the senses break away
    To mix with ancient Night.'

The shell must break before the bird can fly.

    " 'The years that when my youth began
        Had set the lily and rose
    By all my ways where'er they ran,
        Have ended mortal foes;
    My rose of love for ever gone,
        My lily of truth and trust—   160
    They made her lily and rose in one,
        And changed her into dust.
    O rose-tree planted in my grief,
        And growing on her tomb,
    Her dust is greening in your leaf,
        Her blood is in your bloom.
    O slender lily waving there,
      And laughing back the light,
    In vain you tell me "Earth is fair"
        When all is dark as night.'   170

My son, the world is dark with griefs and graves,
So dark that men cry out against the heavens.
Who knows but that the darkness is in man?
The doors of Night may be the gates of Light,
For wert thou born or blind or deaf, and then
Suddenly heal'd, how wouldst thou glory in all
The splendors and the voices of the world!
And we, the poor earth's dying race, and yet
No phantoms, watching from a phantom shore
Await the last and largest sense to make   180
The phantom walls of this illusion fade,
And show us that the world is wholly fair.

    " 'But vain the tears for darken'd years
        As laughter over wine,
    And vain the laughter as the tears,
        O brother, mine or thine,
    For all that laugh, and all that weep
        And all that breathe are one
    Slight ripple on the boundless deep
        That moves, and all is gone.'   190

But that one ripple on the boundless deep
Feels that the deep is boundless, and itself
For ever changing form, but evermore
One with the boundless motion of the deep.

" 'Yet wine and laughter, friends! and set
    The lamps alight, and call
For golden music, and forget
    The darkness of the pall.'

If utter darkness closed the day, my son—
But earth's dark forehead flings athwart the heavens   200
Her shadow crown'd with stars—and yonder—out
To northward—some that never set, but pass
From sight and night to lose themselves in day.
I hate the black negation of the bier,
And wish the dead, as happier than ourselves
And higher, having climb'd one step beyond
Our village miseries, might be borne in white
To burial or to burning, hymn'd from hence
With songs in praise of death, and crown'd with flowers!

    " 'O worms and maggots of to-day   210
      Without their hope of wings!'

But louder than thy rhyme the silent Word
Of that world-prophet in the heart of man.

    " 'Tho' some have gleams, or so they say,
      Of more than mortal things.'

To-day? but what of yesterday? for oft
On me, when boy, there came what then I call'd,
Who knew no books and no philosophies,
In my boy-phrase, 'The Passion of the Past.'
The first gray streak of earliest summer-dawn,   220
The last long stripe of waning crimson gloom,
As if the late and early were but one—
A height, a broken grange, a grove, a flower
Had murmurs, 'Lost and gone, and lost and gone!'
A breath, a whisper—some divine farewell—
Desolate sweetness—far and far away—
What had he loved, what had he lost, the boy?
I know not, and I speak of what has been.
    "And more, my son! for more than once when I
Sat all alone, revolving in myself   230
The word that is the symbol of myself,
The mortal limit of the Self was loosed,
And past into the Nameless, as a cloud

Melts into heaven. I touch'd my limbs, the limbs
Were strange, not mine—and yet no shade of doubt,
But utter clearness, and thro' loss of self
The gain of such large life as match'd with ours
Were sun to spark—unshadowable in words,
Themselves but shadows of a shadow-world.

  " 'And idle gleams will come and go,   **240**
   But still the clouds remain;'

The clouds themselves are children of the Sun.

  " 'And Night and Shadow rule below
   When only Day should reign.'

And Day and Night are children of the Sun,
And idle gleams to thee are light to me.
Some say, the Light was father of the Night,
And some, the Night was father of the Light,
No night, no day!—I touch thy world again—
No ill, no good! such counter-terms, my son, **250**
Are border-races, holding each its own
By endless war. But night enough is there
In yon dark city. Get thee back; and since
The key to that weird casket, which for thee
But holds a skull, is neither thine nor mine,
But in the hand of what is more than man,
Or in man's hand when man is more than man,
Let be thy wail, and help thy fellow-men,
And make thy gold thy vassal, not thy king,
And fling free alms into the beggar's bowl, **260**
And send the day into the darken'd heart;
Nor list for guerdon in the voice of men,
A dying echo from a falling wall;
Nor care—for Hunger hath the evil eye—
To vex the noon with fiery gems, or fold
Thy presence in the silk of sumptuous looms;
Nor roll thy viands on a luscious tongue,
Nor drown thyself with flies in honeyed wine;
Nor thou be rageful, like a handled bee,
And lose thy life by usage of thy sting; **270**
Nor harm an adder thro' the lust for harm,
Nor make a snail's horn shrink for wantonness.
And more—think well! Do-well will follow thought,

And in the fatal sequence of this world
An evil thought may soil thy children's blood;
But curb the beast would cast thee in the mire,
And leave the hot swamp of voluptuousness,
A cloud between the Nameless and thyself,
And lay thine uphill shoulder to the wheel,
And climb the Mount of Blessing, whence, if thou   280
Look higher, then—perchance—thou mayest—beyond
A hundred ever-rising mountain lines,
And past the range of Night and Shadow—see
The high-heaven dawn of more than mortal day
Strike on the Mount of Vision!
                              So, farewell."
                                        [publ. 1885]

POETS AND THEIR BIBLIOGRAPHIES

OLD poets foster'd under friendlier skies,
    Old Virgil who would write ten lines, they say,
    At dawn, and lavish all the golden day
To make them wealthier in his readers' eyes;
And you, old popular Horace, you the wise
    Adviser of the nine-years-ponder'd lay,
    And you, that wear a wreath of sweeter bay,
Catullus, whose dead songster never dies;
If, glancing downward on the kindly sphere
    That once had roll'd you round and round the sun,   10
You see your Art still shrined in human shelves,
You should be jubilant that you flourish'd here
    Before the Love of Letters, overdone,
Had swampt the sacred poets with themselves.
                                        [publ. 1885]

DEMETER AND PERSEPHONE

(IN ENNA)

FAINT as a climate-changing bird that flies
All night across the darkness, and at dawn

Falls on the threshold of her native land,
And can no more, thou camest, O my child,
Led upward by the God of ghosts and dreams.
Who laid thee at Eleusis, dazed and dumb
With passing thro' at once from state to state,
Until I brought thee hither, that the day,
When here thy hands let fall the gather'd flower,
Might break thro' clouded memories once again   10
On thy lost self. A sudden nightingale
Saw thee, and flash'd into a frolic of song
And welcome; and a gleam as of the moon,
When first she peers along the tremulous deep,
Fled wavering o'er thy face, and chased away
That shadow of a likeness to the king
Of shadows, thy dark mate. Persephone!
Queen of the dead no more—my child! Thine eyes
Again were human-godlike, and the Sun
Burst from a swimming fleece of winter gray,   20
And robed thee in his day from head to feet—
"Mother!" and I was folded in thine arms.

Child, those imperial, disimpassion'd eyes
Awed even me at first, thy mother—eyes
That oft had seen the serpent-wanded power
Draw downward into Hades with his drift
Of flickering spectres, lighted from below
By the red race of fiery Phlegethon;
But when before have Gods or men beheld
The Life that had descended re-arise,   30
And lighted from above him by the Sun?
So mighty was the mother's childless cry,
A cry that rang thro' Hades, Earth, and Heaven!

So in this pleasant vale we stand again,
The field of Enna, now once more ablaze
With flowers that brighten as thy footstep falls,
All flowers—but for one black blur of earth
Left by that closing chasm, thro' which the car
Of dark Aïdoneus rising rapt thee hence.
And here, my child, tho' folded in thine arms,   40
I feel the deathless heart of motherhood
Within me shudder, lest the naked glebe

Should yawn once more into the gulf, and thence
The shrilly whinnyings of the team of Hell,
Ascending, pierce the glad and songful air,
And all at once their arch'd necks, midnight-maned,
Jet upward thro' the midday blossom. No!
For, see, thy foot has touch'd it; all the space
Of blank earth-baldness clothes itself afresh,
And breaks into the crocus-purple hour   **50**
That saw thee vanish.

                    Child, when thou wertgone,
I envied human wives, and nested birds,
Yea, the cubb'd lioness; went in search of thee
Thro' many a palace, many a cot, and gave
Thy breast to ailing infants in the night,
And set the mother waking in amaze
To find her sick one whole; and forth again
Among the wail of midnight winds, and cried,
"Where is my loved one? Wherefore do ye wail?"
And out from all the night an answer shrill'd,   **60**
"We know not, and we know not why we wail."
I climb'd on all the cliffs of all the seas,
And ask'd the waves that moan about the world,
"Where? do ye make your moaning for my child?"
And round from all the world the voices came,
"We know not, and we know not why we moan."
"Where?" and I stared from every eagle-peak,
I thridded the black heart of all the woods,
I peer'd thro' tomb and cave, and in the storms
Of autumn swept across the city, and heard   **70**
The murmur of their temples chanting me,
Me, me, the desolate mother! "Where?"—and turn'd,
And fled by many a waste, forlorn of man,
And grieved for man thro' all my grief for thee,—
The jungle rooted in his shatter'd hearth,
The serpent coil'd about his broken shaft,
The scorpion crawling over naked skulls;—
I saw the tiger in the ruin'd fane
Spring from his fallen God, but trace of thee
I saw not; and far on, and, following out   **80**
A league of labyrinthine darkness, came
On three gray heads beneath a gleaming rift.

"Where?" and I heard one voice from all the three,
"We know not, for we spin the lives of men,
And not of Gods, and know not why we spin!
There is a Fate beyond us." Nothing knew.

Last as the likeness of a dying man,
Without his knowledge, from him flits to warn
A far-off friendship that he comes no more,
So he, the God of dreams, who heard my cry,   90
Drew from thyself the likeness of thyself
Without thy knowledge, and thy shadow past
Before me, crying, "The Bright one in the highest
Is brother of the Dark one in the lowest,
And Bright and Dark have sworn that I, the child
Of thee, the great Earth-Mother, thee, the Power
That lifts her buried life from gloom to bloom,
Should be for ever and for evermore
The Bride of Darkness."

               So the Shadow wail'd.
Then I, Earth-Goddess, cursed the Gods of heaven.   100
I would not mingle with their feasts; to me
Their nectar smack'd of hemlock on the lips,
Their rich ambrosia tasted aconite.
The man, that only lives and loves an hour,
Seem'd nobler than their hard eternities.
My quick tears kill'd the flower, my ravings hush'd
The bird, and lost in utter grief I fail'd
To send my life thro' olive-yard and vine
And golden-grain, my gift to helpless man.
Rain-rotten died the wheat, the barley-spears   110
Were hollow-husk'd, the leaf fell, and the Sun,
Pale at my grief, drew down before his time
Sickening, and Ætna kept her winter snow.

Then He, the brother of this Darkness, He
Who still is highest, glancing from his height
On earth a fruitless fallow, when he miss'd
The wonted steam of sacrifice, the praise
And prayer of men, decreed that thou shouldst dwell
For nine white moons of each whole year with me,
Three dark ones in the shadow with thy king.   120

Once more the reaper in the gleam of dawn
Will see me by the landmark far away,
Blessing his field, or seated in the dusk
Of even, by the lonely threshing-floor,
Rejoicing in the harvest and the grange.

Yet I, Earth-Goddess, am but ill-content
With them who still are highest. Those gray heads,
What meant they by their "Fate beyond the Fates"
But younger kindlier Gods to bear us down,
As we bore down the Gods before us? Gods,   **130**
To quench, not hurl the thunderbolt, to stay,
Not spread the plague, the famine; Gods indeed,
To send the noon into the night and break
The sunless halls of Hades into Heaven?
Till thy dark lord accept and love the Sun,
And all the Shadow die into the Light,
When thou shalt dwell the whole bright year with me,
And souls of men, who grew beyond their race,
And made themselves as Gods against the fear
Of Death and Hell; and thou that hast from men,   **140**
As Queen of Death, that worship which is Fear,
Henceforth, as having risen from out the dead,
Shalt ever send thy life along with mine
From buried grain thro' springing blade, and bless
Their garner'd autumn also, reap with me,
Earth-Mother, in the harvest hymns of Earth
The worship which is Love, and see no more
The Stone, the Wheel, the dimly-glimmering lawns
Of that Elysium, all the hateful fires
Of torment, and the shadowy warrior glide   **150**
Along the silent field of Asphodel.

[1887; publ. 1889]

PARNASSUS

Exegi monumentum . . .
Quod non . . .
Possit diruere . . .
                              . . . innumerabilis
Annorum series et fuga temporum.

HORACE.

I

WHAT be those crown'd forms high over the sacred fountain?
Bards, that the mighty Muses have raised to the heights of the
    mountain,
And over the flight of the Ages! O Goddesses, help me up
    thither!
Lightning may shrivel the laurel of Cæsar, but mine would not
    wither.
Steep is the mountain, but you, you will help me to overcome it,
And stand with my head in the zenith, and roll my voice from
    the summit,
Sounding for ever and ever thro' Earth and her listening nations,
And mixt with the great sphere-music of stars and of constella-
    tions.

II

What be those two shapes high over the sacred fountain,
Taller than all the Muses, and huger than all the mountain?   10
On those two known peaks they stand ever spreading and
    heightening;
Poet, that evergreen laurel is blasted by more than lightning!
Look, in their deep double shadow the crown'd ones all dis-
    appearing!
Sing like a bird and be happy, nor hope for a deathless hearing!
"Sounding for ever and ever"? pass on! the sight confuses—
These are Astronomy and Geology, terrible Muses!

III

If the lips were touch'd with fire from off a pure Pierian altar,
Tho' their music here be mortal need the singer greatly care?

Other songs for other worlds! the fire within him would not
    falter;
Let the golden Iliad vanish, Homer here is Homer there.   **20**
                                         [publ. 1889]

FAR — FAR — AWAY

(FOR MUSIC)

WHAT sight so lured him thro' the fields he knew
As where earth's green stole into heaven's own hue,
          Far — far — away?

What sound was dearest in his native dells?
The mellow lin-lan-lone of evening bells
          Far — far — away.

What vague world-whisper, mystic pain or joy,
Thro' those three words would haunt him when a boy,
          Far — far — away?

A whisper from his dawn of life? a breath   **10**
From some fair dawn beyond the doors of death
          Far — far — away?

Far, far, how far? from o'er the gates of birth,
The faint horizons, all the bounds of earth,
          Far — far — away?

What charm in words, a charm no words could give?
O dying words, can Music make you live
          Far — far — away?
              [publ. 1889]

TO MARY BOYLE

WITH THE FOLLOWING POEM[1]

I

"SPRING-FLOWERS"! While you still delay to take
    Your leave of town,
Our elm-tree's ruddy-hearted blossom-flake
    Is fluttering down.

II

Be truer to your promise. There! I heard
    Our cuckoo call.
Be needle to the magnet of your word,
    Nor wait, till all

III

Our vernal bloom from every vale and plain
    And garden pass,
And all the gold from each laburnum chain.
    Drop to the grass.

IV

Is memory with your Marian gone to rest,
    Dead with the dead?
For ere she left us, when we met, you prest
    My hand, and said

V

"I come with your spring-flowers." You came not, friend;
    My birds would sing,
You heard not. Take then this spring-flower I send,
    This song of spring,   20

[1] The "following poem" was the early "Progress of Spring," which
is included in this volume on page 118.

VI

Found yesterday—forgotten mine own rhyme
  By mine old self,
As I shall be forgotten by old Time,
  Laid on the shelf—

VII

A rhyme that flower'd betwixt the whitening sloe
  And kingcup blaze,
And more than half a hundred years ago,
  In rick-fire days,

VIII

When Dives loathed the times, and paced his land
  In fear of worse,   30
And sanguine Lazarus felt a vacant hand
  Fill with *his* purse.

IX

For lowly minds were madden'd to the height
  By tonguester tricks,
And once—I well remember that red night
  When thirty ricks,

X

All flaming, made an English homestead hell—
  These hands of mine
Have helpt to pass a bucket from the well
  Along the line,   40

XI

When this bare dome had not begun to gleam
  Thro' youthful curls,
And you were then a lover's fairy dream,
  His girl of girls;

XII

And you, that now are lonely, and with Grief
　　　Sit face to face,
Might find a flickering glimmer of relief
　　　In change of place.

XIII

What use to brood? This life of mingled pains
　　　And joys to me,   50
Despite of every Faith and Creed, remains
　　　The Mystery.

XIV

Let golden youth bewail the friend, the wife,
　　　For ever gone.
He dreams of that long walk thro' desert life
　　　Without the one.

XV

The silver year should cease to mourn and sigh—
　　　Not long to wait—
So close are we, dear Mary, you and I
　　　To that dim gate.   60

XVI

Take, read! and be the faults your Poet makes
　　　Or many or few,
He rests content, if his young music wake‍
　　　A wish in you

XVII

To change our dark Queen-city, all her realm
　　　Of sound and smoke,

For his clear heaven, and these few lanes of elm
    And whispering oak.

               [1889; publ. 1889]

MERLIN AND THE GLEAM

I

O YOUNG Mariner,
You from the haven
Under the sea-cliff,
You that are watching
The gray Magician
With eyes of wonder,
I am Merlin,
And *I* am dying,
I am Merlin
Who follow the Gleam.　　　　　　10

II

Mighty the Wizard
Who found me at sunrise
Sleeping, and woke me
And learn'd me Magic!
Great the Master,
And sweet the Magic,
When over the valley,
In early summers,
Over the mountain,
On human faces,　　　　　　20
And all around me,
Moving to melody,
Floated the Gleam.

III

Once at the croak of a Raven who crost it,
    A barbarous people,
    Blind to the magic

And deaf to the melody,
Snarl'd at and cursed me.
A demon vext me,
The light retreated,   30
The landskip darken'd,
The melody deaden'd,
The Master whisper'd,
"Follow the Gleam."

IV

Then to the melody,
Over a wilderness
Gliding, and glancing at
Elf of the woodland,
Gnome of the cavern,
Griffin and Giant,   40
And dancing of Fairies
In desolate hollows,
And wraiths of the mountain,
And rolling of dragons
By warble of water,
Or cataract music
Of falling torrents,
Flitted the Gleam.

V

Down from the mountain
And over the level,   50
And streaming and shining on
Silent river,
Silvery willow,
Pasture and plowland,
Innocent maidens,
Garrulous children,
Homestead and harvest,
Reaper and gleaner,
And rough-ruddy faces
Of lowly labor,   60
Slided the Gleam—

VI

Then, with a melody
Stronger and statelier,
Led me at length
To the city and palace
Of Arthur the King;
Touch'd at the golden
Cross of the churches,
Flash'd on the tournament,
Flicker'd and bicker'd   70
From helmet to helmet,
And last on the forehead
Of Arthur the blameless
Rested the Gleam.

VII

Clouds and darkness
Closed upon Camelot;
Arthur had vanish'd
I knew not whither,
The king who loved me,
And cannot die;   80
For out of the darkness
Silent and slowly
The Gleam, that had waned to a wintry glimmer
On icy fallow
And faded forest,
Drew to the valley
Named of the shadow,
And slowly brightening
Out of the glimmer,
And slowly moving again to a melody   90
Yearningly tender,
Fell on the shadow,
No longer a shadow,
But clothed with the Gleam.

VIII

And broader and brighter
The Gleam flying onward,
Wed to the melody,
Sang thro' the world;
And slower and fainter,
Old and weary,   100
But eager to follow,
I saw, whenever
In passing it glanced upon
Hamlet or city,
That under the Crosses
The dead man's garden,
The mortal hillock,
Would break into blossom;
And so to the land's
Last limit I came—   110
And can no longer,
But die rejoicing,
For thro' the Magic
Of Him the Mighty,
Who taught me in childhood,
There on the border
Of boundless Ocean,
And all but in Heaven
Hovers the Gleam.

IX

Not of the sunlight,   120
Not of the moonlight,
Not of the starlight!
O young Mariner,
Down to the haven,
Call your companions,
Launch your vessel
And crowd your canvas,
And, ere it vanishes
Over the margin,

After it, follow it,   130
Follow the Gleam.

[1889; publ. 1889]

CROSSING THE BAR

SUNSET and evening star,
    And one clear call for me!
And may there be no moaning of the bar,
    When I put out to sea,

But such a tide as moving seems asleep,
    Too full for sound and foam,
When that which drew from out the boundless deep
    Turns again home.

Twilight and evening bell,
    And after that the dark!   10
And may there be no sadness of farewell,
    When I embark;

For tho' from out our bourne of Time and Place
    The flood may bear me far,
I hope to see my Pilot face to face
    When I have crost the bar.

[1889; publ. 1889]

INDEX OF TITLES